Have a good day

10-6-0

MW01518435

To Wave ...

Thank you for your service and support of the WWP. I have sponsored a young Marine WWP. Soon is our 234th Bday. Nov 7. I will be speaking at St. Augustine, Fl. for the Marine Corps Ball. I speak somewhere most every year, this year I'm close to home. If you are in the area .....

Semper Fi

John "Doc" Hatch

Be Blessed
[signature]

6 Nov 09
Wave!
with deepest
appreciation for your
Outstanding service to
Corps & Country, marine to
marine. You're a marine bond
and I'm damn proud.
Call me anytime Semper Fi.
God Bless and Semper Fi.
Frank Libutti
LtGen USMC (Ret.)

Love,
Semper Fi!
[signature] Bill

The Names NOT on the Wall

The Names NOT on the Wall

by

John "Doc" Hutchings

www.TheNamesNOTontheWall.com

Email: DocHutch@TheNamesNOTontheWall.com

©2006

ISBN 0-9778394-0-0

SAN: >>>>>>>>   8 5 0 – 2 9 7 8   <<<<<<<<<<

First Edition

Graphics & Cover Designed by
Derek Smith

DEDICATION

How do you dedicate a novel of this nature to any one person or group of people? Who deserves it? I believe every one of you who allowed yourself to let go for a while and be taken back to Oct. 1968 deserves part of the credit.

Linda, my young wife, was torn apart from her husband when duty took me to a place from which I most likely would not return. When I did return, she had to deal with the fact that the man she had kissed hello was quite different from the man she had kissed goodbye. Yet she stuck by my side saying, "The man I married is in there somewhere, and I won't give up until I get him back!

My 16-year old **niece Becky** wrote 365 letters of encouragement during my tour!

Vernon and **Rosemary Womack, Leon "Junior"** and **Marybeth Hutchings**, of course, also influenced my early years greatly. From slipping quietly through the woods to outdoor survival, Junior and Vernon, taught me well. Rose and Marybeth made me feel loved unconditionally.

Alpha Co. 1/5, you are **my Marines** - past, present and future. Many of you laid down a line of fire to protect me as I darted to treat a downed Marine. Many took wounds doing so. Many Marines, not just names, will forever be a part of my life, and I dearly appreciate each and every one. You DO take care of your Docs. Semper Fidelis!

Lauren Vincent Hutchings and **Jamie Lynn (Hutchings) Smith**, our children, stayed with me and loved me when my head wasn't yet back on straight. Their spouses, **Derek Smith** and **Johnette Hutchings** and my wonderful grandchildren (**Joylyn, Kailey and**

Lindsey Hutchings, and **Jaden and Koby Smith**) encouraged me to tell my story to help others.

My friend and doctor, **Patrick Harris, D**.O, without whose encouragement in the beginning and throughout this process the novel would not have been published at all.

"**The Bears**": **Eva Harris, Sandra Smith, Terri Anderson**, and the **Phil and Maryellen Brewbaker**. All were such encouragers and I truly believe your prayers were heard. **Marilyn**, my VA nurse and friend was always so supportive and encouraging.

The **Vets** we reunited with in California, and their supportive wives. I never felt anything but respect as a "Doc" among Marines.

To the US Navy, for the superior schools they offer.

To **Casual Company**: If we only knew....

Robin, Sarge, and Stuckey, of course, take up the greater part of this novel, along with my partner **Fred Hemenway, Steve Brit** and **Pat McCrary**. Those we lost: **Lt. Tony, "Bud", Pappy, Tony, Lt. Koster, Doc Hall**, and many others.

Doc Eddie Harren, my best friend in the world in Bethesda, then again when I had my bush time working at 1st Medical Battalion Psyche ward. Eddie, I owe you my sanity, what little there was of it. You taught me it was okay to laugh again

As you walk with me through this dedication, I see **Cheryl Rios**, whom I love to pieces - such a supporter! All the Marines and Corpsmen that served and are serving, all you wives who have stood and are standing with your heroes, strong and long, are such an important part of this novel. I can feel the hearts of many of you now, and I think I've reached a conclusion:

As author, I hereby dedicate "The Names NOT on the Wall" to:

The Names <u>ON</u> the Wall!

Each and every one of you gave your all, and many of us are alive because of you!

Semper Fidelis!

Doc Hutch

*For speaking engagements, personal appearances and book signings, please contact Doc at:

<u>DocBear68@aol.com</u> ;
or

<u>DocHutch@TheNamesNOTontheWall.com</u>
or

John Hutchings
PO Box 249
Crescent City, FL 32112

THE CORPSMAN AND THE WALL

Thirty-two years had come and gone. I needed to see
my friends.
I took a list, a few small gifts, and went to visit them.
I was their "Doc" in Vietnam and silently recalled;
How their names had earned a resting place...
Engraved there on "The Wall".

My bag of gifts was personal – simple things I guess:
Florida sand, hot cocoa, and a pack of cigarettes.
I took my list to the "Lady in blue" to help me find
them all.
Soon I stood there moved to tears -
Staring at "The Wall".

Slowly approaching the massive "Wall", my list of
names in hand;
I touched each name; mourned them all; and traced
"Bud's" name with sand.
"Did you know him well?" asked a lady's voice,
Whom I turned around to face.
She was there to mourn her fallen son – I saw it on
her face.

"Was he family, or did you serve with him? You
know he's now at rest."
I smiled and held my palms toward her, "These
hands were in his chest.
I was his Doc in Vietnam... couldn't save them all."
Recalling my Field Med Instructor's voice,
I turned back to "The Wall":

"Rule 1: Good men will surely die when all is said
and done.

Rule 2: You do the best you can, but you won't
change Rule #1!"
I spent the night there with my friends - the ones who
gave their all.
When the sun rose bright, I had wept all night....
Staring at "The Wall".

I went to my room, but soon returned just after a few
hours sleep.
To deliver the cocoa and cigarettes...a promise I'd
yet to keep.
As I sat and watched the mourners file by
With names they sought to find,
A heartfelt peace fell over me
As I opened up my mind.

As I saw them point and search for names, "The
Wall" came alive to me!
In my mind appeared a list of names – names THEY
could not see.
I recalled the men I'd treated – every casualty!
Each Marine I had given back life!
Names NOT there........because of me!

Chris would not tremble here searching for Lauren's
name!
Janie would not weep here mourning Fred!
The list grew long – lives and limbs now saved...
Among the living –
Not here with the dead!

I sat the third night all alone.
With my heart at peace I saw....
My tour in 'Nam was justified........
By the names NOT on "The Wall"!

"Doc Hutch"
September 30, 2000
Alpha 1/5
2nd Platoon
'68-'69
An Hoa Basin
1st Marine Division

TABLE OF CONTENTS

Introduction		Page 11
Chapter 1	July '66	Page 14
Chapter 2	So This is Vietnam	Page 28
Chapter 3	The Fighting 5th	Page 40
Chapter 4	The Bush	Page 53
Chapter 5	First Patrol	Page 59
Chapter 6	The Wonderful World of Ambushes	Page 68
Chapter 7	Chasing the Orange Bag	Page 77
Chapter 8	Mercy, Doc	Page 86
Chapter 9	Knowing Captain Compton	Page 93
Chapter 10	Sarge	Page 101
Chapter 11	Doc Bear	Page 113
Chapter 12	Sometimes They Get You	Page 122
Chapter 13	Liberty Bridge	Page 134
Chapter 14	Seagrams and Oberle	Page 139
Chapter 15	Go Noi Island	Page 150
Chapter 16	Blocking "Farce"	Page 157
Chapter 17	Ambush	Page 168
Chapter 18	Point Man	Page 175
Chapter 19	The Plan	Page 186
Chapter 20	Dear Field Med Instructor	Page 202
Chapter 21	Back to the Bush	Page 215
Chapter 22	The Old Man and the Well	Page 222
Chapter 23	Nothing is as it Seems	Page 231
Chapter 24	Elephant Grass and Army Pilots	Page 243
Chapter 25	The Change	Page 250
Chapter 26	Losing Control	Page 258
Chapter 27	February 6, 1969	Page 264
Chapter 28	How Do You Like Your Eggs	Page 271
Chapter 29	Brave Little Soldier	Page 278
Chapter 30	Tet 1969	Page 286
Chapter 31	Year of the Monkey	Page 296
Chapter 32	The Deadliest Weapon in the World	Page 303
Chapter 33	What Did He Say?	Page 310
Chapter 34	Chi Com and Chi Coms	Page 319
Chapter 35	A Peek at the Future: Hawaii	Page 330
Chapter 36	Saving Private Brian	Page 340
Chapter 37	The Longest Night	Page 348

Chapter 38 Platoon Commanders and Squids   Page 355
Chapter 39 Whale of a Surprise   Page 362
Chapter 40 Letting Go   Page 368
Chapter 41 A Plan for Closure is Born   Page 374
Chapter 42 Dream Team   Page 379
Chapter 43 Leaving An Hoa   Page 387
Chapter 44 "Are You Going to San Prancisco?"   Page 391
Chapter 45 Stuckey   Page 396
Chapter 46 Sitting on a Dime Dangling My Feet   Page 402
Epilogue   Page 413
Afterword   Page 425
Author Bio File   Page 426

Introduction

July 3, 2002

It is appropriate (and somewhat planned) that I write the introduction to this novel while aboard a flight to reunite with three main principles of this book.

This is not a biography, rather a novel based on actual events. Time and many years trying to forget these events force me to claim this as a novel of fiction. Very little is. Two of the Marines are based on real people, and forever friends.

Sarge is based on my dear friend Vince Rios. The "best point man in the world" is based on Lauren Alvin Stuckenschmidt. My wife and I did, in fact, name our first born Lauren Vincent. The last Platoon Commander I served under is based on a true hero by anyone's standards, except maybe his own – Robin Montgomery.

Due to the respect (and often awe) I have for these men, I tried to keep the events of their characters as factual as possible. If my memory has faded on some patrols and ambushes, and it surely has, please forgive me. Some have intentionally been enhanced to provide the reader with more excitement and humor. For this reason and due to a constantly fading memory, only Sarge and Stucky's (stookie's) real names are used. This in no way means I don't appreciate the Marines I served with that aren't mentioned by their real names. Some, in fact, at one time or another were responsible for saving my life.

In reality, some of the days in the "bush" were flat-out boring. I chose to share a minimum of those with you.

I spent my tour as a "bush Doc" with Alpha 1/5. The intent of this novel is to take you back to Quang

Nam Province, October, 1968, An Hoa Basin in the Republic of Vietnam.

      The principle character is Doc Bear. As I mentioned, this is not a biography and I was not called Doc Bear by my Marines. I was Doc Hutch. My real name is Hutchings, not Kenner. Still, most of "Doc Bear's" experiences are based on my own, though not all of them. For the purpose of making this enticing entertainment, I used some experiences (actual experiences) of other Corpsmen I knew. I either went to Field Med School with or fought along side of these men.

      Perhaps you will notice the reader begins his/her "tour" in Vietnam 1968-1969, knowing very little. I didn't provide a glossary in the front of the book, or detailed maps. I wanted you to have the experience of learning terms, customs, rules of engagement, enemy territory and friendly territory much as I did - through living it. Picture this: A Navy Corpsman- attached to a Marine unit- sent into the jungle to save lives.

      My chief objective is to put you there with me and make you feel what the Marines, and especially bush Corpsmen, lived and felt. If you laugh, cry, lose a good night's sleep worrying about the safety or future of these Marines you have come to care a great deal about, then I did my job. If not, I failed.

      I have read many novels about Vietnam. Most I couldn't identify with at all. "Fields of Fire" by James Webb hit very close to home for me. He served with my sister Company and, though I don't recall meeting him, we were there about the same time. "Fields of Fire" brought a lot back to me that I had forced myself to forget. When I read it, I basically "relived my 365-days in country".

      This novel will be different from other books on "The Nam". Though most patrols, ambushes, and adventures are based on actual experiences, they are presented "from a Doc's point of view". I hope, in a different way and from a totally different perspective, to have you join me and the Marines of Alpha 1/5.

For those who have lived these experiences, remember: It is over.

For those who ran to Canada, this is what you were running from.

For the rest of you...for the next 46 chapters...welcome to Vietnam. It could quite possibly change your life forever

Doc Hutch
Alpha Co.
2nd Platoon
1st Battalion 5th Marine Regiment
1st Marine Division
1968/69

Chapter 1
<u>July '66</u>

I stood in the corridor in front of Ward 3C, Bethesda Naval Hospital, (National Naval Medical Center), Bethesda, MD, awaiting the whirlwind that would soon be coming around the corner. A "whirlwind" pretty well described the last eight months of my life.

December 16, 1965, I took my oath to serve in the US Navy. Navy boot camp was somewhat of a culture shock for a 20-year old boy from southeast Missouri. The frozen terrain of Great Lakes, IL, was a definite eye-opener. The temperature dipped well below zero as we stood outside "on watch" guarding what must have been a dangerous Dempsey dumpster. We were armed and told to, "Guard it with your lives!"

The D.I. was an angry Petty Officer First Class, who seemed to warm his body temperature mostly with the aid of Jack Daniels, or perhaps a more economic version of the same beverage. I wondered many times if brain damage perhaps was a by-product of this economic decision. He stood about 5'5", weighed all of 120 lbs., but had an ego that would tip the scales at least at twice that. He delighted in our humility and took every opportunity to let us know we were the lowest things on earth - with the possible exception of an Army recruit. This, of course, was his job. Knowing that in no way improved my early opinion of serving in the Armed Forces.

The truth was I was there because I didn't want to go to Vietnam and die in some wet, dirty rice paddy for a war I didn't believe in.

My Navy recruiter, however, was quite a different character. He told me how bright I was and promised me any school I desired and a safe four-year tour, cruising the seven seas in warm tropical climates. When I mentioned I was going to be married in a year, he assured me if I chose the medical field I would be stationed stateside most of my tour and the Navy would welcome my bride with open arms.

I selected Dental Tech School as my first choice after boot camp, and since "for technical purposes only" I had to pick a second choice, he recommended Hospital Corps School. "Even if you do have to go on a ship for a few months, you would be the 'Doc' - your own boss! But with YOUR I.Q., don't worry! You'll get Dental Tech School!"

Graduation day, Company 758 was leaving the Great Lakes Recruiting Center, and we were all awaiting our new destination. As the names were called out, there was occasionally a laugh or snicker, and I nudged my new buddy Mark.

"Hey, what are they laughing at?"

"He got Hospital Corps School! He's going to be a friggin' Marine!"

The Hospital Corps School thing seemed vaguely familiar, but this Marine crap was nothing I had heard before.

"What do you mean, a '<u>Marine</u>'?!"

"Bear," my nickname mostly because I was 6'2" and 215 lbs., "the Marine Corps has no medical personnel! They get all their Corpsmen and Doctors from the Navy! You know where the Marines are now? Vietnam! Hospital Corps School is a death sentence!"

I suddenly recalled my Navy Recruiter in a very different light and wished I could get my hands on that smiling face. Still, I was going to Dental Tech School…he assured me of that.

"Seaman Apprentice Kenner! Hospital Corps School! Great Lakes, Illinois!"

Damn! Not only did it look like I was going to be a Marine, but I was going to have to spend another four months in this frozen, God-forsaken tundra!

I rode home with my parents and bride-to-be after graduation, and told them I was going to Hospital Corps School in Great Lakes, but didn't mention the possibility I could be sent to the Marines. I just didn't know enough about the situation to worry anyone yet, but vowed I would sure as hell find out as soon as I got back to Great Lakes.

"I am Chief Hospital Corpsman Valdosta. I am your Company Commander, one of your Instructors, and Drill Instructor." He, too, was about 5'5" and 120 pounds, but quite the opposite of my D.I. in boot camp. He looked very intelligent, "squared away", and so far hadn't kicked or hit any of us.

Chief assigned section leaders, squad leaders, MAA (Master at Arms - another word for the guy making the rest of us sweep, swab, and sweat), and Platoon Leader. There were around 100 in our new Company 12. I had no extra responsibilities, and that suited me just fine. My basic goal was to get through the school, get through my four years unscathed, and return back to civilian life. There I would become more assertive and try to build a comfortable life for my wife and future children. As far as the school went, I was content to "just get by" as I did in high school and my one year of college. My grades were passable and I prided myself in the fact I'd never taken a book home or studied. I was often told I could be an honor student, but I didn't believe it.

Hospital Corps School was unlike anything I had ever seen. Rumors were flying, and they weren't pleasant:

"The lifespan of a Corpsman after we hit the beach is 30 seconds."

"In six months, anyone who doesn't have a major school assignment will be in a Marine uniform stumbling through the jungles of South Viet Nam."

Week two of school, we were in Chief Valdosta's class in which he was teaching us First Aid. To be exact, he was teaching us how to treat a pneumothorax ("sucking chest wound").

Chief paused for a second and said, "Gentlemen, I will never lie to you. In six months many of you will be in Vietnam treating wounds just like this. You'll be doing amputations, treating gunshot wounds, AND you will be doing it in the bush, just seconds after the wounds are inflicted. Many of you won't come back. Many of you will be wounded, and med-evaced. But what I DON'T want to happen to you is for you to lay there in the middle of a firefight with a bleeding Marine in your arms and watch him die because you don't know what the hell to do. The choice is yours. You can learn now, or wish you had in a few months. Men will die if you don't learn now, and you will have to live with that the rest of your life!"

Chief had my attention. This scared the hell out of me. I pictured myself there with a Marine dying, depending on my skills to save his life, and my not knowing what to do.

For the first time in my life, I applied myself. I studied. I took books back to the barracks and studied more. I was scared shitless.

About two weeks later, I was in another of the Chief's classes, and when it ended we were dismissed.

He said, "Bear, I want to see you after class."

I was wondering what I did but couldn't think of anything, so I sat there until the room was empty. Then I stood and said, "Yes, Sir! You wish to speak with me?"

"John, what are you doing tonight?"

17

"Well, Sir, I was going to study, then maybe go shoot some basketball with a few of the guys."

"I would like for you to come to my house and have dinner with my family. Would you be open to that?"

I stuttered, "I guess so, Sir. I don't know what to say."

"Don't say anything. Be in civvies at 1800 in front of the barracks. Don't tell anyone where you are going. I will pick you up there."

"Yes, Sir!"

At 1800 hours, I was outside the barracks wondering what the hell was going on. He pulled up and I got in.

"Relax, John! We're going to have a nice dinner my wife is preparing, you'll meet my two children, and we'll talk."

All I could say was, "Yes, Sir!"

I met Priscilla, an attractive lady in her mid 30's. She was very hospitable and the two children were very energetic but disciplined.

The dinner was very nice, Italian, and a pleasant change from the swill we were used to eating on base.

We did talk a while, but not about school, war, or the Navy. We talked about us – them and me. It was actually a very pleasant evening and I felt very good about it, but still wondered what the hell I was doing there.

When it was time to go, I told the kids and Priscilla goodbye. As I was turning around she said, "I'm very glad to have met you, John. From what I hear you are the backbone of the Company."

I stood there for a second, not having any idea what was going on or why Chief would tell her such a thing. I had decent grades, was second in the class, but I was still a "peon" and content with being just that.

On the way back, Chief said, "See, Bear, Navy life is a pretty good way of life once you have some time in and rank. It's a great career."

Suddenly it dawned on me he somehow thought I was a potential career man.

"Sir, may I speak freely?"

"Certainly, John."

"I'm afraid you have me all wrong. I hate the military. I don't want to be a Corpsman or a sailor, and I sure as HELL don't want to be a Marine. To be honest, I am trying to figure out some way of getting out of this school honorably. If I can't, I will still do my best to stay out of the Marines and Vietnam. The only reason my grades are up is because you scared the shit out of me when you told me I may have a Marine die in my arms in a few months...and..."

"And...John, that's what makes you a leader. You have honor. You took an oath to serve your country, and you WILL be a Corpsman. I think you will be a damn good one. It doesn't matter what you want; it matters what you signed and swore. Leaders excel, John, because of the situation they're in. You may or may not be a Marine, time will tell; but if that is what you are ordered to do, that is what you will do. The military is NOT a democracy. You gave up your civilian rights when you took that oath. I'm not trying to scare you. I'm trying to explain the way life is in the military. I am being honest when I tell you the time I spent with the Marines is the most incredible part of my career. My job is to sift through the personnel and find leaders. From them, I build the best Company possible. You can screw up and get kicked out of this school, but you won't. And why not? Inside of you there is a leader waiting for a chance to surface and excel - an opportunity. And that opportunity is here. I need a new

Section Leader starting Monday. Will you do that for me?"

"Well, yes, sir, I guess, so."

"Good, we will talk more then."

Three months later, Company 12 graduated from Hospital Corps School. I took pride in the fact I graduated second in my class, and that I was the Platoon Leader as I barked out commands and marched the newly graduated Company in front of the visitors and families of the new Corpsmen. Chief Valdosta had changed my life in that second week. He got my attention, and he gave me the motivation to learn and excel - motivation I really never had before. He was a man of honor, character, principle and a credit to the Corps.

After graduation, I once again went home and had a week before reporting to my new duty station, National Naval Medical Center, Bethesda, MD, where in one year I would start Neuro-Psychiatric Tech School. I hoped that would keep me out of combat even if I did go to 'Nam. But I was beginning to think more and more "fate" had been set into motion.

I was assigned to ward 3C, what they called a "dirty orthopedic" ward while awaiting my school. We had 33 beds, a montage of patients ranging from wounded Marines to sailors who got drunk and fell down a ladder or whatever it is they call those things on a ship.

To the Marines, we were "Doc's" and to some of the sailors as well. To others we were just Corpsmen. You could see the respect in the eyes of the Marines. I had never experienced anything like it - instant respect and immediate confidence.

I worked hard the first three weeks, learning all I could, and thought I was doing okay. I was still looking forward to getting married in December and to starting my primary school.

One day, after the doctors made their rounds, I was called into Captain Green's office. He was a Navy Captain, equivalent to a Marine Corps Colonel. I approached his office, knocked on the door, and was called inside. There sat Captain Green, Commander Sanders (Charge Nurse of the whole wing) and Lieutenant Adams (the 3C Ward Nurse). I was shaking like a dog passing razor blades. I was told to be seated and Commander Sanders began.

"H.A. Kenner, we are losing our Charge Corpsman. He has orders to FMF First Marine Division. We need a new Senior Corpsman and think you would be best suited for the job."

My mouth dropped open for two reasons: 1) I was happy as a "puppy-with-two-peters" I wasn't in trouble; and 2) I was once again scared shitless.

"Ma'am, Sir, I am honored, but I am the junior man on the ward. I have only been out of school three weeks and am a Hospitalman Apprentice. You have E3's and two E4's on the ward who are much more qualified for this."

"Let us worry about qualifications. We think you are the man for the job. Will you do it?"

I stood a few seconds, overwhelmed once again and said, "I will do what you want me to do."

I walked out of the office the new Senior Corpsman. HM3 Collier was leaving in two weeks so he trained me in my new role. I was afraid there would be others who resented that I was put ahead of them. If they did, they didn't show it. It was an awesome responsibility. I was in charge of the Ward. I had to see that everything was done and done right. It was my job to order meds, Make sure they were given as prescribed, go on rounds with the surgeons, make sure sterile techniques were followed, do the major dressing changes myself, do pre-op, post–op, assign all duties, make sure they were followed up on, take all the doctors' orders, and even make sure the autoclave was working. It was an amazing responsibility for a Corpsman with three weeks experience.

One benefit was I was on four-section duty, (duty every fourth weekend), instead of port and starboard duty (duty every other weekend) and also every fourth day instead of every two days.

It forced me to learn quickly. I also slowly began to fall in love with Orthopedics and was no longer looking forward to Neuro-Psych School.

In June, we got a new patient, HM2 Brown. He was a Doc with a Marine guerrilla unit in 'Nam and was shot through the right femur while running to treat a wounded Marine. He was different. His eyes were different. He was a very nice guy, but when I tried to talk to him, I knew he was not like me. I noticed the respect the Marines gave him. Yes, they respected me and called me Doc and all, but when they talked to Doc Brown, I saw in the Marines something that ran deep. He was one of them.

I tried to talk to him, "Doc, tell me what it's like over there. I'll no doubt be going over after NP school, and would like to know what to expect."

"Bear, you've heard the stories, and all I can tell you is it's worse than you've heard. I've done things I'd never even SEEN done before, and done them because if you don't that Marine would die. I was with the Fifth Marines and we were in firefights almost daily. I treated every type of wound you can imagine, and it never ended. I hated it, and if you can possibly keep from going, do it. It's pure hell!"

Doc Brown had "seen the elephant". He was quiet and reserved; but one look into those deep brown eyes, and you knew they contained a vault of information, personal experiences, tragedies, victories, and defeats. He seldom asked for pain medication. He would take it if I offered it to him, but mostly he lay quietly in his bed in severe pain awaiting word about his future.

I could hear the whirlwind approaching now. It came in the form of Captain Green, Chief of Orthopedics, and his entourage of surgeons, including the surgeon in charge of my ward, Dr. Dixon. Captain Green was a 6', 250 lb. ball of energy. You could <u>feel</u> his presence coming as well as hear it. Dr. Dixon was on my ward often, and I liked and respected him.

The entourage approached me now, and I greeted them with, "Good Morning, Sirs! Ward 3C ready for rounds!"

As the six surgeons went from bed to bed, my duty was to inform them of any changes, elevated vital signs, lab results, etc.; and to be able to retrieve any information they required immediately.

As they walked by, Captain Green patted me on the shoulder, and said, "Good morning, Bear. Let's see what we can do for these gentlemen today." He had a way about him. Yes, he was military, but he showed his human side despite being a "full bird" Captain. I had known him for a month now, and my respect for him was ever-growing.

I pushed the chart rack along, and had the chart ready for each patient when we got to him. As I handed it to the patient's doctor, I would answer questions and tell them of lab results which, if out of range, I had already "flagged".

As we approached Doc Brown's bed this day, I noticed something about the chief. He slowed a little. Dr. Dixon stepped forward and said, "Sir, this is HM2

Brown. He was a 'bush' Corpsman and was shot through the right femur, shattering it."

"And what does the future hold for this young man, Dr. Dixon?"

I had handed him the recent x-rays and he said, "Well, Sir, as you can see, the femur is gone. We will have to take the leg. And he will have a very short stump, but with prosthesis, he will live a relatively normal life."

"Dr. Collins, what are your feelings about this patient?"

"Well, Sir, I have to agree. There is nothing to work with - nothing much to graft to. I'm afraid we have no choice but to take the leg."

Doc Brown looked straight ahead, quietly listening - no sound - no emotion.

As each surgeon was asked, each agreed.

Then Captain Green turned to me and said, "And what does our Charge Corpsman feel about this?"

I was stunned. I had checked out the x-rays, but was highly unqualified to make such a decision. "Well, Sir, there is very little left to graft to."

Captain Green slowly cleared his throat, "Gentlemen, what we have here is a young Corpsman who put his life on the line to save a wounded Marine; and by God, if there is any way possible, I will have him walking out of this hospital on his own two legs!"

I looked at Doc Brown, and saw a single tear rolling down his cheek.

"Yes, Sir!" I said, realizing probably in the night Captain Green had come in and read about this patient, and was determined to do this.

Two years later, time had marched on. I had been with Doc Brown for the first six surgeries, treating him pre-op and post-op. Though we had become close, he still talked very little about his experiences in 'Nam.

One year and one day after I had taken my oath to serve in the US Navy, I took yet another oath. I married Linda, my childhood sweetheart on December 17, 1966.

I also had left my beloved Orthopedics, and graduated from Neuro-Psych School. I was working the officers' ward one day, charting on my patients. I looked up and saw a Navy Corpsman walking down the corridor in Marine Corps full Dress Greens.

I had, in fact, just been thinking about Doc Brown. I now had my orders to leave in three days for the FMF First Marine Division. I had gone to say goodbye to Captain Green just the day before, when he once more surprised and complimented me.

"Bear, when you get back from 'Nam, I want you to look me up. I will get you into any medical school you want in this whole damned country and help you find the money to do it. But first you must commit to me that you will be an Orthopedic Surgeon, not some crazy damn head doctor."

"Yes, Sir!" I laughed openly.

Now a product of his work and dedication was almost to my desk.

"Doc Brown! Damn, man! You look great! How's the leg?"

"I'm fine, Doc. They just discharged me. I'm going home and I had to stop by and thank you for all your care and support."

"You're leaving right now?"

"Yes."

"Hang on, I'll get someone to cover my desk and I'll walk out with you."

The elevator was descending as I said, "Doc, I have my orders: FMF First Marine Division."

"Damn, Bear! I hope you don't get the Fifth Marines."

25

"Why? Are they that bad?"

"No, Doc. Don't you watch the news? They're just finishing up in Hue City, my old unit. They're always in the shit. They're going to the An Hoa Basin now, I think."

"I try not to think about it, but yeah, I've seen the pictures."

"Well, did you see the nine men left from Alpha 1/5? They climbed the citadel wall on the last day. That was all that was left of the whole unit – nine men!"

"Yes, I saw it."

Little did I know that October 27, this same year, I would be on my very first ambush with one of these last survivors of Hue City, Corporal Bob Carrel?

We walked under the huge rotunda to the main entrance to Bethesda Naval Hospital. Even now I was aware that Doc Brown was so different from me or anyone else I knew. What was going on inside that head? What guilty feelings and horrible nightmares did he recall when he let his defenses down?

We descended the steps, and I smiled as he negotiated them with no apparent pain or limp. What had this young man experienced in the jungles of Vietnam? At the base of the steps, we paused and faced each other.

"Congratulations, man, you made it! You are going home!"

"I never thought I'd see this day, Doc! Thank you so much for all you've done."

"No, Doc, thank you!"

We embraced, and I watched as he walked solidly toward the bus stop. We both tried to conceal our tears of happiness. I walked back into the hospital, stood under the rotunda, and looked up.

Right up there three stories was my old ward, 3C. Two years ago, a very special Corpsman had come to my ward shot all to hell, with little to no hope of ever walking again. Today he was whole! How many more stories did these walls contain? Countless accounts of lives that had been forever changed!

I walked back to the Psych Department humbled and overwhelmed. I had been honored to know Doc Brown. I knew I would never forget him. I also knew there was a very special Chief of Orthopedics that this rejuvenated Corpsman would always be grateful to have known: The wise, the talented, the dedicated Captain Green!

My time here was finished. After fifteen days leave, I would have to kiss my wife goodbye for the first time and depart for Fleet Marine Force (FMF) Field Medical School, San Diego, California. It looked like it was going to be one hell of a ride!

Chapter 2
<u>So This Is Vietnam</u>

The terminal at Camp Hansen Okinawa was overflowing with Marines going to and returning from the Republic of South Vietnam. It seemed there were significantly more going to than returning from.

I horsed my Marine sea bag on the right shoulder of my new Marine Corps dress greens, making my way to be manifested onto the flight that would take me to my final duty station of my four-year tour.

As an FMF Corpsman, I had earned the right to wear the uniform of a US Marine. Our right sleeves were bare; our left bore our US Navy rank and Corpsman caduceus. My heart was racing as I felt the insecurity of what was in store for me. Doubts and fear filled my mind as I struggled with the sea bag. It would accompany me to that final duty station First Marine Division, Vietnam.

Though I had lost 15 pounds in Field Med School and Marine boot camp, I still tipped the scales at 236. Since our wedding day, 22 months ago, I had gained 37 lbs.

I noticed two Marines coming off the plane as I was walking through the manifest area and overheard them. One said, "Look! That big bastard is a private! He doesn't stand a snowball's chance in hell of making it home!" I turned to look at them and the other Marine saw my Corpsman caduceus and replied, "No, he's a Doc! And you're right - not a snowball's chance in hell!"

It was my size that concerned me the most. I was raised in the Ozark Mountains, was an accurate shot with almost any weapon, and very comfortable in the woods - at least the woods of the serene Ozark Mountains. By the time I was 12 years old I had killed deer, turkey, fox, coyote, and of course a variety of small game. For a large man, I was well coordinated and moved quietly in the woods. I had been doing it since I was 6 years old.

What concerned me, however, was in all probability I would soon be treating wounded Marines under fire, and I was myself a significantly large target.

"Continental Airlines flight 743 now boarding," came the call. It was a commercial flight in a civilian aircraft, but the passengers were all Marines.

The stewardesses were beautiful and the "welcome aboard" was strained. They did their best to make us comfortable, but it must have been difficult for them to deal with the situation. I was shown to my seat and met Mike, a Marine Corporal who was a Clerk, anxiously returning for his second tour. We talked a while and he was very friendly, and even a little sympathetic, knowing the odds were I would be fighting my way through the rice paddies and jungles in a few days to try to save the life of a wounded Marine. I still carried the fear planted there by Chief Valdosta that a Marine could die in my arms if I didn't know what to do. Already I had nightmares hearing, "Corpsman up!" I was also afraid I would die there. It would take an idiot to ignore the odds and possibilities after all the training we had received in the last four months. Marine boot camp was tough. Field Med School was brutally hard and honest. They pulled no punches with us. They gave us no illusions. If sent to the "bush", the first six months in Vietnam would be sheer hell. If we survived that, which only about 20% did, we would be among the elite in the Corps.

Mike was a nice guy and we talked a little about home, some about 'Nam and our families. He was single and was flirting with the pretty stewardesses, who seemed not to mind in the least. I asked him about the

Fifth Marines and told him what Doc Brown had told me. He pretty much agreed. The Fighting Fifth seemed to be always in the "shit". I had no idea at this point where I would be assigned, but "The 5th Marines" sure seemed to be coming up a lot.

"Continental Airlines flight 743 wishes you a safe tour and return trip home," said the stewardess on the intercom. I saw the look in her eyes. She was thinking, "How many of these guys will go home in a box?" I was wondering the same thing.

I was still hoping the completion of five medical schools would help keep me out of the bush. Most Corpsmen had only been through two. I could be assigned to an Orthopedic Unit as a tech at First Hospital, a Plaster Room Tech at First Med, or maybe even a Neuro-Psych Tech at First Med Battalion.

The plane made a routine landing and we began to unload. I could feel the pumping of testosterone and adrenalin. I gathered my carry-on and followed Mike toward the exit. Fear was also a reality as I was about to take my first step onto Vietnamese soil, or in this case, concrete.

We got to the door and I saw a pretty young stewardess hand Mike her phone number and address. Mike gave her a grateful smile. We were at the door and stepped onto the ramp where I was immediately aware that this wasn't the good ol' USA. The heat and humidity were smothering. You could SEE the heat and the smell was the first thing that hit me. It was putrid. It was explosives, fear, heat, filth, shitters burning, petroleum, and oppression. My first thought, "So, this is Vietnam…"

We were going down the ramp where we would wait for our sea bags to be unloaded when Mike turned back to me and said, "Doc, look over there." I looked but didn't see anything out of the ordinary.

"What?"

"Those three Marines, Doc, over there by themselves. Look at their eyes."

Then I saw it. It was what was referred to over here as the "1,000-yard stare". I remembered Doc Brown and my feeling upon meeting him when he was first admitted to my ward. I had known I had nothing in common with him. These men were different. They didn't look AT you - they looked THROUGH you. I had a sensation that these guys could read my thoughts, knew my fear, and they were above such things.

There was a story about a young native in Africa, in the desert area, who took it upon himself to leave the tribe. He traveled weeks and months to explore the amazing continent. He heard along his travels about a great beast. He had to see it. He decided to go on a journey. Finally one day he found a huge set of footprints unlike anything he had ever seen. He followed them and eventually settled in at dusk near a waterhole. When he awoke, there it was - the huge rogue elephant! His giant tusks were glistening in the morning mist. His call to his mate trumpeted, and the sheer bulk and power of this beast overwhelmed the young man. He couldn't wait to get home to tell his loved ones. He traveled back to his village, and finally as he approached the small ville he was so excited he ran the rest of the way. He had to tell them of his big adventure. With joy and enthusiasm, he ran into his home ville screaming, "I have seen the elephant! I have seen the elephant!" But, his people had never seen an elephant. They knew not of what he spoke. They looked at him blankly and did not understand. He was not like them any longer. He had seen things they had not seen. He knew things they did not know. He had "seen the elephant".

31

These three Marines had "seen the elephant". They were not like me. They had seen things I had not seen, and hoped I never would. Statistics told us one in five who served in Vietnam actually saw combat...I mean real combat. Most everyone at some time or another probably heard an incoming rocket or mortar, or a distant firefight. That isn't combat. That isn't what I saw in the eyes of these three Marines.

As I looked around while going down that ramp, I saw maybe eight or ten out of the 150 or so Marines waiting to board the great Freedom Bird home who had the "1,000-yard stare". About 140 of them were jubilant, excited the big day had come, their tour was over and they were headed home. They were laughing, grab-assing, and joking, as they should be. They had done their duty and were going home to their loved ones: mothers, fathers, wives, girlfriends, daughters, and sons.

The eight or ten Marines with the "1,000-yard stare" weren't laughing. They were watching. They were seeing things the rest of us could not see. They were feeling things we could not feel. They had earned the ability to be aware. I had the feeling each of these Marines knew exactly what they would do in any given situation. They had already planned how to react in the event of an unlikely attack on the airfield. They knew where they would go for cover. They knew what they would do to defend themselves. They had scanned the Marines around them, and had a pretty good idea who they could count on. These men had "seen the elephant". They knew what it was like to kill up close and personal. They knew what it was like to put a dear friend in a body bag. They had wiped the blood from their hands of both friends and enemies. They knew the stink of decaying bodies, the aroma of a fresh wound, the putrid smell of the newly dead, and the repulsive odor of the neglected dead.

Yet, these Marines had families, too - families who would have a hard time dealing with this great transformation. Wives, lovers, fathers and mothers who had no idea what these men had had to learn to cope with the last 13 months, the tour of duty for a US Marine. People who truly cared about them would have to learn to deal with the nightmares of their newly returned heroes. Yes, these men were heroes. You could feel it in their "presence". You could see it in their eyes. They probably did not think of themselves as heroes, but they were. They had put their lives on the line for others. They took assignments they didn't have to take. They went on missions where they didn't have to go. The eyes told the story. They had "seen the elephant"…and it consumed them.

I descended the ramp and stepped on the ground. The first three Marines were close by and I dared to look in their eyes. They looked right through me. I felt they knew my fear, my desire to be anywhere but Vietnam. I felt they knew what I felt, that I was not like them. Perhaps they thought I might even be a coward.

I turned away, feeling unworthy to be that close to these Marines. As I walked to get my sea bag, my mind wondered, "What would I be like in 365 days (a Corpsman's tour of duty)? If I beat the odds and made it, what would I be feeling? Would I be jumping and joking, waiting to get on that great freedom bird to go home and start my life? Would I even be one of the 20% who made it?"

God, I didn't want to be like those who stood out. I didn't hate the Vietnamese! I didn't want to kill them! Hell, I didn't even want to treat wounded Marines! I wanted my life back! I wanted to go home and be a good husband and provider and start the family I had been promising my wife! And I didn't want that stare!

33

I had one ribbon on my chest. If I boarded this plane in one year and still had one ribbon, I would be a happy man. It would mean I had made it, that I hadn't been hurt, hadn't taken any stupid chances, and would return the same as I was when I got here. "Gentle John" was the name my father-in-law had given me, and it was true. I had always had a kind, gentle heart, maybe sometimes even too gentle. Sometimes I laid back even though I knew I should have been more aggressive or assertive. My family loved me the way I was, but what would the next year bring?

Three-hundred-and-sixty-five days later (to the day) I indeed stood waiting to board the great freedom bird. I had my Marine dress greens tailored to fit my 190-pound body. I had a 44-inch chest and a 28-inch waist. I looked like a Marine. Hell, I WAS a Marine! I watched the newly arrived Marines and thought, "My God, did I look that stupid and scared 365 days ago?"

I stood watching them descend so we could board, and looked right through them. There was no eye contact, yet I was aware of each man exiting the craft. I knew exactly where my sea bag was, what I would do in the event of incoming mortars, and how I would react in any given situation. I ignored the attention as someone pointed at me as they came down the ramp.

"Look, a bush Corpsman! Damn, I bet he's seen a world of shit!"

I thought, "You have no fucking idea!" as I stared straight ahead.

"Look at those ribbons! Purple Hearts and all! Damn!"

I watched and soon a Corporal exited. I sensed we had something in common. It was his second tour. He had many of the same ribbons I now wore, and had been wounded twice on his first tour. I felt for this man I guess because I knew what he knew, but he was here to do it all again. I watched him come down the ramp, and though we were both E-4's he slowed as our eyes met. He came to attention and I saw a tear form in his eye. He snapped a crisp undeserved salute to me and said, "Thank you, Doc! God Bless you!"

I returned the salute out of respect and said, "Good luck, Corporal!"

I could only guess that another Corpsman had kept him alive when he was hit on his first tour. We had never met, but we were brothers. He was black and probably hailed from a city far from the Ozark Mountains, but we were brothers-in-arms. This Corporal was the only new arrival I could identify with. Again I wondered, "Was I that stupid 365 days ago?"

I decided, yes, I was. Three-hundred-and sixty-five days ago, I didn't know the difference between the sound of an AK-47 and an M-16 firing. Now, I not only knew the difference, but I could tell how far away the firefight was and from which direction each burst was coming.

Three-hundred-and-sixty-five days ago, I had only treated wounds in a semi-sterile, safe hospital. Today I could do a cut-down with a K-Bar (Marine fighting knife) under intense fire, tie off bleeders with suture material, make my own trache kit, and do a trache with my scalpel. I used the same scalpel to treat the next Marine after quickly wiping it on my jungle utilities. I knew exactly when and when not to administer morphine syrettes. I could decide whether a limb could be saved or had to be "taken" in seconds. I could start an IV lying on my back protecting a wounded man with my body. I could decide immediately whether I had time to drag a casualty to safety, or have to administer first aid within seconds after the wound. I could look at a "newbie" and tell if he would make it or not with uncanny accuracy. My life and the lives of others depended on these skills.

Three-hundred-and-sixty-five days ago, I couldn't tell the difference between out-going and incoming. Now I knew exactly what was fired, how far away, and in which direction. I could set up an ambush and know exactly when to trigger it to overwhelm an enemy that heavily out numbered us.

Three-hundred-and-sixty-five days ago, I couldn't read a map. Today I could call in a med-evac, call in a gunship, call in artillery, adjust for accuracy, and fire for effect. I had the best teacher in the world - Sarge! I had never been so close to any man. He was my mentor, my best friend, and my hero. He had taken me under his wing 11 months ago, and in his own words, "Doc, we are going to be very close." God, I missed him.

Three-hundred-and-sixty-five days ago, I had never seen a dead Marine or NVA soldier. Now, a year later, I saw both every time I closed my eyes. Then I had never been shot at. Now I was amazed at how many times I wasn't killed.

Three-hundred-and-sixty-five days ago, I had a heart full of compassion. Now, that compassion was selective. Then, I hated no one. Now, I could take a life and feel no regret. I had "seen the elephant". I was not like these new arrivals. We had nothing in common.

The aircraft was nearly empty. There were several more comments about the "bush Doc". I recalled the comments of the two Marines at Okinawa a year ago, "Not a snowball's chance in hell."

Yet, I <u>had</u> made it. It was time to board now, and I ascended the ramp looking only for the stewardess who would show me to my seat. I had beaten the odds. There were two Marines that I knew who were largely responsible for this: Sgt. Vince Rios, my mentor; and the best point man in Vietnam, Lauren Alvin Stuckenschmidt.

I was seated now and thought about the future. What would it be like not to have 150 Marines depending on my skills to keep them alive? What would it feel like not to have that responsibility, duty and respect?

What if the rumors were true, that we were shunned and rejected by the nation we defended? How would I react to this rejection? How would I react to anything? I knew I was different. I knew I had "seen the elephant"…and it consumed me. I knew as much as I hated war, it was forever a part of me. Where was "Gentle John"? Would that kind, gentle, tender heart ever resurface? How would my wife feel about the change? Could I hide it? What would happen to this hatred, guilt and anxiety that raced through my veins? How would I cope in a world where I was "just a civilian?"

Yet, being a career man would never happen. I had adjusted to combat. I still hated it. I hated it every second! But, God, I missed it! I had been out of the bush for four months and I missed it every day. That adrenalin rush! The fear, and yet the feeling of winning a firefight! Putting the enemy to flight! The pride of being the best! Never mind the fear! You won the battle; therefore, you are the best!

The jet engines revved up, and take off drew near. I sat by the window, looking out at what was Vietnam. We taxied to the runway, and we were off. The power of the jet was refreshing. We were off the ground. I was out of Vietnam. Or was I?

There below was Marble Mountain. I watched it go by and knew 23 miles southwest of there was my unit. Go Noi Island…the Arizona Valley…An Hoa Basin…Liberty Bridge.

I thought of the Marines who were gone. I didn't know it then, but one day far too late, their names would be on a Wall in the nation's Capitol. Doc Hall was dead; Bud, Tommy, Lt. Tony, Lt. Koster...and so many more.

It was time to think of the future. As I tried this, Sarge came back to my mind. He was never far from my mind. My firstborn would bear his name. His name and the name of the best point man I knew. Our son would be Lauren Vincent Kenner. Linda was fine with that. She knew because of these two men, I was coming home.

I remembered the Sarge and the way he chose to make me aware we were in danger. Early on he started it, at the beginning of my first Ambush: "Mercy Doc!" And his deep bass laugh always followed. After that first time, I would always reply with, "Mercy, Sarge!" He was telling me, "Doc, we are going to hit some deep shit, but we will be okay." My response was, "Okay, Sarge, I am with you! We will come out of this!" It was a deep bond.

Yes, Linda was fine with the name of our first son. She knew a lot about him... my best friend, my mentor, and my hero. She knew he was a family man. I had told her about Feb. 6, 1969, the day Sarge lost both legs at the hip, and his right arm. The 105 round destroyed his flesh, but not his spirit. When most men would have gone into shock and died, he had looked up and said, "Don't worry about me, Doc! I have a son at home to raise and, by GOD, I will raise him!" He lived. He didn't even lose consciousness!

I could hear him even now. "Mercy, Doc, you are going home!"

Yes, the shore was right under me now. I sat there thinking about the last 365 days. Maybe it would help me prepare, put it all behind me. I closed my eyes and took that journey in my mind now, revisiting the tour that started 365 days ago.   But first, not caring what anyone thought, I looked out the window as we left the land and flew above water and said aloud, "Mercy, Sarge! It's time for Doc Bear to go home!"

Chapter 3
<u>The Fighting 5th</u>

When I was eight-years old, I was engrossed in a war comic book and remember a scene in which a "medic" came running out onto the battlefield to treat a wounded soldier. He was wearing the white cross the medics of that time wore, and a very real fear came over me. I remember thinking, "That will someday be me, and that is how I will die."

This early experience was a part of my decision to join the Navy instead of being drafted. This was the Marines, not the Army, and Corpsmen didn't wear crosses. Instead we did all we could to blend in as a Marine. However, the fear was still there nonetheless.

As I was approaching First Marine Division headquarters in DaNang, this was on my mind. I would soon learn my fate. I stepped inside the "hootch", saluted the officer of the day, and handed him my orders.

"Welcome aboard, Doc," he said as he opened my orders.

I said a silent prayer that my five schools would finally pay off, but in my heart I knew better. "Let me give these to the C.O., Doc, and he will be right with you."

I took a seat, and within a minute, I heard, "Doc, come on in here."

I walked into the inner office, a tent with air conditioning. The Captain said, "Welcome aboard, Doc! I have a great assignment for you." My hopes soared briefly then dropped like a 40-pound bag of rhinoceros shit when he said, "First Battalion, Fifth Marines has lost several Docs lately and they are a great fighting unit. They will be glad to see you."

I saluted and being somewhat less than thrilled, headed for the chopper pad, where I would catch a flight to An Hoa, home of the Fifth Marines.

A "four-by" dropped me and all my gear off at the chopper pad where I reported to the Corporal in charge with my orders.

"Where to, Doc?"

"Fifth Marines, An Hoa, Corporal."

"Damn, Doc, you don't want to go there! No one comes back from An Hoa." As I heard these words I thought they had a "corny", if not redundant, tone to them. But they were his exact words nonetheless. Well, whether he was trying to scare me or not, (which, by the way, he was way too late for), he was right. I didn't want to go there, but it somehow felt right.

I dropped my sea bag and kicked back a few minutes until a CH-47 (a "Chinook" twin screw chopper) landed and I was called on the manifest. My heart was pounding as I shouldered my sea bag and ran up the ramp into the chopper.

"Welcome, aboard, Doc! Headed to the 5th Marines?"

"Yep, I reckon I am."

We were on our way. About 15 minutes into the flight the gunner said, "Doc, you are new in-country, aren't you?"

"Yes."

"Do you wanna see some 'RPG's'?"

I was just weeks out of Marine boot camp and recalled the term, "RPG's" and asked, "Rocket propelled grenades?"

"No, Doc, 'rice propelled gooks'! We got some "gooners" running down there on Go Noi Island."

I grinned and looked out the window. I saw what looked like a group of ants far below making a run for a tree line as the gunner opened up on them with his M-60 machine gun.

"Go Noi Island, huh? How far are we from An Hoa?"

"About ten miles, Doc. But if you are going to the Fifth Marines, you'll learn to hate Go Noi Island."

Go Noi Island, as it turned out was in the northernmost most part of the Fifth Marines' A/O (Area of Operations). Based at An Hoa, the Fifth Regiment consisted of 1/5, 2/5, and 3/5.

In short, three battalions make up a regiment. There are four Companies of approximately 150 each in each Battalion. So, twelve Companies patrolled and set up ambushes in the An Hoa Basin.

The Basin itself was four to twelve miles wide at the widest point, and about ten to twelve miles long, taking it through Go Noi Island. Go Noi, as I could see from the air, was an "Island" only because it had rivers on all sides.

Many thoughts ran through my mind as I was still adjusting to the unbearable heat and humidity. I was soaked. I had changed into utilities, but assumed I would get camouflage when I was assigned.

I had no idea what An Hoa would look like. On my first day in-country I heard more about An Hoa than any other area. With three Battalions based there, it had to be large. Each Battalion had its own BAS (Battalion Aid Station), where the Corpsmen had set up, operated sick call, did minor surgery, as well as some emergency surgery. There was an MD at each BAS, or at least he was assigned there. He may physically be somewhere else, but he was assigned to that BAS.

Below us was a road. I watched as we crossed a river and I saw a small compound below.

"There's Liberty Bridge, Doc, the forward BAS for 1/5. It also had 105-howitzers, 106-mm recoilless rifles, and 81-mm mortars. It is the northernmost firebase for our area of operations." "Also officially it's called Phu Lac 6".

I saw a burned out bridge, and a ferry below. A burned out piling protruded toward the sky. Apparently Liberty Bridge had no bridge at all. The Navy Seabee's were hard at work trying to remedy that. There was a small compound on the north side of the bridge, and the main compound on the south side. Altogether, it was still small. From the air I guessed you could walk from one end to the other in five minutes or less. Six miles south of there was An Hoa, home of the Fighting Fifth.

The chopper began to circle and as I looked below, whatever I had expected, it wasn't this. It was a large spread-out compound with no apparent boundaries. On the west side was a large river. Past that river was a large mountain range going into Laos. On the south side were yet more mountains. On the east side were......mountains. The north side was at the edge of a large Vietnamese ville. I soon learned its name was Duc Duc.

The mountain range on the east side was actually within 300 meters. I was far from being an authority on the military, but something looked pretty shitty about this set up. A large combat base surrounded on three sides by high ground? Who in the hell would set up a combat base where you could be surrounded on three sides without knowing it? The answer was simple - the French. Lest I was mistaken, didn't the French get their ass kicked here?

The chopper was still circling, and I saw a small airport. The compound was very big, and very spread out. I could see what looked like a large ammo dump. On the east side there were a series of small stucco buildings. Tents were everywhere. Even now, I could see sandbags all over the compound, not just on the perimeter.

The compound itself was red. The Jeeps, four-bys, tanks, and trucks had the red clay dust flying on Oct. 23, 1968. The roads wound all around and were seemingly built haphazardly as new compounds were added. The chopper descended and the ramp lowered as I stepped from the chopper. The dust was six inches deep and was flying everywhere. The rotor wash was blinding and breathtaking. The heat and sweat caused this to become mud as it stuck to my soaking wet utilities.

I grabbed my sea bag and ran to anywhere, my goal being to get out of this damn rotor wash. At the edge of the chopper pad were a series of tents. I had no idea where I was going. I questioned the first Marine I saw.

"Where's the 1/5 BAS?"

"Go up this road to the first road on the left and follow it around, Doc. You will see some white stucco buildings and bunkers. The three BAS's are all in that area."

"Thanks, man," and I trudged off.

It was about a mile away, but I didn't know that when I started. It was so hot. This place smelled like the core of hell. Shitters burning, fuel, gunpowder, steel, mildewed tents, and red dirt six inches deep did nothing to help my first impression. On the other hand, every Marine I saw spoke and was very friendly, wanting to help. A jeep went by, then stopped and backed up.

"Hey Doc, just get in country?"

I guess it was pretty obvious. "Yep, looking for the 1/5 BAS."

"Hop in Doc! Throw your sea bag in the back, and I will take you there."

"Thanks a lot, man". This was actually my first duty station with the Marines and it donned on me that maybe I should be calling him by rank. But I could care less, as long as he knew I did appreciate him giving me a lift.

"Where ya' from, Doc?"

"Missouri…and you?"

"Tennessee, Doc! Twelve and a wake-up!"

I looked at him not knowing what the hell he was talking about and he said, "Doc, in twelve days I am going home. I am so damned short I could sit on a dime and dangle my feet."

"Congratulations, man! Been here the whole time?"

"Nah, I was a grunt with Bravo Company. Got popped in Go Noi and had a bad enough wound and enough time in the bush. I have been here the last two months healing and taking out working parties. Do you know what Company you are going to?"

"I don't know shit except I am assigned to 1/5 and will probably be going to a grunt unit in a day or two."

"Well, Doc, I have nothing but respect for you guys, and I hope you make it. Be careful out there and keep your head down. All the Docs I knew were as crazy as a shit- house mouse. Never met one yet that didn't have balls the size of pineapples!"

"Well, you have now," I laughed.

"Well, you will see, Doc. It's different out there. It's pure hell, but I'll bet you that in a few days you will be doing things you never imagined you would ever do."

"You'd lose!"

He laughed and we pulled up to the BAS. "You're home, Doc! Take care now!"

"Thank you, man! I really appreciate the lift."

Nice guy, I thought.

I threw my sea bag over my shoulder and looked for the BAS office. I saw a Corpsman coming out of a door and said, "Hey, just reporting in. Could you tell me where to go?"

"I sure can," said a skinny HM3 with a huge mustache and a big grin. "I'm Roger Watson. Welcome!"

"I'm Bear. Nice to meet you!"

"Hey we got a 'Smokey the Bear' - funny as hell! Have to introduce you! He is the second in charge. Chief is right inside. Put your sea bag over on my rack and we'll fix you up with a rack when you get checked in."

I followed him to the combination Barrack's BAS, bunker and took him up on his offer. I sensed theft was not an issue around here.

"Well, what have I gotten myself into?"

"Well, Bear, you are looking at six months in the bush, and the Chief is really good about that. He will do his best to make sure you only do 6 months. Then when you get out, you can either stay here or go to DaNang and finish your tour in a nice secure area. The bush is rough, but be careful. Do your best and you'll have a good shot at making it. Main thing is, don't do anything you don't feel you have to do. No unnecessary chances, if you know what I mean."

"I plan on being careful, Rog. Thank you. How do the Marines treat you?"

"Ever been a celebrity, he smiled? It's kind of like that. The Marines are the greatest. I am dead serious when I tell you they will do anything for you, and I mean anything in their power."

I felt a little better after talking to ol' Rog, and it was refreshing that when you asked about the bush, you actually got an answer. Stateside, the issue was avoided.

Here, they wanted to help. I guess they figured you would need all the help you could get.

I went to meet the chief, and Rog went along.

"Chief, we're going to need another steak tonight and maybe a beer or two. Got a new man for you."

I stepped inside and was face to face with Chief Foldner. I was greeted with a big smile and a "Welcome aboard. Have a seat."

I sat and Rog said, "I'll catch ya later, Bear. We'll have a beer tonight after you get all squared away."

"Thanks, Rog! I'll catch you later." I was feeling a little better about all this crap, but was still scared shitless.

Chief was looking through my records, "Wow four tech ratings! After you get your six months in the bush, you can go anywhere you want to in-country."

"Yes, Chief, to be honest it's those first six months that concern me - not the last six.

"I understand that well. I know you are wondering what to expect, so I will do my best to fill you in. The guys here have all completed their bush time, and they will do their best to fill you in on what to do out there, what to carry, and so on. They are great guys, like Rog there that you've already met. He's up for the Navy Cross and will probably get it. He was hit twice by machine gun fire while dragging two Marines to safety! A hell of a good Corpsman!"

Suddenly, I wasn't feeling so good again. This same Rog who told me to be careful and not to take chances had two Purple Hearts and would most likely get the Navy Cross; the second highest medal the Marine Corps gives out? But, I didn't feel Chief was trying to scare me.

"You will probably be assigned to Alpha Co., an excellent unit with a good Company Commander, Capt.

Compton. They have lost three Corpsmen in the last few weeks. You will be here for two days, getting acclimated and issued all your gear, and then you'll be choppered out to Alpha Co. They are currently about five miles northeast of here near the Dog Bone. As for now, going through your records, I have seen nothing but straight 4.0's; so I assume you have your shit together. These guys here do, too. You will like them all, and of course, when you get your six months in, we would love to have you stay. Bear, why don't you go on up to Supply. I will give you a chit, and you can collect your gear and start getting used to it. You will get a lot of advice on what to carry in the bush. Listen to it all, and select what suits you best. I don't go for a lot of gung ho shit here. I want my Corpsmen carrying the T.O. (standard issue) weapon, a Colt .45 automatic pistol. But if you feel you have to carry an M-16, I won't bust your ass for it. A lot of guys carry 16's. We were given some steaks to grill tonight, and we will start them around 1800. So try to get back and we will have a steak and beer waiting for you along with some other trimmings. The Marines treat us great, one of the advantages of staying here when your bush time is in. The first two beers are on the Marines. If you want more it's ten cents MPC (military payment certificates) per beer. I'll see you later. Maybe Norm will serenade us with his guitar tonight. He's really pretty good if you like country music."

"Thank you, Chief. You have been very helpful." I meant it. I already liked this man. He was a young Chief - maybe 30 or so - and had already made Chief Petty Officer. I would come to like and respect him even more.

I walked up to supply carrying my sea bag, which I would put in storage. I had a weird feeling when the Marine in charge said, "Doc, if you have anything in here you don't want anyone to see if you get killed, better get it out now." I just looked at him.

"I'm not trying to scare you, Doc, but it's amazing how many of these damn things I send back to the world. Just trying to help."

"Well, if you were trying to scare me, you are way too late anyway. I'll turn my sea bag in as is."

I suppressed the fear that in a few weeks my wife would be opening up my sea bag with my Mom bawling in the background. It was an unsettling feeling.

Next was supply. I was issued my Colt .45 automatic. Personally I would have just as soon had a big granite boulder. I was a very good shot with rifles and shotguns, but was never into handguns. Oh, I had fired them, of course; but I was comfortable with rifles or shotguns and mediocre at best with a pistol.

I got jungle boots, three pair of green socks, jungle utilities, helmet, helmet cover, four canteens, web belt, Corpsman unit one (which I was told by every Doc there to get rid of) and five magazines and all the ammo I wanted. I asked about skivvies and learned that there was no such thing as underwear in the bush. Tee-shirts, yes. But boxer shorts would make you miserable. That would take some getting used to.

The grill was fired up when I got back, and cold Falstaff was the beer of the day. I met the nine Docs that were at the BAS. They were all very helpful and full of advice. The advice differed, but they were all willing to talk and to help and this was something I needed. I asked a lot of questions and found out a lot about these men. All nine had at least one Purple Heart. None of them were bragging, in fact they were all quite humble and I found myself liking them a lot. At first appearance they were just average guys, doing their job, putting in their time. But when I put all the facts together, it was impressive. Nine Corpsmen, 15 Purple Hearts, two up for the Congressional Medal of Honor, several Bronze stars, Silver stars and one Navy Cross! I was literally surrounded by heroes. Actually that wasn't quite right. The Marines they'd served with were heroes. These guys were heroes' heroes! What the hell was I doing here? I didn't belong with these guys. I was no hero and didn't want to be. I wanted to go home.

Norm sat and played his guitar and sang. He was also up for a Silver Star and had two Purple Hearts. This guy looked like he belonged at the high school prom; but here he was, a decorated veteran. I felt very out of place, but not because they made me feel that way. They were more than friendly, and extremely helpful. They told a few stories; not bragging, but recalling things they had shared in Hue City, Go Noi Island, and Arizona Valley. And I went to bed more afraid than ever.

The next day I was sent with some newly-arrived Marines out to a rifle range to throw hand grenades. I was the only Doc. Now, why was I being taught yet again how to throw hand grenades? The others went first. We were maybe 200 meters from An Hoa and I took the three grenades handed to me by the instructor.

"Doc, now you have done this in boot camp, right?"

"Right!"

"Pull the pin, let the spoon fly and lob it towards the barrel."

I pulled the pin, let the spoon fly, and threw that sucker half way to An Hoa. I didn't give a damn about the barrel; I wanted that thing AWAY from me. I did the same thing with all three grenades. The instructor said, "Damn, Doc, An Hoa is going to think they are having incoming!"

I returned that night and again we had beer and steaks. Chief asked how I was doing and I said, "I guess

I'm fine.   The guys have been very helpful." They had
been.   I had rigged up a homemade trachea kit and one
Doc gave me a doggie pack he had carried (Army pack)
that would hold a lot more gear and was also easier on
the back.   By that night I had a pretty good idea how I
would at least start out.   I listened to each man and took
the advice that best fit me.   I would hump an M-16 after
my first med-evac.   I would use claymore mine bags
instead of the Unit One issued.   My gear was arranged
so I could get to my field surgical kit and battle
dressings quickly.   I would carry IV's and two canteens
in my web belt.   I would have each squad carry another
IV.   I filled up on meds, decided what to take, and took a
lot. I wanted to have everything I needed. I knew I had
too much gear, but figured if I couldn't hump that much,
I could adjust later. I wanted to be prepared.

"Bear, tomorrow night, you'll saddle up and go
to the Alpha Company tent.   First thing the next
morning, you'll be choppered out to your unit."

"Okay, Chief, thank you for your help."

"Be careful out there, don't take chances."

I had no intention of taking chances. I had heard
all about things these guys did and had decided "not this
little black duck". They could bring the causalities to
me.

The next evening I caught a jeep to the Alpha
Company tent. There were five guys going out in the
morning besides me. I was, of course, the only Doc.
Three guys were "newbies" (Marines just in-country).
Two others were coming back from R&R (Rest and
Recreation).

I talked to all of them, but was more interested in
the ones who had been there a while. Stape was just
back from Australia. He had been in the bush ten months.
He was at Hue City. He has seen some shit, so I talked
to him a lot.

51

"It's a good Company, Doc. Good Company Commander, but a lot of guys are new. We lost so many at Hue City. But we have a new Platoon Sergeant that was with this same Company on his first tour. He was written up in "Stars and Stripes" as a point man. And, Doc, he has his shit together. He is going to turn this Platoon into a fighting unit, mark my word!"

I felt Stape was a straight shooter, and I was right. We became good friends. I would be assigned to his Platoon the next morning.

Tomorrow I would become a bush Corpsman with Alpha 1/5, Second Platoon.

Tomorrow I would meet this 23-year old Platoon Sergeant.

Tomorrow I would meet the man whom I would name my son after.

Tomorrow I would meet a leader of men.

Tomorrow I would meet the man who would teach me to be a Marine.

Tomorrow I would meet my best friend, my mentor, my hero.

Tomorrow I would meet Sergeant Vince Rios.

Chapter 4
The Bush

It was a night of tossing and turning on a small cot. Swatting mosquitoes, listening to everyone else swat mosquitoes, until around 0300, a large "BOOM" brought everyone out of their rack. I followed suit, "What the hell was that?"

"Incoming!!!!! Incoming!!!!!!!! "

I bailed out of my rack and ran behind the others to a nearby bunker, actually sandbags piled up with no top on it. We huddled in there a while, and there were four more "booms".

I was in a Tornado once when I was 12. I lived three blocks from a railroad track where freight trains passed in the night. The screaming sound immediately preceding the "boom" sounded like a tornado carrying a screaming freight train. It was deafening and horrifying. I had seen war movies. I had seen "incoming" in war movies. I had never heard anything like this. There was a squeal, then a whistle, then a scream, which I thought was my own at first. Then there was the terrifying "boom" and flash. I didn't know how close it came to us so I just listened.

"Sounds like they are after the ammo dump"

"Where is that?"

"It's ok, Doc. It's about 200 meters from here; they missed it and are probably done for the night."

There were no more "booms" that night. And soon we all went back to the tent. I couldn't help but think as I lay there wide awake on that cot, "Even the 3 little pigs had enough sense to put bricks in the walls! What good is it to be in a damn tent?"

I noticed everyone else went back to sleep shortly. I lay there and thought, "This is hell, and I'm still in the rear!"

Then it occurred to me everyone at the BAS was talking about how you had it made after your "bush" time was in. I knew a few hundred meters away they were just going back to bed, too, after the incoming rocket rounds. The veterans calmly said as we huddled in the bunker,"122-mm rockets."

I didn't say anything because I didn't know anything, but the damn thing sounded HUGE!

If this was "having it made", then what would the bush be like?

It was hard to imagine a place where I would "wish" I was back here, but that would be exactly what would happen.

I would soon dream of being back in An Hoa. In fact, I would have given anything I had to get back here.

I must have dozed off. I heard Stape stirring, and I asked, "What's going on?"

"Get your gear together, Doc. We're going to breakfast and then will be catching the chopper in about an hour."

How did he know this? I had no clue, but we went together. The food was edible. In a few weeks I would give my left testicle for a meal like this.

We got back to the Alpha Company tent, and the 1st Sgt, was there.

"Okay, men, the chopper will be here in 15 minutes. Let me call off your names. Answer when called." He went down the short list.

"Doc, you here?"

"Yes, Sarge"

"Good luck, Doc." Now why didn't he say that to the others?

Soon the thumping of chopper blades filled the air. Then, the red clay dust started flying and I had already forgotten how thick it was, how deeply you had to breathe to get air, and the side effect of all this was you just more deeply inhaled the shitty smells of An Hoa. Gun powder, fear, dirt, shitters, fuel! Maybe at least it smelled better in the "bush".

I had my pack. I had my Colt .45 and was ready to go. Soon the chopper landed and the ramp came down. Everyone ran towards the chopper gasping for air and ducking from the whipping blades. I ran up the ramp and we were off.

Many things went through my mind: Home; family; my wife; fear; doubt; and anger at being put in this situation! Damned recruiter!

We turned north, and started up. I saw a huge village below that I had learned was Duc Duc.

I looked out as we flew and saw a road running under us. It looked like we would be east of the road to An Hoa. It wasn't 15 minutes and we were descending. You could feel the adrenalin pumping. Not only mine. The newbies looked as scared as I was and somehow that made me feel better.

The chopper was almost on the ground. I saw a swarm of Marines ducking and awaiting the chopper. We had their supplies and mail. It was a green section of high ground probably a mile east of the road. The ramp came down and everyone prepared to exit. I made sure I had everything. I had no idea what I was getting into. I knew it would be bad but that was all I knew. One thought kept running through my mind. One ideal! One thing I had predetermined! The words were on my lips as I took my first step onto the ground that was the "bush". I remained silent but inside my mind the words echoed loudly, as if I wanted all to know: "Okay, assholes, listen up! I DON'T Make HOUSECALLS!!!!"

I ran hunched over towards the group of Marines. I saw a redheaded Marine-looking guy watching me and then I saw his Corpsman caduceus. He held out his hand.

"Hi, I'm Harry Warren, and I hope you die out here."

I thought I heard him wrong. I looked at him not knowing what to think, and realized I heard him right.

"Well, asshole, if I do, I'm taking you with me." Not a smile.

This was the senior Corpsman with the Company, the one who assigned us to whichever Platoon, and who we gave our orders to for meds, battle dressings, etc.

"We had a Corpsman shot yesterday in Second Platoon. You'll replace him." I wondered if this was true.

"Okay, where do I go?"

"Doc Hal will be your partner. He will fill you in." I saw a black dirty Corpsman walking my way with a big smile on his face. "I'm Doc Hal." He held out his hand and I shook it.

"I'm John, where do I go?"

"Damn! You are big! Do you have a nickname?"

"Seems to be 'Bear' most everywhere I go. I'll answer to anything, though, now. What the hell is that asshole's problem?"

"Who? Oh, 'Weird Warren'?"

"Yeah, the senior Corpsman told me he hopes I die out here."

Laughing, he said, "That's Weird Warren. Actually he's okay. He just doesn't deal well with others. He doesn't know how to handle the loss of a Corpsman...thinks it's his fault. He's not a bad guy really."

"He told me ya'll had a Corpsman shot yesterday. Is that true?"

"Actually, yeah. Just took an AK round through the femur, piece of cake."

"He just took an AK round through the femur and that's okay?!"

We talked a while, and I liked this doc from California. He seemed to have his shit together, and I felt I was fortunate to have a good partner.

"Come on, and I'll introduce you to the platoon. They're right over here."

He took me to the platoon CP (Command Post) and the first one to greet me was Lt. Propst.

"Welcome aboard, Doc! We need you. We don't go too far around here without a Corpsman."

"Well, Lt., I won't be going too far without a Marine either! You can bet on that!"

He laughed and so did I. My first impression was we would get along fine. For the most part, we would, but not without a few rough spots.

"Hi, Doc! I'm Chicken Man!" The black enthusiastic Marine caught my attention right away. I wondered about the name "Chicken Man", and then recalled a popular radio entity, named "Chicken Man", whose introduction for the radio show was, "It's Chicken Man! He's everywhere! He's everywhere!"

Next was a Marine who had an air of confidence about himself. He was 23, about two months my elder, and was about 5'10", maybe 180 pounds, barrel-chested, and looked very squared away. He had a neat flattop haircut like mine, was Hispanic, and simply said, "Nice to meet you, Doc. I'm Sergeant Rios."

I had met "The Sarge".

I settled down next to Hal, asked some stupid questions, and then noticed a Bible study going on nearby. I wasn't exactly a religious man, but thought at this point in my life I wouldn't take any chances. So I ambled on over there.

I had become a member of a denominational church so I could marry my wife in the "eyes of the Church", but whatever they were talking about was beyond my comprehension.

I sat, listened, and as I walked back to my gear thought, "Damned Protestants! They think they're better than us, but they are no different than we are."

Hal was waiting for me. "Well, Doc Bear, we have a patrol going out in a few minutes. Do you wanna get your feet wet?"

I hadn't been in the bush two hours and was about to go on my first patrol.

"Sure, might as well."

They were gathering, and I saw Stapes' gun team was going, so I was at least going with a guy who had survived Hue City, one of the worst battles of the war. I decided I would walk close to him and watch him. I also recalled that most of these guys were fairly new to the bush as well. I heard the squad leader call out, "Saddle up," and quickly grabbed my gear.

I hoped I had everything I needed and was suddenly grateful for the help and advice I had received from the Docs back at the BAS. I was about to disembark on my first patrol.

Chapter 5
<u>First Patrol</u>

It was to be a four- to five-hour trek southwest of our current position to recon the area for enemy activity and to select possible future ambush sites.

The squad leader, Lance Corporal Collier, briefed us before we saddled up.

There would be four check points. All this meant little to me at this time. I was a Corpsman with eight-weeks of Marine boot camp; and other than that, my butt had basically been in a classroom or behind a desk for the last three years.

I decided to establish my routine for patrols, like having a specific way to hump this gear.

It was a short-range patrol, so my pack would be left at the platoon CP area.

It was well over 100 degrees, so I would wear only a cammie t-shirt over which I would don the hot 14-pound flak jacket. I strapped on the Colt .45 automatic, web belt with two IV solutions, and two canteens filled with hot "pissy" water taken from the rice paddy with two Halazone tablets dropped in to purify it.

First over the flak jacket I put three ammo bandoleers. However, the ammo had been replaced by battle dressings - one of the many tips from my new friends at the BAS. I needed to do all I could to look like a Marine - not a Doc.

Next I put on my main medical bag, which was a claymore mine bag I would use to replace the much too obvious Unit One. In this I carried a menagerie of medical gear: The home-made trachea kit I had made up in An Hoa; an assortment of meds; painkillers; morphine syrettes; tape; gauze; and scissors. On the strap of this bag I had snapped my "Field Surgical Kit", which had scalpel, hemostats, 5.0 silk, suture material and a variety of things I hoped I wouldn't need.

My other claymore mine bag had my bulk meds, malaria tabs, salt tabs, and other things I shouldn't need on a short range patrol. So this was left behind, except I did pop a small bottle of salt tabs into my main bag.

Chicken Man was on point, and we slowly moved out of the tree line to begin the patrol. I stood there and let them go by, watching and waiting for Stape. I had decided to walk behind him, mostly because I knew him best and had the impression he was a good Marine.

As Stapes gun team went by, I said, "Hey, Stape, mind if I tag along?"

He laughed and said, "Hell no! Always wanted to have my own personal Doc with me!" and off we went.

The squad spread out as I had been taught in boot camp, basically 15 meters apart. We walked a paddy dike going southwest and moved slowly.

As we got to the first tree line I noticed a change. The space between men got shorter, the talk got louder and the cigarettes were lit up. It took on the look of a damn Disneyland tour! These guys were talking and shooting the bull and laughing, so I looked at Stape and said, "What the hell is going on? This doesn't look right."

"Like I told you, Doc, we have a lot of new guys and they don't have their shit together yet. Be careful, do what's right and we will make the best of it."

I knew nothing about the bush and very little about being a Marine; but I did know unless we were going to a picnic that I was unaware of, we were a disaster waiting to happen.

We reached check point 1 and took a water break in a small tree line. Fifteen minutes later Chicken Man took off, and like 14 obedient ducks we followed. We crossed the road to An Hoa and went into what was known as "booby trap alley"- the Phu Nhans.

We went through a small ville where the people tried their best to ignore our presence, and that was check point two.

We crossed a larger rice paddy. I was beginning to get a feel for the land, and these paddies were "a bugger". By the time ten men in front of me had walked across them, they were as muddy and slippery as a "minnow's dick". I had always wondered if I would be scared...well, looking at my hands confirmed that. The heat was incredible. Even my utility trousers were totally soaked with sweat. The smell of Vietnam changed very little in the bush. We were outside the realm where the bitter "burning shitter" aroma could reach us, but the smell of filth, oppression, feces (both animal and human) was a part of life here. Ahead loomed a large piece of high ground, which would be check point three.

There was a tree line perpendicular to us and another one running parallel to us. Chicken Man headed towards the smaller one - also the nearest. As we got inside the tree line Collier said, "Okay, check point three, take five."

He got on the radio and the rest started getting out canteens. I looked at Stape and he stayed back which convinced me to do the same.

"Damn, Doc, they are all cluster-fucked! One" heat tab" would wipe them all out. Stay back here with me and we will move out after they do." This man had been through some crap. If he would have told me to stand on my head and whistle "The Marine Corps Anthem", I would have considered it.

"Movin' out!" came the call. I looked around and saw Chicken Man turn right (starboard in "Navy", I guess), heading out of the tree line. All around us were other tree lines.

Now, I was not a religious man, nor did I consider myself a spiritual man, but I was about to become a believer in "guardian angels". As Chicken Man headed out of the tree line, something impressed me so strongly as if someone had smacked me in the head and said, "LISTEN TO ME! HIT THE DECK!!" I did literally hear, not audibly, but in my mind a strong voice say "HIT THE DECK!" I did, and for a second on the way down I felt like the stupidest asshole on earth. I dove to the damp ground for no apparent reason. But before I hit the ground, there was a tremendous "BOOM". Then all hell broke loose. Booby trap! Ambush! "CORPSMAN UP!!!" came the dreaded call, and I was up and running without thinking.

Now the smell was truly horrible - blood, powder, smoke, fear and destruction filled the air. I looked as I ran to the call and was amazed that this squad of Marines was already laying down a line of fire. Stapes' M-60 machine gun was set up and lighting up the tree line with tracer rounds. The Marines were returning fire, too, even the wounded Marines. I looked to my left as I ran to the cries for help and in the deep recess of the dense growth I saw muzzle flashes. It was all there. My biggest nightmare, AK-47's firing full automatic, M-16's returning fire, machine guns, "spoon's flying", grenades going off, the squad's M-79 grenade launcher pumping rounds into the tree line. "Bloop!" Then "BANG!"

I saw AK rounds digging into the dark rich ground in front of me, heard them flying by my head as I ran and recalled my statement a day ago when Doc Norm at the BAS told me, "You are like a free agent, but you WILL go out after the wounded, and you WILL do it because those men would put their lives on the line for you." I had said, "Not me, man! They can bring the wounded to me!"

I was aware as I ran that these men were doing just that. "Cover Doc, God-dammit! Put out rounds!" These same guys that I was maybe a little pissed at for walking too close and talking on patrol were "covering" my ass. They were fighting like the bunch of professionals they were.

Time both stood still and went 100-miles-per-hour. I saw a man down and dove beside him. He was returning fire with 1 hand as his left arm spurted bright red blood in the air. Severed radial artery - piece of cake! I started to apply a pressure dressing and then thought, "Okay, Doc, get your shit together. Triage. Triage. This man will make it. Go to someone hit worse." I said, "Have someone put a pressure dressing on this as soon as possible. You'll be okay!" and took off.

Cries filled the air - cries of all types.

"I'm hit, Doc!"

"Corpsman up!"

"Cover Doc!"

"Put out rounds!"

"Knock out that gun!" This was hell on earth.

I saw where the booby trap had gone off and dove down beside the lump of a man that was "Chicken Man". He was hit bad, but still alive. Triage, right? I rolled him over. He had tripped the booby trap that was the key for them to set off their ambush. Pneumothorax! That was life threatening. I quickly plugged it and rolled him over on his wounded side so only the injured lung would fill with blood. He was bleeding very badly.

Rounds were still flying by my head, and then suddenly it slowed. They had repelled the ambush and the enemy had taken off.

Chicken man was covered with wounds. I took out my K-bar and cut off his trousers and his legs were a mess. He had wounds twelve inches long, three inches deep and spread wide open. I clamped bleeders, applied probably 15 battle dressings and got the bleeding under control. I said, "Chicken Man, stay just like that! Don't move! I'll be right back."

Then I went to other wounded. Two gunshot wounds, which I treated; many, many shrapnel wounds, including the first I saw as I ran - the severed radial artery. I had three IV's going.

"Collier, get me a chopper in here stat, four emergencies, five priorities, one routine, no KIA's!" (Killed in action)

"On the way, Doc!"

I went back to Chicken Man now that everyone was taken care of, to make sure I didn't miss anything life threatening.

According to CBS, I should expect a chopper in here in 30 seconds, but this was the real world, and it would be at least 30 minutes.

The men had set up a quick perimeter to protect the wounded, which was basically everyone. Ten out of 15 were hit. Stape was fine.

I checked out Chicken Man now in depth. I cut off his utilities and as I ripped them off, I saw something else. His scrotum had been slit by shrapnel and his testicles had fallen out. I didn't recall a class covering this particular injury. I thought about what to do with them as I continued to check his many wounds, still putting on battle dressing when needed.

As I cut a sterile battle dressing open, I had an idea. His balls were still attached; they simply fell out when the scrotum was slit open. I took a battle dressing casing, opened it neatly with my knife, and took his balls and dropped them inside it. Then I broke open a bottle of Ringer Lactate and poured some of the salty solution inside. Then I sealed it as best I could and taped it to his inner thigh. I didn't tell him about that, the surgeon would find it, but I did say, "Chicken Man, now I want you to listen." I had given him pain meds but not enough to knock him out, I wanted him alert as possible to avoid going into shock with a breathing problem.

"I want you to stay on this side, just like you are laying now. If you do, you will live! You have my word. If you don't, you will die. When we put you on that chopper no matter what anyone says, you lay on that left side and don't move until you see a surgeon coming after you with a scalpel, got it?"

"Got it, Doc! Thanks." A finger was gone, and I was pretty sure one eye was lost, but he would make it.

"Is everyone else okay? All bleeding stopped?"

"Yeah, Doc, we'll make it."

The chopper came in and ten men of a fifteen-man patrol were choppered out.

I came to an understanding at this point. There was NO way I would get out of this place alive. I decided I would try to save as many Marines as I could and the sooner I was killed the better. I didn't want to go through six months of this shit, and then get killed on my last day in the bush. That would piss me off.

The remaining five of us headed back. Collier, Stape his gunner and another Marine I didn't know.

The M-16 felt good in my arms. The radio man now had my .45.

We hit checkpoint four and I was gulping from my canteen of crappy water when the guys were talking about Chicken Man.

"Poor Chicken Man, he is so fucked up."

I said, "Hey, Chicken Man will be back in the world drinking beer and getting pussy in two weeks. If you want to feel sorry for someone, feel sorry for ME! This is my first day in this hell hole and I won't see a beer OR my wife for a year!" They laughed and I smiled.

I had a feeling of respect and acceptance, and these guys had my respect. They were very young. But, man oh man, they were fighters.

We got back to the Company and the Lieutenant and Sarge were waiting for us. I gave my report and Collier gave his and we got a "Well done!"

Doc Hal wanted to know if everyone would make it.

"Yes, Chicken Man lost a finger and an eye, but with the exception of possibly shooting blanks for the rest of his life, he will be okay."

"Shooting blanks?"

I told him about Chicken Man's slit scrotum, and he laughed.

Yes they would all make it. They had to. Through no choice of my own, I was now a bush Corpsman and these were my Marines.

I began to see things maybe just a bit clearer. I had been a Corpsman nearly three years and had never understood this bond between Marines and their Docs.

There was an unwritten law. It was a law of survival and respect and it had been in existence nearly 200 years.

Marines take care of their Docs. Corpsmen take care of their Marines. It may as well be written in stone. That was the way things were, and had always been since the birth of the Marine Corps.

In a few days, a Marine would come up to me informing me he had something for me.

"What?"

"I got a letter from Chicken Man, Doc. He told me to give you this." He handed me a state-side ten dollar bill. I took it and gave him a confused look.

"Chicken Man said to tell you the Doc said you saved his balls - I guess in more ways than one!" We both smiled.

66

I had a vision and a tinge of pride at the thought of a few years from now a bunch of little "Chicken Men" running around his house.

It was my first Patrol. It would be the last time I would receive monetary rewards.

There would, however, be many rewards.

They would come in many forms.

There would be namesakes.

There would be bonds stronger than life itself.

There would be friendships.

There is a Marine saying, "Pain is temporary; pride is forever."

This was my first patrol. There would be many more.

And from them would evolve relationships that would last decades after the bullets stopped flying.

Chapter 6
The Wonderful World of Ambushes

I sat at the Platoon CP (Command Post) talking to Hal and trying to adjust to this new life. My first patrol ended two hours ago, but I knew it would be with me forever.

I heard a gruff voice outside our two-man poncho shelter we had put together for shade. Sarge was talking about the ambush that would go out that night. Bob Carroll's squad had the honor.

Each platoon had three squads. These squads rotated patrols and ambushes. So every three days a squad would go on a patrol; not counting, of course, the regular daily platoon-size patrol. Every third night each squad had an ambush. There were, if we were fortunate, two Corpsmen per platoon. So we were to alternate as well. But since there were only two of us, we would have a patrol one day and an ambush the next. If there was only one Doc, then he went on every patrol and every ambush. This was one reason so many Corpsmen were killed or wounded, and also why we Corpsmen served six months in the bush. Uncle Sam got his money's worth out of us, for sure.

Hal had been alone the day before so had been on both a patrol and an ambush. I guessed it was only fair that I go on the ambush tonight. I wasn't looking forward to it.

I guess one way to avoid the horrors of the world was to ignore them. I pretty much did that the first three years of my Navy career. I watched little TV about the war and, in general, pretended it was just another game the "lifers" were playing.

Bob Carroll didn't have that luxury. There was a handful of Marines in this company who survived Hue City eight months ago. On the final day, one of the few

68

to climb the citadel wall was Bob Carroll. He would lead the ambush tonight.

It was nearly dark and I gathered my gear, pretty much the same as I did earlier on the patrol, only this time I took three M-26's,(fragmentation)grenades, my poncho and poncho liner.

I crawled out and went to the briefing. As I walked toward the gathering, I wondered what Corporal Carell would be like, a man who had seen things so terrifying they were practically unspeakable. I slowly meandered over that way and as I got there a Marine stood up and said, "Hey Doc! I'm Bob Carroll! Want to go with us tonight?" He was smiling like he was inviting me to a college panty raid.

"Sure, Bob!" as I shook his hand. I was greeted by everyone and just had a hard time with how casual and calm everyone was. As I watched, though I got a better insight on Bob. Behind that boy next door smile there was a lot going on. That brain was churning, planning, recalling all resources, and anticipating the night ahead. If I had to go, I was glad I was going with his squad. It wouldn't last. In two days, Bob was going home. He was one ambush away from returning to "the world".

I liked him already. I respected and admired what he had endured and hoped I would never have to. Bob was maybe 5'8", 155 pounds soaking wet and tough as hell. He was a typical marine, one who had "seen the elephant". He was also friendly as hell, and I couldn't imagine anyone not liking him. Everyone seemed to. They were kidding him about being "short" and joking about him going home. He was wired. I could almost see the adrenalin pumping through his veins. Mine was pumping at a pretty fair pace as well as the briefing began.

"We are going over to the road and set up an ambush along the west side here at this curve. Hopefully, we will catch some gooks setting booby traps and can ambush them.

Also be very careful for the same reason: They booby trap the hell out of that area! If we are lucky, we can catch a sapper team setting landmines for the convoy that comes through every morning. We will have three fire teams on the road: one guarding our rear; squad CP will take the middle one."

Sounds like a plan to me, and soon we were on our way. It was about a mile to the road and we got there shortly after dark. We set in quickly and within two minutes of our arrival we were set in, had claymore mines set out, gun team covering the road, a fire team covering our rear, and we were quietly waiting for "Charlie".

I lay back in the thick grass and watched the road a while with Bob. Him, the radioman and I made up our fire team, and Bob asked me which watch I wanted.

"Third," I said for no real reason. That would put me on watch from 0200 to 0400. After a while I tried to sleep. The damn mosquitoes were like miniature helicopters. If they could train these damn things they could use them for medical evacuations and supplying the troops. I had my plastic bottle of "bug juice" and I guess it helped; but it smelled so bad I was afraid the gooks could smell it a mile away, and they probably could.

I lay back, hoping there would be no ambush, and finally dozed off. I had my head inside my helmet for a pillow, and covered with the best invention of the war, the poncho liner. I was awakened around 0200 by Bob.

"Doc, it's your watch! Just key the handset when they do a security check and wake me if you see anything."

"One more sound and I'll blow your damned head off!" came from our rear. I looked at Bob. He was as cool as I was scared. "I'll take care of it, Doc, just watch the road."

I did, and when Bob came back a few minutes later I didn't even bother to ask what the hell that was all about.

I was on my first ambush, watching for a sapper team and I was wide awake. I was blessed with great vision and with my adrenalin pumping; I didn't think I would miss anything.

The mosquitoes were loud. A fire mission went out from Liberty Bridge two miles north of us. And then another from An Hoa four miles south of us. Neither was landing very close to us. This went on for my entire watch, but I was surprisingly relaxed. I checked my watch and it was 0400. Time to wake up the radioman. Then I lay back down but couldn't go back to sleep.

At first light, we saddled up and took off towards the platoon. It was dark and the fear of hitting a booby trap or ambush was very much a reality. We got back with no problems, and I must admit I felt a little better about it all. That first patrol had pretty much given me an outlook of doom, but last night went off fine. Well, as far as I am concerned "no causalities" equals "good news".

I crawled into our two-man hootch and took a nap.

"Saddle up, moving out." The Platoon was moving again. I donned my gear again, putting my doggie pack on last in case someone was hit, so I could drop it and get to the men quicker. We were moving a few hundred meters to our new night position.

I learned we operated differently than most of the other units in country. We seldom stayed in the same place two nights in a row. We didn't dig foxholes. The reasoning behind this was when you left an area the gooks would come in, see how you set up your perimeter, and could more easily figure out how to overrun your position; or at the very least, where to fire their B-40 rockets and mortars. We instead would recon an area during the day on patrol, then move out and set up a perimeter; and then send out an ambush that night or at least a LP (listening post).   Hal took the patrol earlier and I would have the ambush that night.

We got set in as a platoon, and soon heard a heated discussion about tonight's ambush. Some "genius", obviously one who wasn't going out on it, decided we would have a "roving ambush".

Corporal Provost came over to the platoon CP to be briefed. I noticed a lack of enthusiasm in Sarge. I was a "boot" to the bush, but I had sure as hell never heard of a "roving ambush".

We were to hump about 500 meters to a specific tree-line; set in for an hour; hump another 300 meters; set in there for another hour; hump back in a circle towards the Platoon CP; and set in for yet another hour. Most of this humping, according to the map, was across wide open rice paddies, and then we would move into the dark looming tree- lines.

Now, not knowing about tactics or Marine theology, I was thinking, "What the hell are we going to ambush?" We were going to parade around all night in the wide open, give the NVA ample opportunity to listen to us splashing around in the mud, and then set up their own ambush. This is a 'roving ambush'?

In the Ozarks where I was raised, we have another term for it – "BAIT!" But, what did I know, so off we went.

I fell in behind the radioman, a Georgia boy named Arthur. We got about 200 meters from the platoon when Art falls into the rice paddy for the first time that night. The radio was the cause and also this also went with him. I would give the dive a score of about a 1.2. Way too much splash and his feet weren't together. There would be many more splashes to follow. The radio was heavy, the paddy dikes slick and the night black as a witch's heart. I kept pulling him out of the mud and off we would go. We got to the first check point and set in. Actually that's not exactly correct. We found the piece of high ground, approached it, and when we weren't blown away by a waiting NVA battalion, we all piled in. I was thanking God we weren't shot down as we approached the tree-line.

I lay down in the dark grass and trees keeping my gear on, thinking I probably couldn't find it if I took it off. I lay my head back in my helmet and within seconds I was fast asleep.

Now this surprised me because, because no two ways about it, I never expected to see daylight again. Someone woke me up saying, "Moving out, Doc!" and I lay there a second thinking, "Who the hell dreamed this up? It couldn't be someone on our side!"

Off we went again. Art was pretty well dried out for the first 100 meters and I saw this dark piece of high ground ahead. To the left was a stretch of tree-lines. On the right, another smaller piece of high ground. This dark tree-line straight ahead was check point two.

My mind went back to Marine boot camp and I remembered being taught to avoid "L" shaped ambushes and even more so "U" shaped ambushes. This was an upside down "U" if there ever was one and "F Troop" here was roaming right into the center of it. What amazed me most was someone actually PLANNED this! My ass was puckered up like a possum in a persimmon tree as we got closer and closer. When we were within 50 meters I thought, "What are they waiting for? They have us right now, and we wouldn't have a chance." To my amazement, nothing happened. We marched right into that tree-line like the seven dwarfs following Snow White, only we were 14, and the point man looked nothing like Snow White.

This time we set up a quick perimeter and I set in next to Provost.

"Let me ask you a question" I whispered. "Have you ever been on one of these roving ambushes before?"

"Doc, this is the stupidest thing I have ever seen. I have been on at least 100 ambushes but this is a damned suicide mission!"

I felt relieved. At least I wasn't the only one who felt like a guillotine blade was going to fall on us any second.

Soon we moved out again. I got to know Art rather well. I felt sorry for him, falling and splashing around with everyone saying "SHHHHHH!" It wasn't his fault. That radio was heavy, the dike slick, and he couldn't see shit. If I had that extra weight on my back, I am sure I would be doing nose dives myself.

After two more check points, I saw day breaking. I wanted to kiss the ground, something, anything. I never thought that patrol would end.

We slipped into the perimeter of the Platoon. Sarge and the skipper were there to meet Provost. I headed for the CP. On my way, I decided to make my feelings known.

"The fucking genius who thought this up can go on the next 'roving ambush' and he can take my Unit One, because I have been on my first and last one!"

I went to lie down and fell asleep. I was inwardly pissed. I had figured it out, and I am sure Sarge already knew. That's why he didn't like the idea of a "roving ambush". Some asshole Colonel in An Hoa wanted some "numbers" and decided if we went on a so-called "roving ambush" we would get hit. They would know from where, and had artillery and air strikes all ready to call in on certain co-ordinances. They were willing to let us get our shit blown away so they could retaliate with air and artillery.

I woke up after a while and as I walked past Sarge I saw him grin. I didn't know why, but I came to learn he was glad I had made that comment. Nothing scares a commander more than having a patrol or ambush and no Doc along. Also, perhaps Sarge saw I would stand up and speak my mind if I thought something was screwed up and would get good men killed for no good reason.

I was getting to know the ol' Sarge, and knew he cared about his troops - all of them. He expected a lot of his Marines, but he would fight tooth and nail to keep injuries from happening unnecessarily.

I had learned something else from this ambush: A Doc can and did get away with almost anything. Things a Marine wouldn't dare voice would just bring a small look of disapproval from an officer when we said it. In the next few months I would insult Company Commanders to their face, as well as Platoon Commanders – well, all but one.

In a few months I would walk by the Colonel's tent and make sure he heard me as I called him an "Elmer Fudd-looking son-of-a-bitch". These comments were, however, justified. He did look like Elmer and pissed me off in a big way when he came into the bush during an operation for one day then put himself up for the Silver Star. I had been in the bush two days. I only had 363 more to go. During this time no one would mistake me for a career man.

Chapter 7
Chasing the Orange Bag

A week after the "roving ambush" we were off on a major Company-size move. It was a long hump. We would cross the road, continue west through the Phu Nahns and make our way to the river and set up a company-size ambush as well as recon the area across the river. The river was a boundary for all practical purposes. The area on the other side of the river was called "The Arizona", named so because it was considered "Indian country".

There were several "areas" of the basin: Phu Nahns, Arizona, Go Noi Island (the large area with rivers on all four sides), Charlie Ridge, Cu Bans, and Dog Bone. There were many areas but these were the most talked about - especially Go Noi Island and the Arizona. These two areas were where "Charlie" seemed to be most active. I had been to neither so far.

It was a long hump and my mind drifted as I wiped the constant sweat from my face so I could see. The helmet and flak jacket seemed a part of me now. They were hot as hell, but I reached for them automatically when we were moving or going on patrol. I also noticed my vocabulary had changed a lot. Of course I had learned more military terms and Vietnamese slang, but even my southern drawl had adopted a lot more "Fuck it!" and "Kiss my ass!" I also noticed I talked rougher, not always like a gentleman as I usually tried to be. I guess there was something to the ole saying, "Ya bark like the dogs you're runnin' with."

I watched Sarge as we slowly moved along. One hundred and fifty or so Marines spread out in a long column snaking our way to the river. Sarge impressed the hell out of me. I watched him now, his eyes constantly moving, alert, knowing how he would react in any given situation. I more or less had no clue what I would do in any given situation other than to try to get my ass down if we were hit.

We were the "point" platoon and were nearing the river. Sarge was directing the "point man", telling him which way to go as we crossed the last large rice paddy before the tree-lined river bank. I had no doubt he was the best Marine in the platoon. In short, he had his shit together.

The point element entered the tree line and I could almost hear the running water. Visions of a nice bath and a swim ran through my mind as a possibility. I could see the point squad moving in quickly and setting up a quick perimeter.

"BOOM!" One hundred and fifty men braced themselves trying to anticipate the next move. "BOOM!" "Corpsman up!" came the now familiar dreaded call. "Marine down!" I ran with my head as low as possible not knowing what to expect. No small arms fire yet - just shouts of pain and confusion. I ran by the Marines ahead as they made way for me. They were crouched, awaiting orders to assault the tree-line or set up security. I just ran toward the blast. I watched and was aware even as I ran that these Marines were waiting to "cover" me. As of yet, we hadn't taken any fire. I broke through the tree-line and saw and smelled the effects of a booby trap. The point man was down. I saw him lying on the ground, his body jerking as I dove next to him to examine him. It was Woody, and he was laughing.

"Are you hit?"

"Yeah, Doc, I'm hit in the neck"

"Why are you laughing?"

"It's my third Purple Heart, Doc! And it's not bad! My ass is out of the bush! I'll spend the rest of my tour pushing chow in An Hoa or guarding some fucking lifer, but I am out of the bush!"

He was right. A pretty good size chunk of shrapnel hit his neck, but missed the carotid artery. He would be fine and would be placed in my memory as the happiest causality I would ever have to treat.

In a few days I would be asked about this wound. The Marine Corps centers itself around pride: Pride in your Unit, Corps and Country. A lot of things can be forgiven in the bush. One thing, however, can't: Self-inflicted wounds. They were the mark of a coward and a disgrace to the Corps. I didn't think this was a self-inflicted wound, mainly because it was the neck. It made sense that if you were going to shoot yourself or "frag" yourself, the self- imposed target would be the leg or possibly an arm.   I discovered later that sometimes a guy will stab himself in such areas to take away suspicion from himself. I hate to even mention events like this because I hate to think any Marine is capable of such cowardly actions. My personal opinion, at least in this case, was the injuries were due to a booby-trapped grenade. However, self-inflicted wounds unfortunately did happen.

The Company moved in and set up a perimeter. The bad news was there was no doubt the enemy knew exactly where we were. I called in the "med evac" chopper and a jubilant Woody waved good bye to his buddies.

Second Platoon had the right flank and despite the certainty that there were probably more booby-traps around, it was a beautiful place. The river was fast and deep, maybe 40 meters wide and we could see the "Arizona" clearly on the other side - at least a portion of it.

Second Platoon was set in now; I put my gear in with Sarge as we set up in a hootch. It was maybe an hour before dark and we were aware they knew exactly where we were. Instead of moving, we were sending out two "LP's" (Listening Posts) in case they came too close. First Platoon and Third Platoon would send out squad-sized ambushes.

Stape's gun team was set up facing the "Arizona".

Soon I decided to walk around some, checking out the area. We hadn't tripped any more booby-traps, but that still didn't mean it was safe. So I tried to walk in the footprints where others had walked before me. I was approaching Stape's team when sniper fire opened up on us. The rounds were close and I hurried over to his gun team and set in. We were returning fire, though I didn't really see a target at this point - just a general area where the sniper had fired from. Stape worked out with his M-60 machine gun and it was an awesome weapon.

"Doc, look here!"

I crawled to him, "What?"

"Look on that bank right across from us."

I looked and soon saw the biggest gooks I had ever seen. They looked six-feet tall and were heavy as well.

"They're 'Mountain' people!"

"What the hell are 'Mountain' people?"

"They're from the mountains up north. They're big and very good fighters."

In the darkness, I could make out three of them and Stape's team opened up on them. They returned fire, but our M-60 was a superior weapon. They were no longer visible and I assumed were dead.

I asked Stape if I could shoot that sucker and he said, "Sure, Doc. Go ahead and fire where we saw the gooks."

I did and it was a feeling of raw power. I got it to eight-round bursts and felt pretty good about it. I sat there a while "shooting the shit" and decided I would go back toward my hootch, thankful I wouldn't have to go out on an ambush tonight.

As I was walking back, I noticed a sniper in a Vietnamese hootch taking aim through his scope. I didn't even know we had a sniper with us, but I recognized his weapon, a Remington 700 ADL 7-mm Magnum. This was a very fine rifle. I watched a while and he was still looking through his scope. I walked up to a Marine standing there.

"What's going on?" he asked.

"He's got a gook about 800 meters out sitting on a stump; I think he's going to pop him." I looked through the binoculars and, sure enough, there was a gook on a stump.

Now I had killed a lot of deer in my life, but none of which was 800 meters away. The sniper took a long aim, and I just didn't think he could hit him. Hell he was so far away and only partly visible.

"CRACK!"

The 7-mm Mag popped loud and I watched for a second and the guy was still there.

"Missed him," I said. And just then he disappeared from the stump. He dropped like a box of rocks. One hell of a shot! I had always thought I was a good shot, but I didn't think I could have made that one.

Right before dark we got a chopper in. This meant mail call, supplies, and we knew they knew where we were. The cargo was always a treat, but this time more than usual. New uniforms! I had just worn mine ten days and they looked new compared to most, but they were big on me. I had lost about 20 or 25 pounds in ten days. I slipped into my new utilities and thought I would maybe recommend the bush for Weight Watchers.

We all changed and turned our skuzzy ones in, piled up high. Then I saw a big orange bag coming around. The chopper was already gone, but none of that registered in my mind yet. We all put our dirty utilities in the bright orange mail bag.

Night was coming on us and the call came, "Moving out!"

I had mixed emotions about this. It was late for a company-sized move, but on the other hand, I knew we were likely to get hit that night. We didn't dig in and we were for sure not going to surprise anyone tonight. We saddled up and moved out. First Platoon dropped off. Then we took off to a piece of high ground leaving Third Platoon with the Company CP. We had only gone about 300 meters but still we had moved and I was glad.

Sarge said, "Doc, we'll set the Platoon CP right there covering that trail, so find us a soft spot." I laughed. Now I did something I was supposed to do, what I preached like a Southern Baptist minister to my Marines to do, but I myself had never done it this quickly. I picked out a spot and sat down and took off my boots and socks. The socks were new, but I still don't know why I did this so fast. My feet weren't even very wet. I sat there a second and decided I would get up and take a look around so I stood up and quickly said, "Ouch! Damn!"

"What's the matter, Doc?"

"Damn thorn I guess."

I went on and looked around. It was nearly dark. I got back to our POS (position). No poncho hootch tonight - too visible. And then I stepped on it again!

"Ouch! Shit! I hope I don't lie down on this thing!"

"What is it, Doc?"

"It's a damned thorn or something!"

Sarge came over and we dug around looking for the "thorn".

"'Bouncing Betty'! Engineer up! Check carefully this area is booby trapped!!!"

Everyone came to attention quickly and searched for more booby traps. Except for the fact that in the bush you don't wear skivvies, I would have filled mine. I had stepped on a "Bouncing Betty' – not once, but twice! Had I not taken off my boots and socks I would no doubt have been compost for the local villagers.

A "Bouncing Betty" is a mine that has three prongs that stick up. When stepped on, it causes a small explosion - usually enough to take a leg off. Then the mine pops up about three feet and a big explosion takes place, usually large enough to take out a whole squad.

This shook me up. Sarge called the engineer and he came and blew the mine and the visual I had when that thing went up brought many things to mind, the first of which was that apparently my guardian angel was still with me. I am not mocking when I say for some unknown reason, it wasn't my time yet.

Secondly I realized we were always a breath away from death.

The night went by without further problems. The next morning we saddled up and were off. We were heading towards the Phu Nans. I was walking behind Sarge. As we snaked our way out into a huge rice paddy, I happened to look behind us. There was a Marine who usually walked point and considered by all to be an outstanding point man, carrying a huge orange mail bag - our old dirty uniforms. I thought about this and I guess it made sense not to leave them behind because the gooks could use them, but I still thought we could have burned them before we moved out.

The Marine carrying the bag was called "Stuckey" (pronounced "stoo-key"). His name was Lauren Alvin Stuckenschmidt. I was about to get to know him and in two years my son would be named after him and the Sarge.

The rice paddy was enormous and the company had joined us and 150 Marines were stretched out across it.

"Doc, look at those villagers." It was Sarge and I listened and looked.

"See them moving out of the rice paddy?"

"Yes."

"We are about to be hit. Look at them. They are nonchalantly getting to high ground, either to hide or to shoot at us."

In about ten minutes, his prediction came true. Snipers! A lot of snipers! They were all firing single rounds, aiming at a target - not shooting randomly. I dove behind a paddy dike and we were returning fire, though we had no real target.

Soon here came the object of the snipers' attention in the form of Lauren Alvin Stuckenschmidt and his big orange bag! He ran by me and said, "Doc, they are zeroing in on me and this damn bag!" Off he went and I took off after him. They opened up again, rounds kicking up dirt in front and between us. Stuckey hit the deck. I dove behind him.

"Doc, they are using this bag as a target!"

"Okay!"

Off he went with me on his heels.

Again they opened up on us, the rounds getting closer and closer, and we both dove for cover in the mud behind a paddy dike.

"Doc, they are shooting at ME!"

"Okay!"

Off he went again and again I took off after him. It didn't occur to me he was telling me to stay away from him. My thoughts were simple: If he gets hit, I want to be close to him so I can get to him before he dies. So, I followed Stuckey over 1,000 meters under sniper fire all the way with him constantly telling me

The Names NOT on the Wall

they were shooting at him and me agreeing and following him!

The point finally got to high ground and the M-60 was set up and opened up on the snipers. Stuckey got to high ground with me right on his ass. He dove behind a grave and I dove in beside him. He looked at me seemingly bewildered.

"Doc, why did you keep running behind me? They were targeting me and this bag?"

"I know. That's why I was running behind you. If you got hit I wanted to be close by!"

"Damn, Doc! You either have balls that wouldn't fit in this fucking bag or you are crazy as hell!"

Actually, it was neither. I was ten days into the bush and didn't know shit. Someday, if my guardian angel stayed on duty, I would learn.

85

Chapter 8
<u>Mercy, Doc</u>

Nearly three weeks in the bush now and although still scared shitless, I felt a lot more comfortable. I really was beginning to like these guys. I also loved the respect I got from them though never felt I deserved it. I was also more comfortable in the fact that I was no longer quite as big a target as I was three weeks before. I was around 200 pounds now – 36 lbs. lighter than when I came here.

Other things had changed, too. I smiled as I watched Stuckey on point. We were still in the Phu Nans about three miles north of An Hoa and I felt much more at ease when Stuckey was on point. The orange mailbag incident had been the start of a friendship that, though I didn't know it at the time, would last a lifetime. Stuckey and I were getting close. We talked a lot when we were able to, and got along well. He had asked me if he could be my "apprentice". So I was teaching him first aid, names of drugs, how to treat various wounds, and we both knew it was all just because we liked and respected each other.

I was walking behind Sarge and we were getting closer, too. He was two months older than me so I called him "the ole Sarge". With the exception of "Pappy", a 25-year old fire team leader, we were the two oldest men in the platoon - Sarge at 23 and I would be 23 in a couple of weeks.

I carried a map now and knew where we were at all times. I had to call in med evacs and such, but that was pretty much all I knew about map reading. I knew where we were. I knew where Liberty Bridge and An Hoa were on the map. Everyone talked about "the Bridge", knowing there wasn't actually a bridge. It was, though, where we hoped to go to get some time in the rear, hot food, a shower, so it was that "carrot dangling in front of us". It gave us something to look forward to. Right now I could hardly imagine what a canteen cup of cold milk would taste like - or eggs. These "C" rations (more appropriately called C-rats) had already lost their appeal to me. The little stoves we made out of empty C-rat cans with heat tabs in them to light and warm up the "balls and beans" or "ham and mother fuckers", were hardly worth the trouble. They still tasted like salty crap.

"Gooks in the tree line!"

Stuckey had gotten close to them before they knew we were in the area and they panicked and opened up on us than run the other direction. Sarge immediately had a plan in mind.

"Gun teams up! Online assault! Shoot anything that moves! Frag all bunkers!" We were going to take the ville the gooks were in. I heard Sarge call in artillery, 105's, on the high ground where the gooks were retreating. The Sarge had his shit together. Within seconds of the call, "Gooks in the tree line!" he had us organized and deadly. I looked over the Platoon as I went online with everyone else. Things had changed there as well. We assaulted the tree line and fired all the way, ripping into the hootches and banana trees. I recalled my first patrol and saw a big difference. This was becoming a well-oiled, deadly machine. The guys respected Sarge. They had confidence in him. These 18 and 19-year old kids never lacked courage or ability. Now they had a leader. Yes, our Platoon Commander was in charge of the Platoon, but Sarge seemed in control, at least for the most part. He had been through all this shit before and it would take a fool not to take that into consideration. The skipper was no fool.

I was capping into the tree line that made up the village boundaries but we were not receiving return fire any longer. Our tracers were red every fifth round; the gooks' were green, also every fifth round. At night it was quite a show.

We moved into the ville and set up a quick perimeter.

It was a small ville - maybe 20 hootches. All hootches in the Basin looked pretty much the same: grass sides, sometimes supported by bamboo, and for shelter purposes reinforced with C-rat cardboard. They all had a bunker where the Vietnamese slept and where they went for protection. They all had a cooking area with usually a pot hanging over a fire with a chimney made of dried mud keeping the smoke from infiltrating the hootch. There were also clay water jugs usually filled with rice paddy water, although some of the villes had wells.

We moved in and set up a CP area within the perimeter and I dropped my 100 pound pack with a thud and lay back on it. I was exhausted. We all were. It was a long Platoon-size hump. The rest of the company was doing the same thing a few hundred meters north of us.

The last week or two, we had an addition to our Platoon CP, which gave us another man to stand watch when I wasn't out on ambushes. His name was Jack and he was an interpreter. Jack spoke Vietnamese fluently and it was almost comical. I had been around him a lot, of course, and had come to like him. He was a country boy, a blonde-headed, grinning, "Opie-Taylor" kind of guy. He was always grinning. That was what made it comical. Picture a blonde-headed, fair-skinned, Tennessee boy with a grin like a possum in a persimmon tree, who walks like Opie Taylor, with a southern drawl as pronounced as mine, speaking Vietnamese! Jack was with us for a reason, and it was time for him to do his job.

"Hey, Doc, I'm gonna mosey around here and talk to some villagers, want to go with me?"

Had to like this guy! "Sure" I said as I grabbed my M-16 and medical bag, leaving everything else at the CP.

Jack was going to interrogate some locals and try to get some information on the fleeing NVA. We went inside the closest hootch which was pretty much like all the others I had seen.

Now my Vietnamese vocabulary consisted of maybe three Vietnamese words, none of which would be permitted in my home. So I basically came along to watch, listen and possibly learn a word or two.

The first thing the grinner did was pull his .45, grab mamasan by the arm and put the barrel of the Colt automatic to her temple, grinning like Opie all the while. He started screaming questions at her, pumping her for information, and the whole situation brought reality to me.

"Holy, Shit! He's going to kill her!" was my only thought. Mamasan wouldn't talk, so the grinning blue-eyed Opie grabbed a little girl, maybe five-years old. Still smiling, he put the .45 to her head and again, started asking mamasan questions. At this point, I mentally put Jack on my "most-likely-to-become-a-serial-killer" list. He was enjoying this shit! Mamasan got the message, but kept saying, "VC number fucking TEN!" (Vietnamese slang for bad!) "Marines number fucking ONE!" (Vietnamese slang for good!) That was about all she would say. Jack threw the little girl to the deck and grabbed a young boy, maybe three-years old. Again, he put the .45 automatic to the boy's temple and began questioning mamasan. He cocked the hammer. This time she started cackling like a Rhode Island Red hen laying a goose egg.

I noted 3 things mentally at this point:

1) Jack was nuts and he loved this. I would never go with him again, not just the two of us.

2. It was obvious the boy's life was much more important to mamasan than the girl's life, and this fact left a sick feeling in my stomach.

3. We weren't finished at this ville. Jack got a lot of information.

We soon left the hootch and I let out a silent sigh of relief that he hadn't killed any of them. We got back to the CP and I didn't say a word, just lay down on my pack and watched things unfold as Jack talked to Sarge and the Lt.

There was some discussion and soon, Sarge had a plan. We moved out of the ville, went about half a click (500 meters) and set in - the whole platoon. I had overheard and knew I didn't have to go out on an ambush. There were other plans for us.

At 0300, we saddled up and moved out again, all of us. We were going back to the ville where we had interrogated the villagers, but by a roundabout route. I could see Sarge was pumped. He was excited about this move. As we got close to the ville, Sarge sent out the three squads to their assigned positions. It amounted to an upside down U, with the Platoon CP in the center of the U with a squad. The other two squads had the two M-60 machine gun teams. It was a large U. There was maybe 500 meters between the 2 squads on the side and we had the other squad and a blooper-man with us along with Frank who carried a 3.5 rocket. We were spread out in fire teams with Sarge, the radioman, Lt. and I making up the fire team in the very center of the U. We had about an hour until the sun would rise. I dozed off about the time the "morning star" appeared and was asleep when Sarge nudged me.

I was pumped as I lay there waiting for Sarge to say something. I knew in my mind the way we had set up the ambush and it looked like a good plan. The adrenalin was flowing even as I slept and it amazed me I could sleep knowing soon, if all went well, we would be killing other humans. The never ending fear was still with me as well as the damned mosquitoes, but my pulse was racing with excitement. It reminded my of a deer drive back in the Ozarks. The only difference was.... these deer carried AK-47's. I was awake, leaning against my pack when I heard these words for the first time.

"Mercy, Doc!"

These words were followed, as they would be many times in the next few months by Sarge's deep bass laugh.

I got to my knees behind the brush next to Sarge and looked out across the field.

There they were, about 30 hardcore NVA soldiers coming straight at us. Their AK-47's were glistening like a southern belle's cheeks on a sultry day.

"Mercy Sarge!" escaped my dry mouth.

He laughed that bass roar once again, and from that time on it was a personal thing between the two of us. The words "Mercy, Doc!" would speak volumes to me from now on. The deep low laugh would always follow. It would become his way of telling me, "Doc we are hitting the shit, but we will come out of this okay."

My "Mercy Sarge!" would mean, "I'm ready Sarge! You can count on me!"

It was a term we would use to signal each other from now on. There and even back in "the world" when we would reunite. It would bring a lot of strange looks at times, an unspoken bond.

Now the NVA were closing in on us. They were right where we wanted them. Sarge looked at me and smiled.

"Let's get some, Doc!"

We opened up on the oncoming NVA soldiers. Several dropped at the initial burst. They were within 100 meters. I was firing on semi-automatic and noticed Sarge was, too. Accuracy was more important right now than fire power. The gooks, what was left of them, turned north and the right flank opened up on them. More dropped. One gun jammed, but we had position and surprise on our side. I kept firing, amazed how fast I could now reload a magazine. Most fire fights last maybe two or three minutes. This one didn't. This one was like shooting trapped fish. They turned south and the other squad opened up on them along with an M-60. Tommy was pumping blooper rounds into what was left of them.

We ended up taking five prisoners and the rest were KIA's (killed in action). That's the way you want an ambush to go, wipe them out or capture them! And we didn't lose a man. My kind of ambush! It didn't happen that way often but, we rejoiced in it now.

The Company was near and I heard the radio as Capt. Compton asked and listened to the skipper tell how it went. Capt. Compton was very pleased. Tomorrow we were going on a company-sized move. As a reward, Second Platoon would have the company CP with us.

Tomorrow I would meet Capt Compton and his crew.

Tomorrow I would get to know Capt. Compton very well.

Tomorrow, I would have my hands in his chest.

Chapter 9
<u>Knowing Capt. Compton</u>

We moved out of the ambush area shortly after the firing stopped and the prisoners were secured (bound and gagged), not to mention severely threatened against trying to escape or try to warn their comrades, by Jack the potential serial killer. I noticed a bounce in the step of the whole Platoon, including my own. We got some! We planned an ambush, set it up and set it off, plus we just finished killing 25 men! The fact that they were men with wives, children, sisters and lovers hadn't hit me yet. Minutes ago I had gone out with the others, walked up carefully to a dead NVA soldier, quite possibly one who had one of my rounds in his torso, and took the AK-47 from his still warm hands and thought, "Gotcha, Motherfucker!"

Twenty-five men dead! Twenty-five men would make up the entire male population of many Ozark mountain communities. The bodies were in absurd positions of death. We checked each body carefully, removing anything of value, securing weapons, letters, knives pictures and supplies, as well as souvenirs. The funny thing about it was it didn't bother me. It seemed the right thing to do - appropriate behavior, like taking out the trash, or putting a large mouth bass on a stringer. They were ours. We were the conquerors. The spoils belonged to the victors.

We moved about 300 meters and set in. We would get supplies, rest for a while, and then move out on a company-size move. The Company CP would join us and we would have them in our ranks, almost doubling the size of our Platoon due to the "Weapon's Platoon" (60mm mortar team, 3.5 rocket team, interpreters etc.) We set in on a piece of high ground awaiting the chopper that would bear C-rats, smokes, candy, coffee and whatever else we were lucky enough to get. This would be done now so we would move afterwards and the chopper wouldn't give our POS away.

Around 1000, the blades beat the thick smelly acrid air as the chopper descended. We would also load up our five POW's to probably be set free in a few weeks as "chu hoys" (enemy soldiers who converted to our side, at least until they could escape).

It had been a week since we had supplies or mail, and it was a welcome sight. Mail call was the highest point in the life of a grunt. I leaned back on my poncho and counted my letters. TWENTY-ONE! Eight from my wife, eight from my 16-year old niece, three from Mom, one from my Dad and one from my step-Dad.

It is hard to describe what getting mail means to someone on foreign soil, fighting a stupid war no one really believed in, but it was the ultimate stimulant. I was very fortunate, and didn't take it for granted. In my three weeks in the bush I had already had a few Marines come to me about their "Dear John" letters. I didn't worry about getting one. I knew it wouldn't happen to me. That was very comforting. Linda wrote every day, and I was doubly blessed in the mail department. My 16-year old niece wrote me every night before going to bed to say her prayers for me. Now this is a high school junior with her first car, first "real" boyfriend, who without fail wrote her "Uncle Funny Bunny" a letter every day. They were light, funny and I cherished them. It gave me an opportunity as well to keep my sense of humor alive. I would answer, not everyday but at least once a week with letters on C-rat boxes, prescription pads, or anything I could find unusual. I even wrote on the writing tablet I always made sure that I kept dry. I was and am a sentimental man. I kept all my letters. My bulging pack was a testimony to this and I often got teased about it. I "humped them on my back" until I could send them to the rear with someone I knew would put them in a safe place for me until I could ship them home.

Now, if you don't think as an individual that you can make a difference in someone's life, let me assure you the innocent love of my 16-year old niece for her "Uncle Funny Bunny" made a difference in mine. Thank you, Beck, I will always love you.

"Saddle up, we're moving out!" came the now familiar call. It was noon and we were to hook up with the company CP and contain them on the Company move. It was a sort of reward for executing a successful ambush. First Platoon had point. We had the center with the Company CP and crew, and "third herd" brought up the rear. In the center of our Platoon was Capt Compton, his radio man and the rest of his CP. I was about eight men behind them with Bravo squad behind Sarge as usual. We were still in the Phu Nans, heading toward, though not going into, the "Arizona". We were going to set up in the area close to the river that separates "booby trap alley" from "Arizona". There is a lot of high ground here and we humped several hours without incident or contact.

As we were crossing a relatively open area (which always made my ass pucker), I saw a huge graveyard ahead. We were heading straight toward it. At least there were mounds there, and I was soon running to one as the point element was ambushed.

"On-line assault! Shoot anything that moves! Frag all bunkers!" The ambush had spread. The whole tree line was spewing hellfire and brimstone at us. Automatic weapons, rockets, and tracer rounds were cutting through the air around us. I dropped behind a grave and returned fire. No call for "Doc" yet, so I kept capping, checking out the route I would take to assault the tree line when the inevitable call came.

Suddenly there was a huge explosion. "Boom!" Then another. "Boom!!!"

"CORPSMAN UP!" came the dreaded call. I had my pack on last and as I ran to the call, I reached in front and released the convenient snap on my "doggie pack". That allowed it to fall to the ground so I could get to the wounded faster. Later that day when the action had slowed or stopped, a Marine would bring me my pack. It wasn't something I would worry about for a second. The pack wasn't important at this point, but the respect and knowing my Marines would look out for me was ever present. We ALL wanted me where I was needed ASAP. It was unspoken, unwritten, but etched in stone. We looked out for our Marines; they looked out for their Docs.

I had my medical gear very much at my disposal now and M-16 in my right hand as I ran toward the screaming.

"Doc! Corpsman up!"

"No one move! Land mines!"

"Mine field!"

As I ran, I knew the "no one move" didn't include me or Doc Hal. We were both hauling ass to the wounded by different routes.

The NVA had seen us crossing the open ground and had set off an ambush, on the other side of the mine field, knowing we would assault their position. We were now being hit by AK's, SKS's, B-40 rockets and a recoilless rifle.

I was running as hard as I could, watching the muzzle flashes from the tree line. I hit a small knoll and pushed off towards the cries as it donned on me....... "Mine field!?" I was in mid-air as this revelation came to me. Suddenly I became very aware of where I was going to land. I quickly searched for a foot print, or a place that looked safe to land, and then push off again.

The company was pinned down now and the mine field a major worry, which temporarily stopped our assault of the tree line.

"Put out rounds! Shoot anything that moves! Assault the tree line! Frag all bunkers!" Doc Hal was ahead of me in the column and as I topped a knoll I saw him treating a downed Marine. There were several hit. I saw one Marine laying face down, writhing in pain, blood seeping from underneath him, so I dove beside him hoping I wouldn't land on yet another landmine. I grabbed the wounded Marine and rolled him over. I was looking straight into the eyes of Capt Compton.

"I'm dying Doc. They got me in the chest. I can't breathe." It was more a statement than a cry for help. It was as though he had accepted his fate and was okay with it.

I opened his flak jacket and cut off his t-shirt. His chest was bloody and I saw bubbles frothing from his left lung.

"Skipper, you will make it. It's your lung. Listen to me and you will make it."

"I can't breathe, Doc. I'm dying."

"Skipper, listen to me! Do you remember in first aid class about a "sucking chest wound?"

"Yes, Doc."

"Well, right this second I am plugging yours off and you have to listen to me!" I was working quickly on him, distracting him while I worked by talking to him.

"I trust you, Doc. I'll do what you say. Just tell me, is it my heart?"

I couldn't help but chuckle, "No, Skipper, if it was your heart we wouldn't be having this conversation. I almost have it plugged. I will bandage it tight and then roll you over on your left side. I'm not giving you morphine. I want you awake and alert. Your left lung will fill with blood, your breathing will be a little heavy but you will breathe. Your right lung will get you through until a surgeon repairs your left lung. Skipper, it's as simple as this: If you stay the way I have you, you will live. If you roll over or lay on your back, both lungs will fill with blood and you will die. Do NOT move from this position until you see a surgeon coming at you with a scalpel, got it?"

"I got it, Doc. Thank you."

There was other wounded so I moved on. Ever since that first patrol I had given in to a silly superstition. I would not now, or ever wash the blood off my hands. Stupid, I know, but it didn't matter. I wouldn't do it. I felt if I did then it would be like saying, "Okay, I am done with this. Let whatever happens happen to him." By keeping his blood on my hands, he was still my patient; I felt I wouldn't let him go until he was safe. I feared if I did, he would die. My hands had been in Capt. Compton's chest and they were bloody as I moved to the next causality. I wiped them on my utilities, but would never wash them.

Capt. Compton stayed the way I had put him. He would make it. He was an Annapolis graduate who took the Marine Corps option (which I could never see why anyone would), but an intelligent man.

I heard him as I worked on the radio man, "I owe you, Doc!"

I smiled, "No, Skipper, this is what I do for kicks!"

I ran to another wounded Marine, applied pressure dressings then on to another. The company had taken the tree line and the enemy had fled. The problem was, I was still in the middle of a fucking mine field and had to have a chopper brought in to put the wounded on. It was on the way, and shortly it landed. As he was being carried aboard, I heard Capt. Compton say, "As my last act as Alpha Company Commander, I appoint Lt. Propst Company Commander of this Company."

An hour ago, Lt. Propst was our Platoon Commander, Capt. Compton our Company Commander and Sarge our Platoon Sergeant. That was all out the crapper now. Everything had changed.

I grabbed my gear and started looking for my Platoon, making my way to the tree line that had been secured. They had gone on ahead, taken the high ground and set up a perimeter.

Well, hell! When this patrol started we had a chain of command - now it was all different. It donned on me Sarge was now Platoon Commander and I felt good about that.

I found my unit and plopped down to take a swig of hot pissy water. I lay back, thinking how the Marines I treated would make out, and soon Sarge was walking toward me.

"Hey, Sarge, looks like you have it all under control."

"Mercy, Doc! I need to talk to you."

"Sure, Sarge, what's on your mind?"

His voice was lower than usual, at least in volume and he had a troubled look on his face.

"Doc, it looks like I will be Platoon Commander for a while."

"Good, Sarge! I can't think of anyone more qualified!" and meant it. Actually, I was glad he was in command. The man had his shit together.

"Well, Doc, I need you to help me out."

"Sure, Sarge, what do you need?"

"I need you to make sure the patrols you go on and ambushes are set up right. Check lines, make sure everyone knows what to do, have their claymores set out, good fields of fire, and make sure no one falls asleep on watch."

I was staring at him now.

"Sarge, are you on drugs?" I continued, "I'm a Doc, not a Marine. With the exception of eight weeks of Marine boot camp, I have been sitting on my fat ass in a classroom for the last three years!"

"I have been watching you, Doc, and I think you are valuable to this Platoon - a leader. I've seen you learn and watch the last three weeks - and I need you. You are a Doc. You are older than the others. They will listen to you if you make suggestions."

"Shit, Sarge! I don't know what to say."

"Say you will help me."

"Sarge, I will do my best, but you are going to have to teach me what to do. I don't know shit about this Marine crap."

"Doc, trust me on this. You and I are going to become VERY close."

I was in a daze.

"Doc, I'm taking out a reactionary force after the gooks that ambushed us, and I lost my helmet in the fight, can I borrow yours?"

"Sure, Sarge. Want me to go with you?"

"No, just your helmet. Do you mind if I take this target off of it?" He was talking about a plastic bottle of "bug juice" I kept in the band around my helmet.

I had just received my first lesson from the master. The fucking white bottle was like a target to a sniper.

"Sure, Sarge!" and he handed me the bug juice which I now put in my claymore mine bag.

He would joke about this for some time - the target on my head. Along with the joke was always a lesson. Along with the smiles, he would teach me to be a Marine. In the process, he would save my life.

Chapter 10
<u>Sarge</u>

Sarge was a Texan, born in September, 1945, in the San Antonia area. I liked the fact that he was two months my senior and now usually referred to him as "The Ole Sarge". He was an E-5 Sergeant and now Platoon Commander. Normally a Platoon Commander is an officer, usually a Second Lieutenant, or as we called, "boot Louie". Even a Platoon Sergeant was supposed to be an E-6, or Staff Sergeant. Not being militarily-minded, I put little or no faith in rank. Nor did I care for "lifers". My favorite saying (not original) was, "Lifers are like flies, they eat shit and bother people." Sarge was an exception. He got respect by deserving it. Wise beyond his years, he excelled in Marine tactics. I found he was also an out standing teacher.

"Honor; duty; Corps; and Country" WAS the Sarge. "Doc, it's all about honor. If a man will lie to you, he will steal from you. Learn who you can trust in the bush by observing his character. Look how he treats others, does his duty, helps his comrades. When you find a man with honor, you can trust him in the bush. Oh, he may get blown to hell and back, it can happen to anyone, but he will do it with honor."

"If a man has no honor, he will lie to you. He will fake fire fights, sandbag ambushes (go out on an ambush and set in at a "safe" place, or not go out at all and give radio checks like they were on the ambush site), and eventually get good men killed. It's all about trust, Doc. Learn who to trust by listening to what they talk about, like about duty, and how the treat others of equal or lesser rank."

I know this is a sensitive area so I will simply state this as my point of view. I guess I knew Sarge was

101

Hispanic, but the only time this ever came to my mind was when I was trying to figure out why this man excelled in the bush. Some of the following I know to be fact. Some I am piecing together just from observation.

I imagine it wasn't easy in the 1950's and early 1960's being Hispanic in the Deep South. We never talked about this, but I felt Sarge had at least one, maybe both parents that were strong role models. Sometime, probably in early adolescence, Sarge decided, "I will show the world no one is better than me." He stood out in practically every area: Sports, academics, and popularity, and was determined to be the best. He boxed, played football, ran track and still kept his grades up.

At 5'10", barrel-chested and handsome, getting the attention of the opposite sex was less of a problem than getting the approval or her parents. He was a natural born "protector". In my personal opinion, any parent who wouldn't want this young man as an escort for their daughter is a parent who had their priorities screwed up.

In 1963, Vince decided to serve his country. I am sure there was no other consideration. He would do this as a Marine: One of the few, the Chosen, the Proud. He would excel here as well. On his first tour, he would be on the cover of "Stars and Stripes" in a story titled "Point Man". Ironically, he was a point man for the very same Company he was now serving as Platoon Commander, Alpha Co. First Battalion Fifth Marines, First Marine Division.

If "Jimmy the Greek" were to figure the odds of this they would be astronomical. If he were to figure the odds on my trying to learn to be a Marine, they would be off the chart. That in itself is an example of the leadership of this man. I had no intention, EVER of learning tactics or how to kill the enemy. I was a

Corpsman, and I had taken an oath to serve my country and that I would do to the best of my ability. But this man, just by saying, "Doc, I need you to help me," had changed everything. Now I wanted to learn. Now I had to learn. The Sarge needed me.

It had been nearly a week since I was told about the "target" on my helmet. Every hour was a learning experience. Sarge was a teacher, a living example. On a move, before we would saddle up he would say, "What do you think, Doc?" This would get me thinking about the move. As we humped our way to the next A/O (Area of Operations), he would say, "Hey, Doc, if we were to get hit right now, what would you do?" Or, "Where do you think they would hit us from? Do you think this would be a good ambush site?" He had me thinking all the time, watching, learning, getting into this Marine shit. Before this, all I really thought about was, "Where is the best place for me to walk in case we get hit."

Today we moved into the "Dog Bone". It was a large ville four miles NE of An Hoa. It was called the "Dog Bone" simply because on the map it looked exactly like a dog bone. The ville was used by both sides. Today, it was our turn and there was no sign of the enemy in the ville as we quickly moved in. As soon as we got inside the ville, we were swarmed by children running to offer to fill canteens with well water, give back rubs, and it was obvious this was a frequented site for different units. Children were begging for C-rats, cigarettes, and shit discs, (a carob chocolate-looking bar of candy we sometimes got when we were fortunate enough to get SP's). I was in column, watching the children when I noticed a little girl maybe four or five years old. She stood back from the others and had a different look. Her face was more rounded. She was a little larger than the other kids her age. She was shy, not

103

begging and offering her services like the others. I had the immediate feeling she was an outcast.

Our eyes met and I felt this strange connection with this little girl. I couldn't explain it and I still can't, but I felt something for her I tried hard not to feel for these people. I was learning to hate the Vietnamese, but when I saw her, there was no hatred. First of all, I was sure she wasn't Vietnamese - at least not all Vietnamese. Her father was probably Chinese and had come to train the men of the ville four years ago to be Viet Cong. I looked at her again and as our eyes met she smiled for me. I found myself smiling back.

We set the CP in a hootch near the center of the southern portion of the "Bone". I was laying out my poncho and poncho liner for a place to relax and saw the little girl was shyly hanging around. I immediately came up with a name for her. From now on, when we came to this ville, she would be "Chi-Com" short for Chinese Communist. I called to her now, "Come here, Chi Com, I have something for you." She cautiously walked toward my hootch and for the first time I looked into those big brown eyes. There was something there in those eyes - innocence, intelligence and fear. She stood back a ways and I pointed to my medical bag and said, "Bacse!" (bok-see, Vietnamese for doctor). She came a little closer. I extended my hand with a "shit disc" in it and she shyly smiled. I kept my hand out and she slowly worked her way to me and reached out for the shit disc. I let her take it from my hand and she smiled for me again and happily ran away. It was the first time since I was in the bush that I could say I really felt something for these kids. It's something you avoid with the rationalization that there is really nothing you can do for them and it is best not to care about them. Keep your distance; don't let yourself care or it would eat you up. Chi-Com had overcome those boundaries.

Maybe it was because she seemed an outcast in her own ville, maybe it was because she looked different from the others, and maybe it was the innocence or the shyness. Whatever it was, I knew this little girl had somehow touched my heart. I knew the next time we came back here I would look for her and have a "treat" for her. I also felt a deep sadness. What kind of future could this little girl possibly have? What would her life be like? It was an unpleasant thought and I tried to get it out of my mind, but those eyes kept hauntingly appearing. Yes, our next time through here, I knew I would be looking for those bright innocent eyes. I also knew they would be watching for me. Somehow, for some unknown reason we had made a connection. I had the same feeling I had the day I got my orders for the 1st Marine Division….. Fate had been set in motion.

Sarge was sharing the grass hootch with me and Phil the radio man.

"Doc, do you have the ambush tonight?"

"Yeah, Sarge, I think I am going with Burke's squad."

"Come here. Let me show you where you are going." Sarge showed me on the map a piece of high ground along a trail that ran through the north western sector of the Dog Bone.

"Here, about 300 meters from where we are now, this looks like a good spot. You will be pretty concealed by banana trees and should be able to slip in there unseen. This trail leads both to the Dog Bone and also the foothills in case the gooks come in tonight to get food or pussy. They could come from either the foothills here, or from the east on their way to the foothills. Make sure claymore mines are out and I am telling Burke I want two men up, one man down on watches. They don't know we are here and we have a damned good chance of surprising them."

"What gun team is going?"

"I think its Berry's turn. Stapes had the ambush last night. I will have Burke put Brice on point. He's a good point man and will get you there without being seen."

"No moon tonight, Doc. Keep your eyes open and keep oriented. If you spot gooks, no M-16's or M-60's unless you know you can take them all out quickly. Use claymores and M-26 grenades, Doc. No muzzle flashes."

"Ok, so we will basically be at this 'T', set in, and cover our rear and the two routes going through there?"

"Yeah, you'll need a fire team covering that big rice paddy just in case, but most likely if they come, they'll come the way you came or from the east or west."

"Okay. Guess I'll see you for breakfast. I'll take my eggs scrambled, light."

"Sure, Doc. If you happen to raid a chicken's ass tonight, I'll scramble them for you myself."

I laughed and checked my gear: M-16 was cleaned and oiled; four M-26 grenades; compass; K-bar; and, of course, my entire medical gear. Tonight I would take my poncho liner and no poncho. They made noise and it didn't look like rain. I checked out my medical bag and bandoleers of battle dressings. I would take twenty pressure dressings, surgical kit, my main bag with pain killers, morphine, anti-histamines, Serax, Lidocaine, tourniquets, syringes, and a small pharmacy. It was a short hump, so I only took a small bottle of salt tabs.

It was nearly dark when Burke came to the CP for briefing. I had been with him a time or two and liked him. He was a tall 19-year old Louisiana boy with a good sense of humor and was a pretty good guy. I listened to Sarge brief him and took it all in once again. I had been on a few ambushes by now and knew things usually didn't go as planned. You can tell a lot by looking at a map, elevation, cover, charted trails, etc. But until you were actually there you didn't know how good a field of fire you would have, how big the trail was, whether or not the trail had been recently used and a multitude of other important factors.

The adrenalin was rushing through my veins as we saddled up. Brice took point and I let them file out and dropped in behind Burke. I could always feel the small hairs on my back and neck stand up when moving at night. You couldn't see bobby traps. You couldn't see shit tonight. It was "black as Coalie's ass", as my step-Dad used to say. Hearing was different. Sound seemed to carry even farther on a dark night. I had made sure my canteens were full to the brim so they wouldn't slosh, but I could hear one sloshing up ahead in the column. We were on high ground with no rice paddies, so booby traps were a possibility, even though this was supposedly a "friendly" ville.

I could barely see and was keeping Burke in sight as we moved through the trees and down the trail. It was always a question of which was better: Should you follow a known trail and risk booby traps or being ambushed; or make a new trail and in the process make a lot more noise. In this case, we followed the trail. As dark as it was, this was fine with me. I heard stumbling and grumbling and smiled as I recalled a "session" I had with Sarge a few days ago before going out on an ambush.

"Doc, when you get set up, if you hear someone coming and they are talking and smoking a cigarette or laughing, don't shoot, it's a Marine." Then he laughed hard at his own joke. I didn't always realize it when it happened, but his jokes usually had a point.

We approached the intersecting trail and were at our ambush site. I slowed and watched Burke set in his squad and gun team. He immediately set the gun team in, facing the huge rice paddy to our front. I thought about this and how to approach him. I had no authority actually. He was the squad leader; I was the Doc. I decided to say something anyway before he got everyone set in.

"Hey Burke!" I whispered, "Don't you think it would be better to set the gun team in on this trail we just came in on?"

"Well Doc they will have a better 'field of fire' here".

I recalled a medical term called "portal of entry", which meant the way a virus or bacteria had entered the body. I didn't know at the time that the Marines had a similar term called "avenue of approach".

"I know, but this is the most likely "portal of entry". If they come in here they will probably come the way we did, or from the east or west. They aren't going to be sloshing around in that rice paddy; and if they did, we would have time to reset the gun."

"Good thinking, Doc. Berry, set your gun team covering this trail we came in on."

I also thought it better because if they came from either the east or west all the gun team would have to do is pivot and they could cover either direction, but I didn't mention this. We had 5-3-man fire teams counting Burke, myself, the radio man and the gun team.

Burke put one fire team covering the rice paddy which was a good idea. The gun team covered the trail we came in onto the south. He put a fire team on both the eastern and western trail. I made another suggestion.

"Ya'll know they will either come the way we did or from the east or west. So do you think maybe we should put two claymore mines on the eastern and western trail and one on the southern trail where the M-60 is? Then we'll have more fire power. And if they would come from the north, we will hear them and can reset the mines."

Burke smiled and said, "Sounds good to me, Doc," and instructed his fire teams. I felt so out of place. Hell, I WAS out of place. I wasn't even actually a Marine and I was making these suggestions to a squad leader on how to set in his squad. The funny thing about it is he listened. There were probably several reasons for this. First, I was four years older than him. Second, Marines are taught from day one to respect their Docs. Third, it made sense. As they were setting in, (we would set in right in the middle, right on the "T"), I let this Marine/Corpsman relationship go through my mind. I was basically in the Navy. Marines basically hated Sailors. We were the exception. For the last 190 years this relationship had existed. Marines hated Sailors unless he happened to be a Corpsman attached to the Marines. Then it was totally different. There was instant respect. Never had I had gotten such respect without earning it. Actually I had never had this much respect even if I DID think I earned it. They took care of us. They expected us to take care of them. That was the nature of things. It had always been that way through 190 years of history together and it would never change.

A few days ago we were on a long hot hump. At the end of it, I sat down on a stump next to Stuckey and said, "Damn it's hot! I would give my left nut for a cold beer."

Stuckey smiled and I thought he had found what I said to be funny. He got up and went off down the trail. A few minutes later, he came back and sat beside me.

"Here, Doc."

He handed me a Budweiser. It was hot as hell, but it was a beer and it had nutrients.

"Where did you get this?" We had been in the bush for a solid 3 weeks and I knew whoever he got it from had been humping it on his back for damned near a month.

"Just drink it, Doc."

"Stuckey, tell me who gave you this. I want to at least thank him."

"Just drink it, Doc."

Now, that may not seem like a big thing to some people; but in the bush, it was.

Someone, and I would never know who, was taking care of "Doc". That was the nature of the relationship between Marines and Corpsmen. Corpsmen were the highest decorated members of anyone in the military per ratio: More Congressional Medals of Honor, Purple Hearts, Silver Stars, Navy Crosses, and on down the line. I think it all boils down to this: How in hell could you let a man lie there and bleed to death who would carry a beer on his back for a month and then anonymously give it to you, wanting no thanks, no recognition, and no gratitude. The answer is simple: You can't. You will get to him, and he will cover you - both willing to die for the other. It had been that way for 190 years and that beer helped me understand why. I had been in the bush a month now. I had never in my life had a rapport with anyone like I did with these guys - even the ones I barely knew. They were my Marines. I was their Doc. For the next five months that was carved in stone. The one thing I had yet to realize is that it wouldn't end in five months. For the rest of my life, these would be my Marines.

Burke asked me which watch I wanted and I took the 0100 to 0300 watch. That was when you were most likely to make contact, and if we did, I wanted to be awake. It wasn't quite 0100 when Burke nudged me awake.

"Doc, we have movement."

I got up and was immediately alert. Burke and I crawled to the fire team who spotted movement on the east trail. They were right. We had two claymore mines covering that trail. As dark as it was, I could make out a long column of NVA. It looked to be about fifty. We were fifteen!

"Are the claymores all out?"

"Yeah, ready to blow."

"They are a-ways off. Think we can move another one over here?"

"I think so, if we keep low and quiet."

We moved three fire teams to cover the trail the gooks were coming down, leaving one on our escape route and one to our rear.

I whispered to Burke, "Man, call Sarge! Tell him what we got and see what he says." Burke talked to him, and then I did as well.

Sarge told us, "You are out-numbered four or five to one. When they get close, like 25 meters, blow your claymores, throw all grenades. And make your "dee dee" back here as fast as you can. Do NOT fire the M-60 or any M-16's. They will know where you are and will wipe your ass out. Blow the claymores, throw the grenades, and while they are wondering what the hell happened, get your asses back here!"

We set in online. We each straightened the pin on our grenades and the claymores were ready to blow. When they were about 35 meters away, Burke set off the claymores. Three huge "booms" went off almost as one and we heard screaming and confusion. They were dying and bleeding. Then we all threw our grenades. I didn't know if they thought they were being hit by artillery, booby traps, ambushed or what, and I didn't care. I just wanted everything blown and to get the hell out of there before they figured what happened.

I threw my last grenade where I saw a clump of NVA on the ground, and whispered "Let's get the fuck out of here!"

We were all soon running as fast as we could go. I was scared as hell but felt an urge to laugh which I suppressed. We just ran the way we had come - no particular order. The platoon knew we were coming and wouldn't fire on us. I heard screaming and crying and shouting...and closer, from within our squad, some giggles. I had a menagerie of emotions running through me. Adrenalin was pumping like hell. I was so pumped it was like I could feel each blade of grass I set foot on. See every movement. Fear started to subside as we got to the perimeter. I realized I was getting into this Marine Corps crap.

Sarge was there to greet us. He was smiling. "Well done men."

I went past him and went into our hootch. I grabbed a canteen and drank deeply. My throat seemed parched. I took off my flak jacket and lay down on my poncho liner. There would be no sleeping tonight. I was wired. I lay there a while and Sarge came in the hootch. I could see him smiling in the dark. My senses were sharper than I ever dreamed possible. I felt everything, recalled every scream, each blast, every cry and even the subdued rejoicing as we ran back to the Platoon. I closed my eyes and tried to sleep. Phil was there with the radio, still awake. I heard Sarge lay down, and then heard him speak.

"Get Some, Doc!" and he laughed.

I simply said, "Mercy, Sarge!" and laughed as well.

Chapter 11
Doc Bear

I lay there trying to fall asleep, but that wasn't going to happen. It would be daybreak soon. A few minutes ago we had set off a successful ambush. I had no idea how many we had killed but judging from the screams and crying, there were many, and probably more would die today as a result of our actions. I felt no guilt, which surprised me.

I let my mind examine how things had changed in the last few weeks. As a Navy Corpsman our medical responsibilities were limited. Back in the "world" we could pass meds, start IV's, change dressings, suture wounds, and give patient care. Capt. Green had even had me come to the OR a time or two assist him in a couple of surgeries. I even got to help once on one of Doc Brown's many operations. I remembered watching the procedure and was amazed at the grafting. Capt. Green had taken yet another portion of bone from Doc Brown's Iliac Crest and grafted it to what was left of his femur. When he was finished, he nonchalantly said, "Ok, finished here, close it up, Bear."

I stood there.

"Pardon?"

"Close the incision. You have sutured before. Close him up and make it pretty."

I had sutured before but nothing like this. I was as nervous as a long-tailed cat in a room full of rocking chairs, but did it. It took a while due to the depth of the incision and I had to do both interior and exterior sutures. It actually looked pretty good and I was maybe just a little proud, and very flattered that Capt. Green had such confidence in me.

Two years later, it was a different world. I had grown to love Orthopedics. I missed it. Here, there was no Capt. Green to guide me, to make sure I didn't screw up. Here the responsibilities were overwhelming. Chief had said, "Bear, do whatever you have to do to keep that man alive until he gets to DaNang. That is your responsibility. Keep him alive, and I don't care what you do to do it." In the "world" we maybe held sick call in some places, and routine care. Here, we could do open heart massage, direct transfusions, tracheas, cut downs, tie off bleeders, and tourniquets. The lives and limbs of these men were literally in our hands. It was scary as hell. A few days ago I had done my first trache. It was a matter of life and death and there was no other option. I had never even seen one done. Yes, we were trained to do them. We practiced on mannequins, even oranges, but oranges didn't bleed when you cut into them. It wasn't a hard thing to do; it was just an awesome responsibility. Here it is the graveness of the situation. Your responsibility was to the Marine you were treating. We had no one to call for consultation. There was no MD available. We had no contact with the "Chief" in An Hoa. We were on our own. We had no one to answer to - except our conscience.

Chief had told me we would never be second guessed. We were expected to do whatever it took to keep that man alive long enough to get to 1st Med Battalion, or the "Repose" (a hospital ship just offshore). If a man died we didn't have to answer for it - only to ourselves. And that was the greatest burden of all - living with a bad decision; realizing too late you could have done something to save that life. I had been in the bush only four weeks, and though we had lost men, none had died after I got to them. I hadn't realized my worse fear. No Marine had died in my arms because I didn't know what to do. Not a night went by that I didn't think about that. I thought I had matured a lot in the last three years. I had confidence in my abilities. I also knew I had limitations. Every night I reviewed what I had learned in my schools and from my experience. I have to admit I thought I was probably as competent as anyone else in the bush medically. I knew one other thing: If I fucked up and let a man die because of overlooking something or not knowing what to do, I would have to answer to me. I would never forgive myself.

Serving with the Marines was something I had dreaded and tried to prevent for over three years. Things had changed. I was proud to serve with these guys. I was proud to be a "bush Doc". I was still sure I would die being one.

The ambush was over. Tomorrow we would go check it out. I wasn't looking forward to returning to the scene. Fifteen of us had inflicted death and destruction on maybe 50 men. I still felt the "rush". I remembered how scared I was when we opened up on them. I remembered being relieved when they dropped and wailed in pain and death. I relived running haphazardly back to the Platoon CP area. I was running as fast as I could, looking back and expecting to see the NVA opening up on us from behind. I remembered the laughing of the other guys. Someone had said, "That Doc is a gung ho motherfucker!" I grinned as I thought of that now. If only they knew how scared I was. If only they had a clue how fast I would fly back to the safe Ozark Mountains in southern Missouri. But, the reality was that wasn't going to happen. I was reasonably sure I would never see the sun set over the spring fed Meramac River again. I would never float down the Big St. Francis River flipping a top water lure over by a log where I hoped a small mouth bass was lurking. I would die a bush Corpsman.

My thoughts drifted to my childhood. My parents divorced when I was three. My mom and step-Dad married when I was four. I went back to my very first memory. I was about one-and-a-half-years old, crying on the couch as I watched my dad beat my mother with a broom. I had mentioned it to her after I had grown and she was amazed I remembered that. She told me I had stopped him by throwing my baby bottle at him. I didn't remember that part, but will never forget him hitting her with the broom. Still, I wrote my Dad. We got together two or three times a year, but I had never forgotten that. I don't think I had forgiven it either. I know as an adult I pretty much stayed out of other people's business and minded my own. There was one exception. I would NOT stand by and watch a woman being either verbally or physically abused. That is the ironic part of my first memory. My family all taught respect for women. "Boys don't hit girls, EVER, for any reason." Yet, that was my very first memory.

I remember my Mom and step-Dad's wedding. We all drove to Arkansas to a Justice of the Peace. My new step-Dad was my biological Dad's brother. Yes, I am from the Ozarks. He was also a kind and gentle man, yet a prize fighter and Golden Gloves Manager. I loved him. By example I saw you could be both strong and gentle. You could have the ability to beat the shit out of another man yet treat him as a gentleman.

I learned to box at an early age and wasn't bad. I never liked being hit though, but felt obligated to box for my step-Dad. I did it for three years. There was one thing about boxing I liked more than any other. It kept me out of fist fights. No one wanted to fuck with me. I was very big for my age anyway, weighing 195 and standing 6'1" at 13-years old. Consequently, I usually fought or sparred with guys three or four years older than I was. That helped me develop my skills, but the desire to hurt other people was never there. Oh, I would. When in the ring, I became very aggressive. It wasn't that I enjoyed it, I was doing it for my step-Dad, but the aggressiveness came because I wanted it over as soon as possible. I pretty much reacted the same way in the "bush". I was here because I had no choice and I wanted it over, one way or the other. At the age of 13, I gave up boxing and took up football. The coach was thrilled with this huge 13-year old, solid, 6'1", 195 lb. freshman, who had four years to play. When I graduated from high school, I was 6'2" and 205 pounds. Basically I stopped growing at the ripe old age of 13.

I was an average student at best and was always told I should be an honor student. I did not apply myself at all. I listened in the classroom, did my home work, and that was enough to get me comfortably by, so I never took a book home or did extra studying. I only dated girls from other schools, probably because they didn't flirt with me, or perhaps it was because they did. I had "crushes" on girls at my school, but never acted on them. I wasn't aware of it, but probably I feared being rejected by girls I knew. Teachers liked me because I was a gentleman, even though I rarely studied. Academically I was that way until Chief Valdosta got my attention. From then on, I was a 4.0 student in all my classes.

I went to college one year and didn't take that seriously either. After my freshman year, I took a summer job as a Carpenter Apprentice. A guy that came to my Dad's fishing camp who was a business agent for the Carpenter Local and he liked me.

By June of 1964, I had found a drive-in restaurant I liked. Oh, the burgers were great, but that wasn't what drew me to it. I arrived every morning around 0700, even though it was 35 miles from my home, and got a cup of coffee to go. Later for lunch I would go there and get a "Whattaburger". This I ate. The coffee I poured out each morning. There was a blue-eyed brunette that had caught my interest. I was shy. I was actually pretty popular in high school and college, but had never been "serious" about anyone. It seemed I was always attracted to brunettes but approached by blondes. The waitress was named Linda and I worked with her Dad. I liked him a lot and he was always trying to get me to ask his older daughter out. Linda, it seemed, already had a boyfriend. I wasn't interested in the sister - blonde. I didn't flirt at all. Every morning I would pull up to the drive-in and hope it was the brunette that came to wait on me. It always was. There were two other girls that worked there - twins about my age and blondish with very large boobs, kind of "Dolly-Parton-looking", that got them a lot of attention. Linda thought I was coming there to see them like most everyone else was, but I wasn't.

I had become friends with her Dad and was going to take him on an overnight float trip. He was home one night talking about it. Linda said, "I know him, I see him every morning when he comes in for coffee."

Jim said, "That can't be John, he doesn't drink coffee."

Caught!

The next morning I pulled up in my 1955 Ford and got out to order my coffee. I walked to the window and as usual, was dressed in white jeans and tight fitting t-shirt. Linda came to the window.

"Can I help you?" She smiled.

"Yes, may I have a cup of coffee please?"

"And how would you like that?"

"With everything in it, please".

"Everything?"

"Yes," I said wondering why she asked. I always ordered it that way. I got to the subdivision where we were working. I had been out late the night before and was pretty sleepy. I decided I was actually going to drink the coffee this time. I opened the lid and there staring at me was a pickle with clabbered milk clinging to it. Now I understood what she meant by "everything" and laughed.

I tossed the coffee and that afternoon, she came by, feeling guilty I guess. She brought me a Pepsi and her Dad a coffee. She was embarrassed and I laughed and accepted her apology. I asked her if she would like to go out Friday night, and she accepted. Within a week I was sure I would marry her. Twenty-nine months later, I did.

My step-Dad was a big influence on me. He was incredibly strong with a 50-inch chest. Unless he was in the boxing ring, he was as gentle and kind as any man can be. He had taught me a motto that took a while, but eventually became dear to me: "You can be anything you want to be and you can do anything you want to do; but if you are going to be a bear, be a Grizzly!" Thus along with my size came my nickname: Doc Bear.

The next morning we saddled up and went to last night's ambush site. Sarge had warned me not to expect too much. "Doc, the NVA won't leave a body count for us, they will drag off the dead and hide the bodies so statistics don't build up against them. Don't expect to find much."

We didn't. There were a lot of blood trails, but no bodies and no weapons. They had cleaned it up pretty well, but we knew we had done a lot of damage. I don't know what body count the Skipper turned in and honestly didn't care.

Sarge asked if we could sit in at the same place again that night, and the Skipper agreed. I was surprised at this. We generally moved every day, but Sarge said, "Doc we have a good perimeter here, and I think we can maybe set off another ambush over here," as he pointed to his map.

It was fine with me. Hal had the next ambush so I would stay at the CP. We returned to the ville and later that day Chi Com came slowly over to my hootch. She was such a cute little shit. Those eyes could bore a hole right through you. Her smile was genuine and I had the impression she didn't give out too many of them. I dug in my pack and handed her a can of pear C-rats. The policy was never giving them anything that wasn't opened due to the fact that it would probably end up in the hands of the NVA, but I did this time. I knew she would find a way to get to the fruit when she needed it. As she walked away my heart confirmed my first impression. This little girl was special. She made me smile.

That night the ambush was briefed and went out. I stayed at the CP with Sarge and Phil. I took the 0100 to 0300 watch again and awoke to small arms fire. It was M-16's. I sat up and made my way over to the radio which Sarge was monitoring.

"What's going on, Sarge?"

"I'm not sure yet, Doc."

There were a few M-26 grenades exploding, then a few more bursts of M-16 fire. By now I could easily tell the difference between an AK-47 and an M-16. The AK had a "cak-cak-cak" sound. The M-16 was much faster and distinct.

Soon Cummings came on the net. "Alpha 2, this is Alpha 2 Charlie. Be advised we have been hit. We set off the ambush and threw grenades. The gooks have M-16's." Sarge grinned. "They must think I just fell off the turnip truck, Doc."

"What?"

"They are staging an ambush, hoping I will call them back in."

Sure enough, soon Cummings was back on. "Alpha 2, this is Alpha 2 Charlie. We have lost the element of surprise when we had to return fire and request permission to return to the perimeter."

"Alpha 2 Charlie, this is Alpha 2 Actual (Commander). Request denied. I think we need those M-16's back. See if you can recapture them." Sarge unkeyed the handset and laughed.

The next morning they returned and stuck to their story, but they knew Sarge knew what they had tried to pull.

Some squad leaders would want to do this at times, but it was not a smart thing to do. I had patrols where the squad leader wanted to sandbag, pretend we went all the way and actually stay at the first check point, then come in after a few hours. I wouldn't go along with this. I found it paid to do what you were supposed to do, be where you were supposed to be. I didn't want to be ambushed by friendly troops or hit by H&I because we were in the wrong place. There was another reason I wouldn't sandbag ambushes or patrols.

My mentor had taught me many things all with principle. It was all about honor. It was about trust. I would never sandbag an ambush or patrol.

We were moving out that afternoon. A chopper came in with supplies and mail. It had been a good Platoon Op. No causalities. Today we would hump over to the Phu Nans. Tomorrow we would start yet another platoon-size op. Tomorrow I would learn a very important lesson. Sometimes you get them; sometimes they get you.

Chapter 12
<u>Sometimes They Get You</u>

"CORPSMAN UP!!!" Here we go again. We are getting our asses kicked.

We had left the Dog Bone, humped west, and crossed the road to An Hoa (an wah), to an old CAP (Combined Action Platoon) unit stronghold now called Henderson Hill. The CAP unit hadn't worked out. It kept getting overrun, so they sent the Seabee's in to level it. Now it was a large barren hill with a crater on top and a few scattered fighting holes around it. All around the Hill were "friendly villes" that were considered "wealthy". "Wealthy" meant they had a few chickens running around and several of the villes had well water. It was my first time there. When we approached, I was surprised to see the grinning children. They were offering back rubs, well water and "beaucoup" (boo coo) compliments. "Marines, number fucking ONE!!" They, of course, wanted C-rats in return, and their favorite - cigarettes.

We had linked up with the Company for this move and had all arrived at Henderson Hill together. It was about a mile south of Liberty Bridge (which I STILL hadn't seen), and a little over four miles north of An Hoa. The next morning we were going on a company-size operation. We formed a long wide line and were "sweeping" our way to An Hoa. Theoretically, I guess we were going to "clear out the An Hoa Basin of Viet Cong". What we were doing in reality was clearing out all the booby traps that had been set for us.
This was "Booby Trap Alley" and I was rushing now once again to yet another cry for "Corpsman Up!"

The squad had set up a quick perimeter around the two latest casualties of this screwed up plan, and I slid beside the first one, took a quick look and said, "Get me a chopper in here, emergency med-evac." I knelt beside Frazier and his leg was a mess. I took my K-bar and cut off his trouser legs. Both the tibia and fibula were shattered. He was bleeding profusely so I had to work fast. I also had to make a quick decision. I put a tourniquet on the leg right above the wounds. Without benefit of x-rays, I had to decide whether to: 1) Leave the tourniquet on, take the leg and give him a better chance of survival yet condemning him to a life with one leg; or 2) Decide there was a chance to save the leg, go in, tie off bleeders, and stabilize it so there would be no farther damage in transit. I checked his toes, saw there was blood getting through, and decided to go in and save the leg.

"Someone go in one of these hootches and find me a thick piece of SP cardboard and a couple straight sticks." "SP's" were the boxes of smokes, toilet paper, and other goodies we received occasionally. The cardboard boxes they came in were thick and strong. The gooks used them for their hootches, roofs, wind breaks, or anything they could think of. Three or four Marines took off immediately. They were never reluctant to help a fellow Marine, or a Corpsman and this always endeared them to me. When it came to helping a wounded man, we had no one who shirked their duty.

I briefly thought of all the fine sterile techniques and procedures we were taught both in Corps school and under the supervision of Capt. Green and company at Bethesda Naval Hosp. All of that was out the crapper here. I went in with my bare hands and a scalpel.

"You're going to be okay, Frazier! Hang in there."

"Doc, am I going to lose my leg?"

I said, "How tall are you, man?"

"Five foot 10 inches!"

"Well in six months you will still be five foot 10 inches, and I want you to use this leg when it's healed to kick the ass of the bastard who ordered us to sweep this fucking Basin." He actually laughed through his intense pain.

"You got it, Doc!"

I was working frantically. Clamping bleeders, tying some off, applying pressure on others, and trying to stabilize what was left of this 18-year old Marine's leg. I had to get an IV started stat. I always carried Ringers Lactate. D5&W (dextrose 5% and water) was useless here. It was too hot. The damn sugar would crystallize. We all carried Ringers. I got the IV going and set it fast. He had lost a lot of blood. I kept looking at the other casualty and instructed a Marine to put on a pressure dressing until I could get to him. They had returned with several pieces of thick cardboard and I cut some now and put it under the whole leg. I gave him two Darvon Compounds, 65 mg. I told him I didn't want to give him morphine because it could do more harm than good. The Darvon also was loaded with caffeine which would help keep him awake. With the bleeding stopped, I applied battle dressings with "This side up" written on them. I always had to smile when I saw the "directions" written on the bandage. It was like telling a sod layer to tell his crew, "Green side up."

The battle dressings were tight and secure, so I checked the toes, they were getting blood. I had taken the tourniquet off after clamping the bleeders so all that was left to do now was to make sure the leg was stable. It was critical. If not completely stable, nerves could easily be destroyed with the movement of the sharp open bones. I took the cardboard and completely wrapped the leg with it. I cut and trimmed and it was damned near as good as a cast. Next, I took the two straight sticks and tied the whole mess together. This done, I took

Frazier's M-16 barrel down, and tied it in with the makeshift cast. The M-16 was longer and by tying it high and low, Frazier couldn't move that leg if he wanted to. I checked him for shock but he was doing as well as could be expected. Breathing was shallow and rapid but okay. He was in pain, but the Darvon would kick in soon. I decided to give him a "shot" and pulled out a syringe. I filled it with Ringers lactate and injected it in his good leg. I was afraid to give him morphine, and this would at least help him mentally. I could see relief in his eyes immediately. Your senses were so keen when adrenalin was soaring through your veins. The recall was amazing. Ideas, possibilities and improbabilities sped through your brain. What a rush! I could see him thinking, "Wow two pills and a shot! I ain't gonna feel no pain!" I just wanted to make sure he didn't go into shock on the chopper. I was sure he wouldn't and I was equally sure he would still be 5'10" in a few months.

I went to the other casualty who had caught shrapnel in both legs and his right arm. A Marine had already applied a battle dressing, but I cut it off to take a look before sending him off on the chopper. I cleaned the wounds one at a time. One had visible shrapnel, a large chunk. So I decided to go after it. I gave him a shot of morphine and a battle dressing to bite on and got out the same scalpel I used on Frazier along with forceps and went after it. I thought by doing it here in the field I could save him a lot of bleeding. I removed it easily and sutured (temporarily) the largest wound to slow the bleeding and put on another battle dressing then took care of his other wounds. By the time the chopper was fluttering to the ground, both were ready to go.

We loaded them up, said our goodbyes and good lucks, and they were off... and so were we. It was less than five miles from Henderson Hill to An Hoa, and if we had not had to stop so often to treat the wounded and call choppers in, we could have made it in a few hours. We were into our third day. Morale was shot.

Sarge was pissed. He told me the night before, "Damn it, Doc! This makes no sense. The gooks know what we are doing and they are moving out ahead of us, going over to the Arizona or Charlie Ridge, and coming back at night to set booby traps ahead of us. Not one damn fire fight in three days! And why WOULD they fight us? They are kicking our ass with booby traps! The only chance of getting them is the slim possibility we may catch them either coming or going when we send out our nightly ambushes." So far we hadn't.

Back online again, and after a couple hundred meters, I hear excitement off to the right flank. Sarge is heading that way and I follow. We have a prisoner. We probably caught him "getting a grip" with mamasan. There was also a very pretty young Vietnamese girl there who looked as out of place as a cumber bun at a redneck bar-b-que.

She was lovely, dressed in black and eyes black as the night that twinkled like the stars. You could see intelligence in those eyes. This was NOT a local girl. She looked to be around 20 or so and had pretty soft hands. Those hands had not been pulling seedlings from a rice paddy all her life. She had spirit and a gleam in her eye. Most Vietnamese women even this young (though I had never seen one this pretty) had a, "Well-this-is-my- life-and-I'll-live-it-until-I-die" look about them. Sarge was dealing with the prisoner and Jack the potential serial killer was talking to him.

"Sarge, when you get a chance, come look at this girl. I think she must be a nurse or something. She sure as hell isn't from this village."

Soon Sarge came over and he agreed. "We will send her in with this VC for interrogation." The squad was looking at her like a five-year old at a candy counter. She was toying with them as well. This gal was smart. She would smile, tease, and when the radioman placed his hand on her breasts she yelled at him, then smiled and flirted once again. She was working to get released, but with her dignity. She was definitely not a local.

The chopper came in and off they went to S2 (Marine Corps Intelligence, which I always said was an oxymoron).

Finally we complete the sweep, but not without even more booby traps. We had arrived at An Hoa.

This was our home base which we were never at, and where we were treated like red-headed step-children, quickly shuffled outside the perimeter and were told to wait there for further instructions.

Soon orders came to us. "Wait by the road until the convoy comes by headed to DaNang, then take it to Liberty Bridge and relieve Charlie Company." Relieve Charlie Company? Bet your ass we would relieve Charlie Company. Our Company, what was left of us, was going to Liberty Bridge. As we waited I looked our Company over and we looked more like a large Platoon than a Marine Company. We should have around 180 or so men. I guessed maybe 65 were left - maybe 75, but no more. We were going to the "Bridge" to get back to full strength and get supplies. It was alright with me.

I had heard nothing but awe about the "Bridge". It had a mess hall and that meant cold milk, eggs, maybe even bacon or "shit on a shingle" - food like real humans eat. I felt like I had just gotten a promotion from ape to homosapien.

The convoy came and we piled on the trucks. Off we go. It was early afternoon. I am in a truck with Sarge, our radioman and a few Marines. We get maybe two miles and "BOOM!!!!!!!!!!" A HUGE explosion! I mean it rocked us and shook the truck probably 100 meters back from the explosion. I looked at Sarge and he simply nodded. We had a connection, and he was telling me to go see if I could help out. I bailed out and left my pack with Sarge. I ran hard to the smelly smoke. The words "land mine" were heard many times as I ran past the waiting trucks. Everyone was set to repel an ambush, but there was none. I got up to the head of the convoy, and an engineer had stepped on an 80-pound box mine, meant to wipe out a tank or a truck. This was common and the reason we usually had one company on road security, running patrols and ambushes, hoping to catch and ambush the sappers. Bravo had road security today and they were right here where the mine went off. I got to what was left of the engineer and saw someone treating him. I almost crapped my pants. It was Joe Redding. Joe was one of the original 18 of us at "Casual Company", Marine boot camp and Field Med School. We were very good friends. I knew he was with Bravo 1/5, but it didn't even enter my mind that I would see him out here.

I walked over to him, knelt down beside him and said, "Hey, you got a license to practice medicine in this providence?"

He looked up.

"Bear! Well kiss my ass! No, I'm practicing without a license, KICK MY ASS OUT of here!! The engineer was bad. Both legs were gone at the hip and his right arm as well. This bears repeating. The engineer was being treated by Joe and me as a triple amputation - both legs and his right arm. Joe was working on his leg stumps, though the heat from the box mine had pretty much cauterized the wounds, so Joe was wrapping the stumps and applying some ointment. I did the same to his right arm which also was pretty much cauterized. Soon, I thought the way I could best help was start an IV in the one remaining arm, so I did. His veins had collapsed and I did a "cut down" - my first. I had no choice... he needed fluids.

As I was doing this I heard Joe saying, "Okay, you big pussy! This isn't going to get you off road duty! I'll have your ass out there checking for land mines in two days!" He was trying to "piss him off". This was something we learned together at Field Med School just a few months ago. Trauma often caused shock. Shock frequently caused breathing to stop thus, death. The first treatment was to get the adrenalin going. Pissing him off was a good way to do this. It could save his life. You would rarely give morphine injections to a triple amputee. It would as likely as not kill him. If you gave him morphine, then he went into shock and he would likely never wake up. Most importantly, if you checked your patient out and was sure he was going into shock, he didn't NEED morphine. He would feel no pain. Joe was there first, so it was his call, and he didn't administer morphine. I wouldn't have either. The guy was already going into shock, so we would treat him for that too. I had the IV going. He was patched up as well as we could do it out here, and the chopper was coming in.

Four Marines would carry him aboard the chopper, giving Joe and me a minute together.

I said, "Damn, man, it's good to see you!" We shook bloody hands." You have lost a lot of weight."

"Damn, Bear, so have you! You look like a fucking Marine". We both laughed. He looked like a Marine, too. Joe was a clown and I really liked him a lot. Of the 18 of us, he was in the top four of my best buddies. He was also one hell of a good Corpsman. We had some good times in Oceanside together and an unforgettable night in TJ Mexico.

I asked, "Have you heard about any of our other buds?"

"Well, a few, Bear. Jack Connor was with the Fifth Marines, too - 3/5. His right arm was taken off by a .50 cal round his first week over in Go Noi. Thompson and Henderson are dead. Mac was hit but I don't think very badly. Martin shot himself in the fucking foot to get out of the bush and the silly son of a bitch damn near bled to death. If he doesn't lose his foot he will be in the Brig. Bear, remember when they told us only 20% would make it? I don't think they were bull shitting us."

"No, Joe, I don't think so either."

The convoy was ready to take off.

"Take care of you self, my friend, and in five months we will indulge in a multitude of cold beers in DaNang, okay?

"You got it, Bear! Be careful!"

He went back to his company and me to mine. I felt a deep sadness hearing about lives and limbs already lost of my dear friends from Field Med School. I would see Joe once more. It would be in DaNang, but it wouldn't be in five months. It would be in five weeks.

I got back in the truck and said little to anyone.

Sarge said, "Will he make it, Doc?"

I thought about this.

"Yeah, Sarge, he will live, but he may wish he hadn't."

Enough said. We had done our job. How he coped with it was out of our hands.

I was in deep thought. Damn! So many gone already! Hell it was November. We had been in the bush a month. So many gone - so much time left to go.

The convoy went on without further problems. We pulled into the "Bridge" compound and I was amazed how small it was. An Hoa was huge. This was a tiny fire base with a two-man BAS. The NVA had blown the bridge in the 1968 Tet offensive. "Tet

Nguyen Dan" is the lunar New Year festival and it is the most important Vietnamese holiday. Seabee's were frantically trying to build another bridge. The new one would not be made of wood that was easy to burn. It was going to be lower, probably sometimes impassable during the monsoon season, but made of concrete and steel. They wanted to have it finished by the next Tet in Feb.

We got off the convoy and were greeted by the "gunny". We were to go to the north compound (other side of the river), which was fine with me. It had a mess hall, too. It was also the Seabees' headquarters which meant there was beer to be had. I liked beer, but it was milk that occupied my mind right now.

We walked down to the river and waited for the ferry. The river was deep and very wide. I kept thinking of real food, and I know ya'll are tired of reading this, but MILK!

We boarded the ferry and Sarge and I shot the shit as we crossed to the other side. We had gotten close. We would get closer. I had such respect for this man. Tonight we would down a few beers. The ferry tied up and we were getting off when a fairly tall thin blonde Marine came up to us.

"Where is Sgt. Vincent Rios?"

Sarge said, "That would be me, Sir." He had already determined the man was an officer; I could care less.

"I 'm, Lt. Tommy Peterson, and I am your new Platoon Commander."

Sarge took his hand, "Welcome aboard, Sir."

I stepped up, too, and put out my hand, "Hi, I'm Doc Bear, and you sure are shiny."

He WAS shiny - new utilities, some kind of helmet and flak jacket I had never experienced, and he was white as a ghost. I looked into his eyes, quickly observed as Sarge had taught me his body language, and didn't like what I had seen. I was learning to judge a man quickly. Before he ended our handshake, I had determined this boot louey wouldn't last a month. His eyes wouldn't meet mine - not for long. They wandered. He shifted his feet nervously. I can't say he was scared, but if he wasn't he was a fool. But he appeared, well, uncertain. I got the impression he was spastic, would react without thinking and get good men killed. I wasn't happy as I walked with Sarge to our hootch, leaving the Lt. to watch the rest of the Platoon, what was left of us, unload. We got out of earshot and Sarge began laughing.

"What?"

"Damn you, Doc! 'Boy you sure are shiny!'?? I damned near pissed my pants. You don't talk to an officer like that."

"Well, hell, Sarge, he was shiny! Did you see that hair cut? When he took his helmet off, I was blinded by the light. That fucker must have lived in a cave! He doesn't look like the sun has ever set on his ass in his life."

Sarge was laughing and I did too.

"Well, you tell ME, Sarge….what do you think?"

"About our new Platoon Commander?"

"No about that damn fashion show he put on for us. Did you ever see a flak jacket like that? What the hell was that? It had no plates in it. It was all woven, and wasn't even Marine Corps issue! What the hell was that all about? Of course, I mean about our new Platoon Commander."

"It is an Air Force flight protection jacket I think - useless out here, but it is a lot lighter, and as far as what I think? A month, Doc, tops."

We had an officer for a Platoon Commander again. Sarge was Platoon Sergeant once again. The question was, "Would this new boot louey listen to the experienced Sarge?"

We would soon find out.

Chapter 13
<u>Liberty Bridge</u>

The river was nearly 100 meters wide here at "the Bridge". It had a good current in the center and was relatively clean looking. I could hardly wait to jump into it with a bar of soap.

I was the only Corpsman now in the Platoon. Doc Hal was with "Weapons –Platoon" now Company CP. I wasn't sure why there would be two Corpsmen with the CP and only one with a fighting platoon, but I guess that's the way it goes. I got some soap and headed to the river. It was refreshing and I enjoyed that more than anything else I had experienced in the last month. Skinny dipping in the Song Thu Bon River! What a life! We didn't get new utilities. I guess ours wasn't considered old enough. I had washed my towel I always carried in the bush and made an attempt at drying off. I really didn't care. Bathing in a river with real soap was a luxury.

I went back to our hootch. I was set in with Sarge, Lt. Tommy, Phil and Mark, the right guide. I lay back on the plywood floor of our tent and relaxed as I watched Sarge pick the brain of the new lieutenant.

Tommy, as I would call him, was an Annapolis graduate (Naval Academy) who chose the Marine option.

I could almost see the wheels churning in his head. Sarge was preparing him - testing him.

"These guys have been in the bush for eight straight weeks - no breaks. They don't need to be fucked with by getting "shit" details. Let these pogues dig their own shitters. You have to stand up to the gunny when he comes around and tries to assign us shit details. If you look out for these men, you will have a platoon that will do anything you ask them to. They are a great bunch of guys. They just need a little seasoning."

Tommy said, "Well, what do I tell the gunny?"

"Tell him you are the Lieutenant, and you have things YOU want them to do, and to go get HIS work details elsewhere. Tell him you are sending out an ambush, two LP's and a patrol."

"Do we run patrols and ambushes from here?"

"Hell no, but he doesn't know what we are doing on this side of the river. We have to look out for our men and they deserve to relax and enjoy this break."

"Okay, I'll see what I can do."

The mess hall opened up and I was going to join Stuckey. I could hardly wait for the cold milk. Stuckey and I were becoming good friends.

Docs didn't have to wait in lines in the Marine Corps, but I wanted to eat with Stuckey. So while he waited in line, I took my canteen and walked down to the river to wait until he got to the door. We didn't have to do details either. It was like the "free agent" thing. The only detail we had was if our platoon was assigned to dig "shitters". Then a Doc would have to make sure it was deep enough and wide enough.

I saw Stuckey getting closer to the door, so I walked up that way. Now, when I tell you Docs didn't have to stand in lines, let me explain something. We couldn't if we wanted to.

As soon as I got near the platoon there were shouts of, "Hey, Doc, come on up here with me!" "Doc, come over here!" and so on. It was actually a little embarrassing and really touched my heart. As I was told back at the 1/5 BAS, it was a little like being treated as a celebrity.

I got in line by Stuck (stook), and we were soon served hamburgers, potatoes green beans, MILK, Kool-Aid, and yeast bread. It was like Delmonico's to us.

After a month of C-rats and rice, it was heavenly. I had three canteen cups of milk and took one back to the hootch with me.

Lt. Tommy was there. "Hey. Tommy, getting all settled in?"

A look of confusion left his face as he said, "Yeah, Doc, I think so."

I had been around him two or three hours by now. I was actually starting to like him as a person. He seemed to have a very good heart. I could even see him as courageous. But I still saw him as spastic, someone who would react before they thought. When a commander does that, good men die.

I held to my first instinct, that he wouldn't make it longer than a month. There was one difference. I was already feeling bad that he wouldn't.

Mail call! A grunt's paradise! It was two days before my 23rd birthday. I had many letters and a package. I opened the package from my wife. Homemade peanut butter cookies! I saw a tin foiled tube and opened it up and my heart fluttered. Oberle (o-ber-ly) sausage! It was a special kind of German sausage made only at a little packing plant in the Ozarks. When I killed a deer, I often took it to them and he made me Oberle sausage with venison, pork fat and numerous spices. This was made with beef, but the smell almost brought tears to my eyes. I was so tired of smelling Vietnam. Filth, shitters, smoke, gunpowder, blood, and fear were a constant here. This fragrance briefly removed the rest. I saw a little mold on the sausage as I unwrapped it - a little green, nothing serious. I would leave it on until I was ready to eat it on my birthday. Then I would trim off the mold.

There was also a quart bottle of bleach. I knew what this was. I had told Linda that the pogues would sometimes go through our packages and if there were bottles of booze, slabs of cheese or meat, they would take it. She had filled an empty bottle of Purex bleach with Seagram's VO. I took the top off and smelled it. Yep, bourbon! A little bleachy, but bourbon! I also had fudge and jerky. I put the booze in my pack and the Oberle sausage, and shared the cookies and fudge with the troops.

That night we had lines on the perimeter, but were arranged so at least one squad a night had no watch. That squad bought beer from the Seabees. We had two nights of this when our stay was cut short. November 24, my birthday, we were moving out. The regiment was having a huge operation involving 12 companies. We were up on the morning of my birthday and had a 0400 breakfast: Bacon, eggs to order, grits, toast, MILK, and, for those who drank it, coffee and juice. I had lost 40 pounds in four weeks and it probably looked like I was trying to gain it back in milk alone. So nice and cold!

The orders were given and at 0500 we moved out. I was 23 now, same as Sarge. Hadn't told anyone yet, but would that night.

The plan was not complicated. It was, however, scary. We had in two days received 30 or 40 new men. Alpha Co. would be the center of attention on this operation. We would move off east by ourselves on a small operation east of Liberty Bridge.

We would slowly work our way toward the mountains. Then, before daybreak, in two days, we would disappear into the mountains and head north - hopefully unbeknownst to the NVA. Then we were to continue north to a given destination. We would drop down in the dead of night, then and slip into our ultimate assignment. We would secure a village there and clear it out, trapping all civilians. This village was on the bank of a river. The next morning we were to cross that river and line up in one long line and set in. On the map, it looked like we would be setting up in a long line on the edge of a huge field. That day, miles west of us, eleven companies of combat-hardened Marines would line up as well. Approximately 1760 Marines accompanied by tanks and "am tracks" would begin a sweep designed to drive the NVA, Viet Cong, and any other enemy soldiers or sympathizers into Alpha Co.

The Operation would be called Taylor Common.

The Marines: First Battalion, Fifth Marine Regiment.

The goal? Annihilate the enemy.

The destination? Go Noi Island.

I remembered my first day in country on the flight to An Hoa from DaNang.

The gunner on the chopper had said, "If you are going to An Hoa, you will learn to hate Go Noi Island." The time had come. We would be tested now.

A year ago when someone spoke of "The War", you would hear the names Hue City (way-city) or Khe Sahn (kay-san). Now the hot spots were The Arizona and Go Noi Island.

As we got ready to catch the ferry to the south side of "The Bridge", I looked closely at Lt. Tommy. He still shined. He looked eager, willing and confused. He would be our commander when we were the blocking force for 1760 Marines.

Two words came to mind. "Holy shit!"

Chapter 14
Seagrams and Oberle

We got off the ferry and moved quickly through the southern compound and to the gate. We left the gate and turned east. Second Platoon had point for the Company. It was my birthday. It seemed appropriate that I would spend it in the bush. I was, after all, a bush Corpsman. We humped two clicks and set in east by southeast of Liberty Bridge, just outside the "Cu Ban's".

It was a semi-friendly ville. As we were setting up a perimeter, I heard Sarge tell Lt. Tommy he wanted to send out an ambush that night, just a little way down the trail. Tommy agreed. This eased my mind a bit.

Burke's squad had the ambush that night, just a few hundred meters from the platoon CP. I had a good feeling about this place and decided to stay behind. The four of us were in the platoon CP. As it got dark I said, "I want first watch tonight." Sarge picked up on it right away.

"Doc, you always want the 0100 to 0300 watch."

I reached into my pack and pulled out the bleachy bottle of Seagrams VO and handed it to Sarge.

"Today, Sarge, I am as old as you."

Sarge laughed, "I got second watch."

He laughed again as he dug into his pack and pulled out three cans of 7-Up and set them next to the Purex bottle. Neither of us had said a word about this while in the rear, yet here we were with Seagram's and 7-Up. Tonight it would be Seagrams VO, 7-Up and Oberle sausage.

I stood the first watch and did the usual "Alpha-2-Alpha, Alpha-2-Alpha! This is Alpha-2. If all secure key your handset twice; if not, key it once. Over!"

I heard the two keys.

Two hours later it was Sarge's turn. I would wait for him to finish his watch at 0100.

As the hour approached, I trimmed the mold off the Oberle sausage and mixed us a VO and 7-Up in our canteen cups. It tasted a little of bleach, but was great. The Oberle was outstanding and Sarge was amazed at how great it tasted. Linda had done well. Of all the birthday presents she had ever given me, I enjoyed this the most. We had two drinks and quite a bit of the Oberle and decided to give the rest to the troops. Friendly area or not, we were still in the bush.

The next morning we moved out. I watched Lt. Tommy closely. He was scared, but who wasn't?

I was really starting to like this shiny Lieutenant from Long Island. For some reason, and I don't know why, I always made it a point to put on my best southern Ozark-mountain drawl when I talked to him. This didn't take a lot of effort. I naturally kind of sounded like Gomer Pyle with an education.

We saddle up and I fall in behind Sarge. We are headed for the foothills. I have never been there before and am a little edgy. This country had all possible terrains. The foothills were rocky and steep and, though I had been at the base of them, I had yet to be up in them. As we got closer to the foothills, I thought about Operation Taylor Common. I had no idea who the hell "Taylor" was nor did I think anything was common about having eleven companies of Marines driving an estimated 8,000 NVA hard-core soldiers at us, but I didn't name these things.

We had all heard the horror stories of Go Noi (ga-noy), and some of the men had been there. I had looked it up on my map while waiting for Sarge last night. It was a huge parcel of land surrounded on all sides by two major rivers - thus, an island. It looked to be seven or eight miles long, maybe five or six miles

140

wide and located at the northern most part of the "Basin".

The map showed an old railroad that had at one time run right through the middle of the Island. The word was that the French had built the railroad. When they left the country, the locals dismantled the railroad and used the rails and ties to build incredible bunkers. There was also supposed to be an underground hospital - literally an underground hospital.

We were getting closer to the foothills now, and I paid even closer attention to Sarge as we progressed. I noticed, every so often, he would turn around and look my way.

I saw him pick a small bush twig here, and another one there, and insert them in the holes in the helmet cover. I kept watching, and he kept doing it. Soon, I did the same. By the time we got to the bottom of the foot hills and started up the incline, his helmet had a radius of about 3 feet. I had several in mine as well, and was snapping off yet another when Sarge stopped and said, "Doc, do I look like a bush?" and started laughing.

I was tense about going to Go Noi, and it pissed me off just a little.

"Sarge, stop fucking with me," I said as I started to remove the brush pile from my helmet.

We held up at the foot of the ridge and a supply chopper came in. I saw a few Marines get off (new troops I assumed) and we were issued C-rats and had mail call. I stuffed my letters in my pack and would read them when the hump was over.

We climbed the ridge. It was rough going, but the view was breathtaking. The rocks, clay, ridges and mountains almost made me homesick. The heat was sweltering, the humidity breathtaking, but it sure was beautiful. Once on the top of the ridge, the view to the east was amazing - mountains, valleys and small streams. I imagined streams full of trout and bass - but this wasn't Missouri. The hump was hard, hot and long. I was filthy even though I had bathed in the river just two days ago.

We humped until dusk and just before the sun set it began to pour. I mean "cow-pissin-on-a-flat-rock" downpour. We were soaked to the bone with no sign of a letup.

We set in on the ridge in what would be a piss-poor perimeter at best, due to the rain and the fact that we weren't familiar with the area. You couldn't see two feet past your hands because of the dark and the down pouring rain. No need to send out an ambush tonight. Two 2-man LP's (Listening Post) was about it. There was also no danger of being mortared tonight. There is no way in hell a mortar would fire in this rain.

I had had Linda dye a pair of long-john underwear green and send them to me. I had been carrying them on my back for weeks; tonight I would try them out. One of the biggest problems in the bush during the rainy season or monsoons is the feet. I went around to all the fire teams set in and advised them to take their socks off, rinse them out in the rain, and leave them off tonight. You don't normally want to be barefooted in the bush, but there are exceptions to everything. I went back to the CP and stripped down. As I slipped on the newly dyed long john's I could see I stood out like a whore in church. It was like, "Here, shoot the dumb ass", but they were warm and I put on the long-johns, and then my jungle utilities. I was still soaking wet and, God, it was cold. In actuality, it was maybe 50 degrees up on that ridge. With the rain and wind it felt below zero. I tied my poncho liner to my poncho and wrapped up in it and went into the fetal position. There wouldn't be much sleep tonight. Too wet. Too damn cold. I slipped my head into the poncho and it was all soaked. Body heat was the only source of warmth so I tried to hold in all I could. I lay and shivered all night. It was truly the coldest I had ever been in my life.

Finally the new day broke. I was ready to get on with this, get moving, and set the blood pumping.

We humped the ridge all day. It stopped raining and hit over 100 degrees. Humidity matched the temp. The going was rough even though there was a trail most likely made by the NVA humping rockets and mortars to Go Noi.

We finally slowed near dusk and once again set in near the top of the ridge. I found a rock next to Stuckey and was sitting there guzzling pissy water when I heard someone from the rear of the column approaching.

"Anyone here know Doc Bear?"

I heard several respond "He's right over there by Stuckey."

He walked up to me sitting there and said, "Excuse me, could you tell me where Doc Bear is?"

"You're a lookin' at him."

"You are Doc Bear?" he asked incredulously.

"That would be me, dude. What can I do for you?"

Then I noticed the Corpsman caduceus on his collar. He was a Doc. His next words will be with me until the day I die.

"There is NO WAY I will EVER be that dirty!"

"Well, partner, I hope ya' live long enough to, but guess we'll have to wait and see, won't we?"

I had a new partner. I stood and shook his hand. Good grip. Looked me in the eyes, all good signs. He was a year younger than I but had a few gray hairs. Thus he had a new name. He would be Doc Grey.

We talked a while. He was from South Dakota. Not surprisingly, he wanted to know what I thought about the Marines we were serving with.

"Well, I've been in the military I guess three years now, and never have I been so respected, honored and privileged to serve anywhere." The words came out of my mouth, but didn't sound like something I would say. It was like I was defending these guys, which of course I would. At that moment, I knew I was forever a Marine. Navy could kiss my ass! They attached me to the Fleet Marines and I would never wear a Navy uniform again.

Thinking I may be sounding a little gung ho, I told Gray my favorite joke.
He was sitting on a log across from my rock.

"There were two Marines digging a shitter. They were down in the hole digging away, and they got to talking.

'You know something, I don't understand? I'm an E3, you're an E3 and we're down here working our asses off. And right up there sitting under that tree reading a book is Doc - and he's an E3, too! How come we do all the work while he sits up there reading?'

'I don't, know...why don't you ask him?'

'I think I will!'

So, he climbed out of the hole and presented his dilemma to the Corpsman.

Doc said, 'Well it's hard to explain.' And then he put his hand on the tree he was resting under and said, 'Here, hit my hand with your shovel.'

The Marine said, 'Awww...Doc, I'll break your hand!'

Doc said, 'No, you want to know why you are down in that hole working and I'm up here. Now hit my hand with your shovel.'

The Marine said, 'Okay!' and reared back and swung as hard as he could. Of course Doc moved his hand, giving the Marine a bone-shaking jolt as his shovel slammed into the tree.

Doc said, 'That's why, Marine - intelligence!'

The Marine picked up his shovel, climbed down in the hole and began digging again.

Soon the other Marine said, 'Well?'

The first Marine said, 'Well what?'

The second Marine said, 'Well, what did he say? Why are we down here working our asses off and a Corpsman of the same rank is up there in the shade?'

The first Marine thought a minute and said, 'Well it's kind of hard to explain.' He raised his hand in front of his face and said, 'Here, hit my hand with your shovel!'"

Doc Gray laughed so hard he fell off his log. I guess the tension he was feeling found a release and he continued to roar. I was laughing at him laughing.

"Damn, Gray! Shhhh! You're gonna wake up every gook on Go Noi Island."

He kept laughing. I must say I hadn't made anyone laugh that hard in a long time and it made me feel rather good. I also thought I was going to like this guy. I was right. We would become good friends, and his firstborn son would be named after Sarge and me. I will always be humbly honored.

We were sitting there talking when Sarge came by. "Hey, Doc, got a minute?"

"Why, Sarge? You gonna fuck with me again?"

He laughed with his deep bass roar, "No, Doc. I need to talk with you. You and I are going to take a little recon trip."

I grabbed my M-16 and we walked down the side of the ridge. We got nearly to the bottom when he pulled up and motioned me to sit next to him.

In the fading light of day, I could see this massive rice paddy directly in front of us. To the south was a tree line perpendicular to the ridge. Fifteen hundred meters north was another tree line, also perpendicular to the ridge. Sarge had his map out.

"Okay, Doc, we are right here. See this ville? We need to be set in there on the other side of that upside down "U" around 2300. We will stay there until daybreak and move over here to this ville, clear it of people and that will basically be our headquarters for three or four days."

I said, "Okay."

I looked again at the terrain then the map. Map looked accurate. The rice paddy was enormous. It was around 1500 meters wide and 1000 meters long. On the far side, just over 1,000 meters, was where we were to set in for a few hours tonight.

"Doc, how would you get us to that high ground?" Lesson time!

I looked it over, "Well, Sarge, since we have passed this first tree line and most likely as not we were silhouetted up on that ridge, I guess I would drop down a bit and continue on to the next tree line north of us, take it over to the "T" and head south to the designated ville. Should take us two or three-hours tops."

Sarge looked at the map. "Let me run this by you: See this big rice paddy?"

"Yes".

"We are going right up the fucking middle of it."

I thought I had heard him wrong.

"Are you crazy? A hundred and fifty Marines sloshing through the middle of a rice paddy on Go Noi Island! We'll be ambushed!"

He was silent a minute. "Doc, where are they going to ambush us from?"

146

I looked at the map, the upside down "U" we would be walking into and the answer was obvious. I looked back up at the rice paddy. Then it hit me. Where WOULD they ambush us from?

The rice paddy was 1500 meters wide. The night would be pitch black. If we went right up the middle of it, it would be 750 meters to either tree line. They could hear us, know exactly where we were and how many, and STILL not be able to see us to hit us. If we took either tree line, we stood a good chance of hitting booby traps in the dark and still get ambushed at the "T".

I said, "Damn, Sarge! You're right! That's fucking brilliant!"

Let me tell you, there is no "tactics book" in the world that would have that maneuver in it, but it would work. We may make noise, they may even hear us, but they can't see us. Hell, probably can't even tell where the noise is coming from. They are probably right now sitting near where they set the booby traps waiting for us to come along and trip them, and then ambush us. We would be 800 meters away happily - well unhappily - splashing our way to our objective.

Sarge amazed me. He constantly amazed me. He had his shit together, always looking out for the troops, the best, safest and most effective way to get the job done.
We walked silently back to the company.

At 2200, 150 Marines were splashing our way into Go Noi Island. I heard many comments, "This is fucking stupid! We'll get ambushed!"

I took a little of Sarge's thunder by saying, "This is fucking brilliant! Where can they ambush us from?"

We were soon moving single file quickly into the tree line - no booby traps, no ambush. We set up a perimeter quickly and dug in. We would wait here for three or four hours.

I had just laid down in a hootch inside the barren ville when the now unmistakable sound of an AK-47 ripped through the air. Then another. What the shit?

"CORPSMAN UP!!!"

I was off and running to the call in the dark. Man down! Shot through the neck. Gonzales. He was a fire team leader I both liked and knew well.

The problem was this: We had set in so fast; we caught two NVA soldiers inside our perimeter. They decided to shoot their way out and overran Gonzales' fire team from the rear. Hell! No one would have expected that! Now I had a man hit - head, well neck wound. Gray and I moved him to a bunker. Gray checked the wound. Gonzales was woozy but conscious. He probed the wound, it went straight in, no exit wound and we couldn't find the damn bullet.

"Emergency med evac! Get me a chopper in here!

Lt. Tommy went spastic. He called it in. A few minutes later, Tommy said, "Doc, the pilot won't come in. He said this is Go Noi Island and he is afraid to bring in a chopper at night."

I steamed. "Tommy, I know where the hell we are! Get me a fucking chopper in here, and I want it right fucking NOW!!!"

He called again. "He won't come in, Doc."

Gray didn't know what to think. I wasn't going to let this man die.

"Tommy, get me his name, rank and service number and tell him Doc Bear wants to meet him in DaNang."

Then I said, "Get him back on the net! I want to talk to the son of a bitch!"

Lt. Tommy was going nuts.

Sarge was out checking the fire team that had been overrun from the rear.

148

Lt. Tommy said, somewhat relieved, "Doc he's coming in."

The chopper landed and we quickly got him on board. Sarge was grinning. Tommy was still spastic. He had lost his first causality. Gray had treated his first casualty, and I felt good about that. We had been in Go Noi for less than two hours and already had a fire team overrun, a man shot in the neck and an argument with a chopper pilot.

Welcome to Go Noi Island!

Chapter 15
<u>Go Noi Island</u>

At first light we moved out to what would become known as "People's Village".

Later it would be referred to as "The Christmas Ville". Right now it loomed large ahead of us. We were approaching it single file per usual, and last night's conversation with Sarge came back to me. This ville wasn't chosen at random. It wasn't just picked out on a map. Two weeks ago Bravo Co. (My friend Joe's Company) was approaching this same ville just as we were right now. Sniper fire broke out. One round, then another, and then another. Eight single-shot rounds...eight Marines dead...identical wounds. One neat little hole through the sternum. A 7.62mm round from a sniper's rifle forever changed the lives of at least eight families forever.

I felt the tension in the air. This was a different battleground. There would be booby traps, yes. But here the NVA would fight you to the last man. They were hard-core soldiers - well trained and well disciplined.

We all had heard the horrors of Go Noi: The 6' tall elephant grass with blades that had you bleeding with every step; and the bunker complexes. I had gone into a bunker last night after we med evaced Gonzales and looked around. It was deep and solid, fortified with railroad ties. The old French railroad wasn't far from here. This is where the NVA hauled supplies from the north: Rockets, artillery rounds, mortars, medical supplies, and small arms.

There were rice paddies here, but they were fewer. There was a lot of cover, high ground, ambush sights, trails, spider holes (holes dug along a trail where a sniper would hide and as a patrol went past he would pop up and fire his weapon.) and shelter. There were a lot of banana trees and small gardens in some villes that had the zucchini looking vegetable that was tasteless but filling.

Last night Sarge had told me about the banana trees.

"Beware the banana trees, Doc. The gooks will use the large leaves for mattresses, the trees for shade, and chew the tender stalks like celery. When we move into an area, the banana trees will tell you volumes."

The civilians were very different than what I had seen before. There were no "Chi Coms" here. No children asking for C-rats, cigarettes, or offering back rubs and canteens of well water. No smiles. No friendly faces. These kids, as did their parents, hated us. They ALL were the enemy.

We were entering the ville quickly now, setting the plan into motion. We quickly rounded up all the "civilians" and marched them at gun point to an area in the center of the ville. They would be isolated, restricted to this one patch of ground. We allowed them to take only what they could carry. No trips back for food or pots. The area was surrounded by a trench, sort of like a built-in prison. They were told to stay there or be shot. Anyone leaving there, man, woman or child, would be shot down as a VC. We didn't want them telling the enemy (which was their sons and brothers) of our movements or actions. We would be here a while, at least on Go Noi. After the big upcoming "sweep", Alpha Co. would stay behind and "clean up" the rest of the NVA. This ville would be an area we would keep coming back to, to set in, run patrols and ambushes from, and use as a land mark.

As we herded them up, Steve Britt, a buddy/squad leader said, "Doc, look! They have chickens!" Well, it had been a few days since we had been supplied. The vision of chicken and rice ran through my mind. The villagers treasured their chickens. It was a sign of wealth (not to mention a source of eggs). We knew they would raise hell if we took a chicken. We designed a plan of action. I would be inside the ville with them. Steve would stand on the other side of the trench. I would snatch a chicken, run to the ravine and toss the chicken (yes, I knew chickens can fly) to Steve. I would stun the chicken then toss it to Steve. He would take it to his squad and I would escape from the isolated area of the ville.

Well the first part of the plan went well. I grabbed a chicken, whacked him behind the head and neck with a sort of Karate chop (talk about "glazed "chicken, you should have seen the looks in its eyes - glazed for sure), then ran to the edge of the trench and was about to toss it to Steve when a five or six-year old little girl grabbed hold of its legs. She wouldn't let go. I swung it back and forth to toss it but she hung onto it. Now, I would like to tell you my heart filled with compassion and guilt and I returned the chicken to the family. This book, however, is based on fact. And the fact is I didn't do that. She finally let go and I tossed the chicken to Steve. I will never forget that moment. I will always remember looking at that little girl and thinking, "Gentle John", protector of the innocent! What the hell has happened to me?"

I felt a little shame, but not enough. I knew that if her father would kill me that night, her family would rejoice, shout and cheer. The whole damned ville would rejoice if any of us were killed.

What little compassion I had left (other than for my Marines and maybe little Chi Com) was fast disappearing. As I read this now, I would love to find that little girl and apologize to her. I would gladly take her to a KFC and buy her a BUCKET of chicken! At that time, however, I hated these people. They were why Gonzales was shot in the neck last night. They were the reason I may die tonight. And we were there to protect them? What a bunch of crap! They wanted us dead. They hated us.

I crossed over the trench and found Steve cleaning the chicken. I took my helmet cover off, the liner out, and washed out the "pot". Then I got some C-4 from my pack and filled the helmet pot half way with water. It was a matter of seconds and the water was boiling. Steve dropped the chicken in while his squad was hovering around like vultures. They were drooling for what we hoped soon would be chicken and rice. I let it boil a while then added the ugly brown rice we had with us. I added salt, and someone furnished some Louisiana hot sauce. An hour later we were ready to eat. I ceremoniously took the first bite. It was horrible! I don't know if it was because it was cooked in my smelly helmet, or the chicken was fed on whatever it could find, or if maybe somehow I DID feel a little guilty for stealing that chicken. But I couldn't eat it. Steve and company seemed to not have that problem. I went across the ville and found a squash-looking plant in a garden, picked two green bananas and had lunch. When they were finished with my helmet I would wash it out and be ready for the ambush that night. I wanted the chicken story behind me. Well, it wasn't to be.

In March 2000 my phone would ring. I picked up the receiver.

"Hello"

"Hey Doc, let's go steal a chicken and make some chicken and rice."

"Steve?"

It had been 31 years since I had seen him. He was hit once and I operated on him in the field removing shrapnel. It was from friendly fire and he was the only

Marine I know who went through a whole tour with our Company and didn't get a Purple Heart.

We talked, we met, and we went deep sea fishing together. We live about four hours apart in Florida.

The chicken story isn't over yet.

July 4, 2000, Redwood City, CA, was honoring Alpha 1/5 with a parade and fireworks. I was going so I invited Steve. He went as well. We were all sitting around Sarge's living room talking. I had seen Sarge a few times before this. It was however, the first time any of us had seen Steve.

Sarge recalled, "That damn Steve! Remember the People's Ville?"

"Yes"

"Well he and his squad stole a damn chicken and the village chief raised all kinds of hell! He wanted restitution, money, C-rats, and free medical care - anything he could think of - over Steve stealing that damn chicken! I reamed his ass up one side and down the other."

Isn't it funny when you do something wrong it ALWAYS comes back to bite you in the ass?

"Sarge?"

"What Doc?"

"I stole that chicken. It was me, not Steve. I took it and gave it to his squad."

Sarge roared, "Oh, tell me that isn't so! My Doc stole that chicken?"

"Yep, sure did! Damn thing tasted like paste so I gave it all to them. It was my helmet, and I both took it and cooked it."

Sarge was laughing so hard he was crying.

There is more than one lesson here: I had no idea Steve got in trouble over that. He never told anyone it was me. He took the blame. Yes, it was true then and is true now, Marines look out for their Docs.

After the chicken incident, that night we had our first real ambush on Go Noi. It was platoon-size, and we basically went a half a click (500 meters) and set in by the river and a trail. We hoped to ambush some NVA either coming for water, moving towards "People Village", or crossing the river.

First Platoon had a squad-size ambush out. They had sent a squad up into the edge of the foothills so they had a good view. In case we were hit by incoming, they could most likely see muzzle flashes.

Around 2300 hours, a firefight broke out. First Platoon had set off an ambush. AK-47's and M-16's dueled back and forth. We were about 300 meters away, and could hear the fire fight well, occasionally seeing tracer rounds, both red and green flying into the sky.

The battle was won by First Platoon – not, however, without consequences. They had a man hit in the abdomen by an AK round. We were monitoring the net. Tommy, Sarge, Mac and I listened to the radio traffic.

Doc Holmes called for an emergency med evac. Lt. Propst our old Platoon Commander turned Company Commander, was on the net as well.

"The chopper won't come in. We'll have to wait until morning."

Doc said, "Skipper, he won't make it until morning. I have to get him out of here tonight."

"Do the best you can, Doc."

"Doing 'the best I can' will give him maybe two hours at best. He needs to be in DaNang! Get me a chopper in here or this man will die!"

Skipper told him they wouldn't come in, hot LZ (landing zone), and to wait until morning. I was pissed. I knew Doc Holmes and from what I could tell, he had his shit together. He was trying to save this Marine's life. He was willing to risk his own, but not his patient's.

155

I was on watch around 0200 when I heard Doc Holmes call the skipper. "Skipper, keep your fucking chopper! He just died in my arms...but his blood is on your hands!"

I looked at Sarge and he was pissed as well. There was no reason for this. Doc had told him straight up unless he was taken out he would die. This is what is supposed to separate Marines from other services. Marines didn't let men die. Marines didn't leave their dead or wounded. I was so mad I was shaking. I recalled my fear of having a Marine die in my arms. This one did but not because Doc didn't know what to do. He died because someone was afraid to take a chance to save him!

The next morning after we returned from our ambush, I saw the skipper walking alone towards the company CP. I walked up by him, and greeted him. "Morning, Skipper! Was that your first confirmed kill last night?" I was shaking I was so mad.

He looked confused for a minute, then he knew I meant Doc Holmes' patient. He hesitated and then continued walking. I had gotten my point across. I wanted him to know he was responsible. I further wanted him to know that if he did that to me, he would hear about it. It was Doc's call, and Skipper's responsibility to get the chopper in there. Doc did all he could.

God! I hated this shit! I hated the dying and the fighting! The loss of good men! By all rights these kids should be at the A&W picking up girls, not out here dying! Instead they were here - we all were - fighting a war for Texaco, Standard Oil, and Shell. More would die. More would die soon. Tomorrow, we kicked off Operation Taylor Common. We would be the blocking force.

Chapter 16
<u>Blocking "Farce"</u>

Operation Taylor Common kicked off as expected. We were up at 0400, saddled up and hyped up. We were told we would have a day's delay. Second Platoon would instead go out a ways to another ville and we would run a patrol that afternoon and an ambush that night. Then the next day the operation would be ready to kick off.

Personally, I was in no hurry. We were humping to our new pos for a day and I was watching and thinking about Tommy. I don't think I have ever seen anyone work or try so hard to fit in. We had a patrol out yesterday that Doc Gray was on, and they got back Gray was describing it. He was telling of the movement, how they spotted the gooks running into a tree line, then opened fire. Sarge was listening intently, absorbing all he could. I could see the wheels churning in Tommy's brain. He was so eager, willing and wanted to be a part of all of this. He made a comment about Gray being a Corpsman and shouldn't we get this info from the squad leader. I was pissed at first. I felt Gray was coming right along. I commented back, "Some people catch on fast, Tommy. Gray knows what he was talking about." Then I felt a little bad because I had never gotten anything from Tommy but respect.

It's a hard thing to describe. There is a segment on "Sesame Street" where they ask: "Which one doesn't go with the others?" In a row of five oranges, Tommy was a red apple. Was it because he was a coward? Not in anyway that I could see. Maybe not smart? Nope, he graduated from the Naval Academy, and seemed bright. Out of shape? He was in great physical shape. He was maybe 5'11", but somehow looked shorter. He was well muscled and lean, but strong.

157

Was it that I just didn't like him? No, I think he is a great guy; good personality; a heart of gold. I thought about this during the whole hump. By the time we got to the new pos, I had only one answer. He was the red apple in a row of oranges. He had all the good qualities you would want in a person or a friend. He just wasn't an orange.

We set in at the ville. I had my poncho laid out and was about to lie down when Stuckey came by.

"Hey, Doc, want a couple of eggs?" He said this like we were at a shopping market and he was gathering breakfast.

"Eggs?! Hell yes, Stuck! Where did you get eggs?"

"It's a rich ville, Doc - they have chickens. I found where they laid them." He walked over and handed me two beautiful large white eggs.

"Wow, Stuckey! I appreciate it."

"Not a problem Doc. Do have the patrol today or ambush tonight?"

"Ambush."

"Okay, I'll be back after the patrol and we'll shoot the shit if you feel like it."

"Ok, Stuckey! Thanks a lot."

As he was leaving, he reached into his pocket, got out another egg and was going to throw it.

"Stuckey! Whoa, Man! Why are you throwing that egg away?"

"Oh, I also found three rotten ones. I have two more here that aren't any good."

"Hmmm…Stuckey, can I have them?"

"Sure Doc, but I'm telling you, they aren't any good."

"Ok, appreciate it."

My mind was churning.

158

We had a shit bird Corporal named Crook. He had the patrol this afternoon. I didn't care for him. He was a sandbagger. You had to watch him all the time. I was afraid he was going to get some good men killed because he didn't want to do his job the right way.

I smiled and thought, "Wonder if Crooky likes eggs."

I took out my pencil and marked the two rotten eggs. Then I filled my canteen cup with dirty water and lit some C-4. It was boiling in no time. I dropped the four eggs in. When they were done, I took the two good eggs and put them in my left side pocket, the two bad ones in my right.

That afternoon, Sarge called for Crook to brief him on the patrol. Tommy was there and paying close attention. I watched him a lot and, damn, I was really starting to like him.

While Crook was listening to Sarge, I strolled over, reached into my left pocket, and just like it was a daily routine, I pulled out an egg, cracked the shell, sprinkled some C-rat salt on it and started eating it. Sarge looked at me, but Crooky's eyes got as big as saucers.

"Damn! Where did you get the eggs?"

"Why, Crook? Do you like eggs?"

"Oh! Yeah! I love eggs!"

"Hmm...well, I guess since you have the patrol this afternoon and I'm not going, I'll give you a couple."

Crooky was thrilled. "Damn, Doc! Thank you!"

"Not a problem, Crooky." I reached into my right pocket and pulled out two beautiful white eggs.

"Now I have already boiled them, so you can dig in anytime you want."

I was hoping he would do it then so I could witness his reaction, but he didn't.

He took the eggs. "Damn! Thanks, Doc! I didn't think you liked me."

"Why, I don't know why you would think that! Enjoy your eggs."

Sarge was just watching this transaction.

Crooky was walking back to his squad when he turned around.

"Doc, you're pulling a trick on me, these eggs are raw."

"Crooky, I give you word as a southern gentleman and a Doc, those eggs are cooked."

"Wow! Thanks!" and off he went.

Sarge waited a minute. "Ok, Doc, what did you do?"

Laughing, "Who, Me?"

"Yes, you! Are those raw eggs?"

"Sarge, no! I gave my word."

"Yeah, I heard that. What then?"

"They are two of the prettiest, hard boiled, rotten eggs you have ever seen!"

Sarge laughed, "Damn! What am I going to do with you? Poisoning the troops now!"

"I just wish I could be there when he cracks them."

A couple of hours later, Crooky came back with his squad to go out on the patrol. I was glad Gray was going on this one, 'cause Crooky looked pissed.

"Hey, how did you like those eggs?"

"Doc, you bastard! You KNEW those eggs were rotten!"

"Noooooo, man! They weren't any good? Mine were great!"

He knew and I knew he knew, and that was fine with me. He was a shit bird. He was right, I didn't like him.

160

In a week or two, Sarge would have a chance to send two Marines to the 26th Marines who were afloat. Crooky would be one of them. This probably saved the lives, pardon the pun, of a "few good men".

The next morning, we were lined up like ducks in a row by 0400. The entire Company met on the bank of the river.

Third Platoon had point; Second Platoon had the middle, and First Platoon rear end Charlie. The Company CP was behind Second and in front of First. That was the pecking order. "Third herd" took off and waded into the river. It was wide and I guess four-feet deep where we were crossing. We crossed, and as soon as we stepped onto the bank of the other side, I found what it was to deal with the legendary elephant grass. It was horrible - sharp as a razor and over six-feet tall. Try as you may, if you touched it just a little wrong, it would slice through your flesh. Before we had made it 100 meters, I was bleeding from five or six places. We humped through this crap about two hours. It was about to break day. Then third herd turned south, and we all followed. Finally we were one long line of 150 or so Marines parallel to the river.

The call slowly came down the line: This is it, set in. We were supposed to all face right and then we were a blocking force 150 men strong, able to wipe out 8,000 gooks being methodically driven to us. One problem...I couldn't see 18 inches in front of me. The elephant grass was so tall and thick, what looked good on a map was in reality, probably the worse possible place to set up a blocking force. Around 2000 Marines were lined up around the island, with tanks, Am Tracks, fire support already called in, Phantom's waiting to be called, and we could only see 18 inches in front of us!

"Hey Sarge, you see anything wrong with this plan?"

"Everybody flatten out a spot in front of you, we'll have to make do with what we have."

I got down on the ground and rolled a few yards. I set back in and had maybe a five-foot "field of fire". Sarge was just to my left, and we talked a bit now and then. He got bits and pieces on the radio. Tank stuck. One company was in such thick growth they couldn't see where they were going or where they had been. Many were having trouble with the elephant grass. They were encountering spider holes, bunkers, tunnel complexes, but so far, no gooks.

Operation Taylor Common was under way.

We sat there for ten hours. It was getting dark. Throughout the day, there had been some fire fights and a few booby traps; but, thank God 8,000 NVA didn't come running through my five-foot killing zone. Now it was time to find a night pos.

We were basically going to turn around. First Platoon would be on point, then the CP, Second Platoon, then Third Herd.

We were on the move with about one and a half hours of daylight. We were going to find a place to set in for the night and then the powers-that-be will figure what to do next. Taylor Common was off to a bad start, and was far from over.

On we went, 15 meters apart, through the same elephant grass we had already been through. We went past where we had turned south and we went west. The ground was getting steeper. The grass was thinning. I saw daylight ahead, a place where you could actually see a hundred meters. Now we were in a clearing, a long thin piece of high ground. We were approaching a tree line when the column stopped. I looked around. Not a good place to stop. Tree line to my right 50 meters away. Tree line straight ahead 100 meters away. The river was to our rear. To our port side (left) was yet another tree line, though maybe 200 meters away. We were standing still in this open field surrounded on all three sides by tree lines. I looked all around and there was evidence of a whole lot of shit going down here. Bomb craters all around - some deep enough to hold eight or ten Marines.

It was getting dark and we were still standing out here in the open. I had a very bad feeling. I began yelling, "Get us out of this damn place! We are going to get ambushed!"

Sarge had taught me to always be aware of everything around me, always know exactly what you would do in any given situation - at all times. Being pissed off at being stuck out here in the open had side-tracked me. When the tree line to my right opened up on us with full automatic weapons, I went straight down. I had been in fire fights. I had been on both ends of an ambush. I had never seen anything like this. The fire was so intense it was deafening. Thousands of rounds flying at us! We were perfect targets out in the wide open standing still and 50 meters away. We were, by all rights, fucked like Hogan's goat!

I lay face down waiting for the call, "Corpsman up". It didn't come. The rounds kept coming and coming. I guessed well over 100 full automatic weapons. Occasionally I would hear an SKS (bolt action rifle), but mostly AK-47's and AK-50's. The adrenalin was pumping hard. This is where I would die. This is where we all would most likely die. Still no, "Corpsman up!" I was glad but on the other hand, did it mean they were all dead?

I had been scared before, practically everyday since I'd been in the bush - nothing like this. I had to be hit. There was no way in hell all those rounds could have missed me. They were too close. I felt them. I heard them buzz by my head...and I still heard them. I had my M-16 in my right hand. I squeezed the pistol grip. I could move my hands. I looked at that arm - no blood. I very slowly turned my head to the left; my left arm was stretched out. I moved my fingers. I looked for blood. None! I concentrated on my legs - tried to awaken them, to get the adrenalin to slow so I could feel. I felt nothing. Time stood still. How long had it been? It seemed like we were pinned down here for hours, but surely not over a few minutes. I must be the only one left. I turned my head to the tree line again. Muzzle flashes still pouring out rounds. I thought of moving, diving to a bomb crater and defending it, but knew I would never make it. Even if I did make it I couldn't hold off over 100 NVA alone.

I ran my right hand slowly down my leg looking for blood. I did the same to the left. The rounds were still pouring, kicking up dirt in my face, my back getting sprayed by dirt. I had to be hit. I didn't seem to be. I had to think. The best thing I could do was play dead. When they overran us I would still play dead and hope they didn't bayonet me. Then when they left, I would try to find a radio that worked. If I couldn't, I would make my way back to the foot hills and move only at night until I got close to the Bridge. The thought ran quickly through my mind, "I will never see poor little Chi Com again." Strange thought since I was sure I would never see my wife or family again. Adrenalin still pumping fast!

Soon, I heard an M-79 grenade launcher and thought, "Damn! They have bloopers too!"

I heard another round, and then another. They landed into the tree line we were being hit from. Wait a minute! Someone else is alive! Got to find him! We will team up and fight. I decided to run to one of the bomb craters. I jumped up, emptied my M-16 into the tree line on full automatic as I dove into the crater. I landed on Tommy. Rolled away. "Tommy, you okay?"

"Yes, Doc! You?"

"I think so."

Sarge dove inside, then Gray. We ran to the far side of the crater and opened up on the tree line. I flipped my switch on my weapon to semi automatic. I wanted accuracy. Other men were firing into the tree line. I was dazed. I couldn't figure out what had happened. No one was hit? Absolutely fuckin' impossible! The firing slowed from the tree line, then stopped. It was dark. The monster was going away, or waiting for another chance.

I had never been that scared before. I asked Sarge to contact all three squads for a sit rep (Situation report}. I wanted a casualty report. No one was hit in the whole friggin' Company!

"Sarge, how the hell could they have missed us?"

He laughed. "I have no idea, we were so screwed...and without a kiss."

It was totally dark now.

"Sarge, we can't stay here all night, they know exactly where we are, how many, and other than these bomb craters there is no cover...,"

"I'm going to talk to the skipper."

Sarge and Tommy took off.

I looked at Gray. "Well, Buddy, what d'ya think?"

"Damn, Bear! This isn't anything like what I was expecting."

I laughed, "Hell me either! I thought I was the only one not hit back there - kept hoping no one would call, "Corpsman up!"

"Bear, can I tell you something?"

"Sure".

"I don't think if someone would have called I could have gotten up and gone to them."

"Gray, you just described your own answer. Your first three words were 'I don't think'. Buddy, when the time comes, you won't think, you will just react. Trust me on this one and don't worry about it. Be as careful as you can, but you will react."

I lay there a while and recalled Marine boot camp. On the firing range they had told us, "Aim low in the dark, it is a natural tendency to shoot high at night." Is that what had happened? They had this whole company dead by all rights. Did they just over shoot us? I could think of no other explanation.

Sarge came back and jumped in the crater. "OK, we're setting in here tonight. We're setting up a perimeter here in bomb craters. And because they know where we are, we are calling in "basketball".

Basketball is a flare ship. It circles and drops flares on parachutes. They slowly descend, then burn out. It lights up the night as light as day. Problem is it would light us up, too. We would be okay in the craters, but whoever was on watch was in danger of catching a sniper round between the horns.

Soon we heard the plane coming. He would circle all night. We had "Spooky" on call in case of a human wave attack. Spooky was a gun ship, much the same as basketball, but Spooky dropped 7.62 rounds at an incredible rate of speed – and supposedly could cover an entire football field in 30 seconds.

We lay there in the crater. Tommy was scared but ready - maybe too ready. Gray was shaking like a dog passin' peach pits. I felt good about him, though.

I saw him watching the sky, "Hey Bear! What're all those parachutes?"

I looked and thought a second, "Holy shit! We are in for it now! They must think we are going to get overrun and they're sending in the Green Beret!"

Sarge laughed out loud then joined in. What an absurd idea. Even if we were going to get over run, no respectable Marine would want help from the Green Beret!

Gray lay there looking up and we played with him for a while. Finally, I said,
"Gray, we're fucking with you! Those are the parachutes the flares are on."

He laughed. I thought about how scared he was. I was scared, too. No, he would be okay. I was sure of it. Gray would be scared a lot, but when the shit hit the fan, he was to be counted on. He exceeded my expectations.

I thought we may very possibly get hit that night, but we were dug in now. We had something to defend. We would be okay.

By morning, they would have a secondary plan of action. I hoped it was better thought out than the first.

Chapter 17
<u>Ambush</u>

Shortly after the break of day, we moved out. It wasn't far to the river. Then we would go south a ways and we were back to "People's Village".

Operation Taylor Common would continue, just not as originally planned. On the way back, I was aware that we could be ambushed. They knew where we were last night. The trail could be booby trapped or an ambush set along the trail.

Go Noi Island was certainly different than the Phu Nans or the Dog Bone. At least that part of what we were told was true. It was kind of like back there we were defending An Hoa. Here, the NVA were at home. They were defending their own territory. Go Noi belonged to the NVA.

We reached the river and turned down stream. We hadn't gone far at all when "People's Village" came into view. Of course, now maybe the NVA had moved back in there. That idea was soon gone as I spotted a Tiger (tank) setting on the edge of the ville. We were told to set up a platoon-size perimeter. The Company would go on and set in somewhere else. We would set in here to both guard and use the tank. I liked the idea of having that fire power within our perimeter. It was armed with a 90-mm cannon, a .50- caliber machine gun, and a .30-caliber machine gun. We were to spend the night there, then send out an ambush. It was my turn for the ambush, so I just took out my poncho liner and lay down for a bit.

Sarge and I set into a hootch next to the hootch where the radio man and Tommy were in. Gray set in there as well. The hootches were small, so it was kind of a divided CP. Sarge took out his map.

"Look here, Doc."

168

I crawled over.

He pointed to a piece of high ground. "That is where we got hit from last night. There's a pretty good chance the gooks are still around there. What do you say we take advantage of having a tango (tank) with us, and go drop a round or two on that tree line?"

"Sounds good to me."

We walked down to the perimeter by the tank and Sarge was talking to the tank commander. I looked and, sure enough, I could see the tree line we were hit from. I recognized it easily.

The tank commander sighted in on it and shot out a spotter round. The white phosphorus round exploded just short of the tree line.

Sarge said, "Add 100 and fire for effect."

The tank commander cranked the big gun, and fired off a round - then another. It was right on target.

Sarge and I decided we would go sit by the river and watch the fireworks. The cannon boomed again and again as we sat there watching the tree line explode. It was maybe a click away (1,000 meters).

Sarge had the Platoon CP radio and was talking to the tank commander as we watched. Soon we heard over the net, "Be advised we are receiving incoming .50-cal rounds."

I said, "Sarge, someone named Bravo Tango is getting incoming .50-cal rounds."

"I heard that."

We sat and watched. Soon, the gunner on the tank was aiming the .50-cal machine gun toward the tree line.

"Woohoo, Doc! We are going to get some with the .50-cal! What a show!"

I sat there watching the action. The machine gun was tat-tat-tat-tatting at the tree line. The cannon was booming into it as well. It was quite a display. We still sat on the bank of the river watching the rounds and tracers fly by. The tree line was burning now.

I was watching the smoke, then adjusted my vision and saw something strange. The rounds from the .50 cal was hitting right in front of us - in the water not 30 meters from where we were sitting!

"Sarge, damn! Those guys can't shoot for shit! Look!"

He looked and saw what I was talking about. The rounds were now 30 feet from us and getting closer.

"Doc! Holy shit! INCOMING!!!!!! Take cover! INCOMING .50-cal rounds!!"

The radio we heard was the tank's call sign, Bravo Tango. They were reporting incoming .50-cal rounds. Sarge and I took off toward a bunker. You didn't want to get hit by a .50-cal round. That would screw up your whole weekend.

We jumped into a fighting hole dug long ago and Sarge said, "Mercy, Doc!" and laughed.

"Mercy Sarge!" and I laughed as well. We looked up from the bunker and the battle of the ".50-cals" was still going on. The platoon was well set in and I wasn't worried about being overrun, but I sure didn't want to treat a .50-cal wound.

Sarge was still laughing.

"What the hell are you laughing at?"

"I was just thinking, Doc, maybe we don't have our shit together after all. We were sitting there like a couple of tourists while incoming rounds were coming within 30 feet of us." Then it struck me as funny, well a little funny.

"Mercy, Sarge! Let's not tell anyone about that!"

"Mercy, Doc! I sure as hell won't!"

We laughed. I loved to hear him laugh. He laughed all the way to his socks. That night I had the ambush - Brock's squad, Tex's gun team. Stape was gone now, rotated back to the world. I would never forget him - the straight shooter, telling it like it is. I was happy for him, but I missed him.

The ambush had a simple design. We were to go around 400 or 500 meters down stream, find a trail and set up an ambush on it. We took off at dark. Routine gear – M-26 grenades, a few M-33's, M-16's helmet, flak jackets (which were always used except on three or four-man killer teams), and poncho liners. We got about 300 meters and the point man dropped like 40 pounds of rhinoceros shit.

We all hit the deck. Brock and I crawled up to the point. The point man did well. We had slipped up on a squad of NVA filling flare canisters with water. There were eight of them - three standing guard with AK-47's, and five getting water. It was perfect.

We were across the river from them - less than 50 meters away. Unlike the ambusher's last night, we wouldn't miss. We were elevated above them. I'd had dreams about an ambush like this. We had them outnumbered and all. Everything was in our favor as long as we were quiet, and kept out of sight.

We set up the ambush. A fire team on the left would fire semi-automatic from left to right. Brock, Jack the radioman and I were next, firing full-automatic for fire power; then the M-60 machine gun, which, of course, was automatic as well. Then another fire team would be firing semi-automatic from right to left. The third fire team would protect our rear. Adrenalin was pumping like crazy.

We were in position. Brock was to set it off with a burst of automatic fire. When he opened up, we all did. They never got off a round. It was almost dark, but we could still see the rounds hitting the soldiers, then the bodies. I heard the radio going off - Sarge wanted to know what the hell happened.

"We set off an ambush, Sarge! Caught eight NVA filling canisters with water!"

"Get, some!"

They were all eight KIA's (killed in action).

Brock said, "Okay, we got them. Now let's get back to the Platoon before they can react."

I said, "No, man! Let's get the weapons and canisters, we have time before dark. It wouldn't take us 15 minutes."

"Better not, Doc. They may catch us down there like we caught them. They sure as hell know we just ambushed their men. We had better make our dee dee."

I didn't like it. I was maybe even a little pissed. By morning, everything would be gone. Oh blood trail sure, but the bodies, souvenirs and documents they may be carrying would all be gone.

We moved back much faster than we had come. Brock called and told them to hold their fire; we were coming back inside the perimeter.

Sarge was waiting for us. "Mercy, Doc! Good job!"

"Thanks, Sarge." I went to the hootch while he talked to Brock.

Soon he came in. "You okay?"

"Yeah, I'm fine. Damn it, Sarge! We should have gotten those weapons."

"Why didn't you?"

"It's not my squad. I had no authority. When we go back tomorrow, they will be gone."

"It's okay, Doc. Ya'll should have gotten the weapons...but well, hell, you had a great ambush! Things don't always work out that well."

I smiled. "That part was way too cool. They never got a shot off."

The next morning, Second Platoon went back to the ambush site. As expected, the bodies, weapons, canisters and everything else was gone. Oh there were blood trails, a lot of holes in the bank, and it was obvious that an ambush went down there. They did add the body count to our total, but I still wasn't happy about it. It's not a matter of being gung ho - it's a matter of, "We had it all right there in front of us." It was all ours. All we had to do was gather it up.

We headed back toward the ville. We got about 100 meters and we were hit - incoming rockets, mortars, and AK rounds! It was a hell of a fire fight.

I dove into a bomb crater and Sarge was already there, on the radio, getting ready to call in artillery. He was getting the grids together as Liberty Bridge battery was preparing to fire a mission. Basically it was under control. No one was hit yet, and we had cover and arty on the way. Then I heard the whistle. Incoming round! A CLOSE incoming round!

"SHHHHHHHHoooooooooom! I dove hard into the side of the crater next to Sarge. I closed my eyes, covered my head and waited for the explosion.

"THUD!" It had hit right between the Sarge's head and mine. Dud round! I saw where it buried into the reddish dirt. But, it didn't go off.

"Sarge yelled, "Let's get the hell out of here!" We all bailed out of the crater. Sarge didn't laugh this time, nor did I. As we topped the lip of the bomb crater I did say, "Mercy, Sarge!" and ran like hell to cover. I dove behind a family bunker at the edge of a ville. I saw Tommy beside me. He was wondering what to do and seemed eager to do something. He was excited. I looked into his eyes. I didn't see fear - uncertainty maybe. But this man had heart.

"Shot out."

The artillery rounds were on the way.

The spotter round hit long and to the left of the high ground we were hit from. Sarge adjusted and "fired for effect". The tree line lit up. He had also called arty in on another area in case the NVA had moved to it. We stayed there until the arty was finished. We online assaulted the ville, and took a few rounds. We set up the M-60 and kept going. We took the ville and there was no sign of the enemy that was there minutes before. Tunnels! They must have escaped through tunnels.

We looked all around, in and under everything and found some small tunnels – probably the escape route. Damn this place was amazing! They had been fighting here and in this war for decades and they were ready.

We went back to the ville. Tomorrow another battalion sweep. Once again we would be the blocking force. This time, supposedly, we would be in a position where we could see. This time we knew a little more about the terrain. This time, hopefully, we would do it right. Right or wrong, tomorrow, we would do it.

Chapter 18
<u>Point Man</u>

"Point man" summed up in seven letters is "S-T-U-C-K-E-Y" (stoo-key). The 5'8", 145 lb. Marine from Nebraska was known as the best in the Company - possibly the best in the country. He was also a great guy and our friendship was growing daily. It would be a friendship that would last a lifetime. Lauren Alvin. Now, you would think, given a choice, if you were going to name your son after someone, you would pick someone with a name other than Lauren Alvin. But in two years, almost to the day, my son would be named Lauren Vincent after Stuckey and of course, Sarge. I would never regret that decision.

Stuckey was awesome. It seemed anytime we had a really big move, Stuckey was on point. He was on point a lot. Much of this he volunteered for. He was good at it – "gifted" if you will, and even he knew that. But rather than have some who was married or married with kids walk point, Stuck (stook) would often volunteer to take the other man's place. It was possibly the most dangerous position you could be in.

He could sense an ambush and would automatically switch routes to avoid it; or he'd switch to put us in a better position. He also had a sixth sense for booby traps. He would spot marked trails, and usually go around them. At the very least, he would point them out and also point out booby traps along the trail.

He had been with the Company since August. On his first patrol he was in Mac's squad and walking about the eighth man back. It was before I arrived. But as it was told, after a while at a check point, Stuckey said, "Mac, aren't we going to do anything about those booby traps?"

"What booby traps?"

"We just passed three booby traps on that trail. I was just wondering if we shouldn't tell someone."

Mac said "Where did you see booby traps?"

One by one, Stuck showed them to him. The squad had walked right by them sight unseen. Mac had a new point man.

On one move he had swerved us all around through the same creek three or four times. After the hump, I said, "Stuck, it's a good thing there is only north, south, east and west, because I swear you had us going in every direction possible."

"Trail was booby trapped, Doc. Had to change directions."

"How could you tell?"

"Doc, how do you know what's wrong with someone who is hit without an x-ray? How do you know if he had internal bleeding or whatever it is you do? It's my job to know."

He did know. I don't know how he knew, but he knew. He never once led us into an ambush. He always spotted booby trapped trails. Sometimes we took them anyway, but with the knowledge they were there.

Right now, two hours before daylight, he was walking point - taking us to our new position. We would then set in and supposedly between 2,000 and 8,000 NVA would be driven into our laps. He got us there before daybreak and we set in in the dark. This looked much better than the fiasco we had a few days ago. I set in next to Sarge. We were on a ridge overlooking a fairly open field and had a good field of fire. We also had good cover without doing much digging. I didn't like digging in if it was possible to avoid. It exposed the way you set in to the enemy. Soon the sweep began. We immediately heard small arms fire - AK's and M-16's. The radio was on and we were monitoring it. We could hear everything that was going on. Bravo Company was moving through a ville and searching it. A large straw basket, used to shell rice, was lying between two hootches. An alert Marine lifted it up and spotted a small tunnel.

The skipper called in his "tunnel rat". Armed with a flashlight and a Colt .45 automatic pistol, he went in to check it out. Pretty soon we heard, "Holy shit!!"

They had uncovered a 50-bed hospital. All underground. It was complete with IV's, meds, three nurses, a Bacse (Doctor), patients, weapons and all. This slowed down the sweep, but for a good reason.

Now, imagine if you will, you have a dirt-floored hootch. It is maybe 12-feet in diameter, with a bunker that is fortified and maybe six-feet in diameter. Ten feet from your "hootch" is someone else's hootch. That is your life. That is your sole possession - your home. The rice is for food. You don't sell it - you eat it.

Occasionally, you try to catch a fish in a stream; and when you do, it's a feast. Fish to go in your rice! Then fish heads! Maybe a water buffalo dies, and then you dress it and dry the meat in the sun and have that to get you through. There is no hope for more. That is the best that can happen to you - that and maybe not getting killed by either a Marine or an NVA soldier. Outside your home, the NVA decides to build a hospital. They dig a hole - a very big hole. They carry the dirt away because they don't want it discovered. Neither do you. What would happen to you if the Marines discovered in your "yard" you had a 50-bed enemy hospital? The only access to this hospital is through a hole in your yard that an average size dog couldn't crawl through. This is the life of a civilian on Go Noi. They didn't ask for it. They probably didn't want it. It just was! It is like the sky: Some days it rains rain; some days it rains sun; some days it rains rockets and mortars. Such is life on Go Noi Island.

Inside that hole was another world. A 50-bed hospital! It had food, bedding, medical supplies, medical personnel, and patients. Most of them had been shot or hit by shrapnel. The villagers were taken prisoner away to S-2 and questioned. The medical personnel were taken away as well. All supplies were taken and flown away to be examined and studied.

Soon the sweep was under way again. There were fire fights and booby traps intermittently. They were sweeping our way. We were ready. We had the 60-mm mortars set up to flood the field with shrapnel. The M-60 machine guns were on bi-pods and ready - two per Platoon. Six M-60's. A hell of a lot of fire power! Weapons Platoon had its 3.5 rocket men scattered among the Company. I felt confident we could handle a force five or six times as large as us in numbers. The Battalion Commander (the guy who looked like Elmer Fudd) even flew out and joined one of the Companies - the one escorting the tank. "Elmer" was here to "kill duh wabbit". He would stay three or four hours, fly back to An Hoa and put himself and the First Sergeant up for Silver Stars.

I had a lot of time to think. It's funny what goes through your mind before a battle. You try not to think of anything that may hinder your ability to fight. It is hard to do. Thinking of the things that mean the most to you right now may be the worse thing you can do.

I was thinking about how this would go down. Sarge had me thinking again. We had recently had a talk about tactics. The Army, supposedly, immediately hit the deck immediately if they were ambushed or had sniper fire. They would lay there and call in artillery or fire support or air strikes. But, when we were hit, we would hit the deck and set up an M-60 machine gun, and then the rest of the unit would get up and charge the enemy. I thought this was macho Marine bullshit so I had asked Sarge about it.

"Doc, if you were an NVA soldier and had 20 men with you and you ambushed a bunch of "doggies" and they hit the deck and stayed there, what would you do?"

"I would probably switch to semi-automatic and stay there picking them off one at a time. I would probably do this until we had killed them all or I saw a spotter round come in; and then I would take the men and make a run for it."

"Okay, now what would you do if you had the same 20 NVA soldiers and ambushed a Platoon of Marines; and within 30 seconds they had an M-60 set up firing at you; and the other 47 determined Marines were assaulting your ass online, returning fire and heading right for you?"

"I would probably fire a few bursts and haul ass." He was right. It wasn't just a macho thing; it was tactics. Isn't that what war is all about, tactics?

I asked him, "Sarge, what's going to happen when we open up on them? Will they keep coming? Will they hit the deck and we can cap at them?"

"In a bit, if all goes well, an undetermined number of NVA will be heading right at us. You know what they will do?"

"I hope they will die; but if not, what?"

"Just watch, Doc. They won't break a stride. They will turn and run in another direction, and if hit again, they will turn again. They won't even slow down unless killed or wounded. They will change directions each time they hit resistance until they determine the weakest link, then they will charge it. They'll break through the lines and scatter. They will never hit the deck - they won't even slow down. They will run until they die or figure the best place to escape."

I made a mental note.

About five hours later, we watched 150 hard-core NVA burst through the tree line and head right straight at us. They were armed, in uniforms and looking for a way out. It wasn't 8,000, but it was a lot of gooks. The adrenalin was pumping. Along through Go Noi, there were tunnels and spider holes. By now they were probably filled with the enemy. These 150 were trying to get away. They had no idea we were waiting for them. When they got within 150 meters, the M-60 opened up. Then we all did. I was firing on semi-automatic for accuracy. We didn't need fire power here, we needed accurate shooting. They were returning very little fire. I kept firing and smiled as I saw the column turn to their left, our right. They were hauling ass to that tree line. Just like Sarge said. The only ones that hit the deck were the dead or wounded. We had a right flank out and as the gooks approached, and it opened up. They turned left again and kept running. They were hit by a unit that was headed our way and this time they kept running straight into them, trying to break through. There was a fire fight and many dropped - the survivors breaking through the line. In a flash they were gone. We slowly moved from our pos (position) into the battleground. We took a body count, weapons and wallets, and whatever else from the dead and wounded. I found a dead Corpsman and took his "unit one". I quickly looked through it. All his meds were in tubes in which you had to inject water into the crystals making the needed solution. I couldn't wait until I had time to go through all of this.

We advanced carefully. They could be wounded and playing dead just waiting for a final shot. Off to my right I heard a "bloop", quickly followed by an M-16 round. I later learned the blooper man had approached a body and as he got close, he saw the "body" had an AK-

47 pointed at his chest. He fired the blooper but he was too close. The blooper round has to travel a ways before it will detonate as a grenade. It is set to rotate and after so many rotations only then will hit detonate upon impact. The round simply hit the NVA in the shoulder and didn't go off. A Marine to his right saw what was happening and put a single .556 round through the NVA's head. The body count was 43. There were another seven who were wounded and surrendered. Tommy was excited. The company did well. I always thought we did well when I didn't have to treat a casualty. I watched Tommy's excitement. I knew I would really like this guy in the states, or the rear - anywhere but here. He wanted and tried so hard to do what was expected of him.

We called in the choppers and loaded the dead and prisoners. This done, we still had time to get back to "People's Village". We were there by dark and set in. No ambush tonight. We sent out a three-man LP and that was it.

Early the next morning, we were off on a platoon-size operation. The main element would go to the ville we set in upon our arrival - the one Gonzales had been shot at. It was north of the ville and they would go there while I went with Crooky's squad. We were to go north by northwest and circle around and join the Platoon around dark. We were supposed to recon the area for activity and possible ambush sites. It was a long patrol with full packs and gear. I passed out salt tabs and made sure everyone had Halazone tabs for the water. It would be an all-day hump. We took off, split from the rest of the Platoon and headed west by northwest. Marshall was on point. We went a ways and then turned north. The terrain was just simply Go Noi: Dense growth, banana trees, villes and a few scattered rice paddies. We were walking along a tree line next to a graveyard. We had a good 15 meters between men and that is what saved us. We were ambushed. It was an upside down L, the short leg to our front, the long one to our port (left) side. There was little cover. Two men were hit right away immobilizing us. To the east of us was a grown up field. We returned fire, trying to hide behind the grave yard mounds.

Two men were hit. I ran to the first - gunshot wound right thigh. I put on a tight battle dressing and gave a shot of morphine. There was an estimated 50 to 75 NVA shooting at us. The fire intensified as I ran to the second casualty. He was hit in the lower leg and shoulder. I patched him up and gave him morphine as well. Two men both would make it, neither could run. We were hugging the ground returning fire, trying to blend in like chameleons with the terrain. We couldn't advance; couldn't withdraw. We were holding our own, but they were dug in and not going anywhere. Fire superiority would eventually prevail, and they had it. I got on the net, "I need the Papa Sierra (Platoon Sergeant)!"

"I hear the fire fight, Doc! What's going on?"

"We are fucked. Two men down! They will live but they can't run and I can't med evac them unless we move, and we can't move. We're pinned down just outside a graveyard with very little cover. If they decide to attack us, we will get some, but they would eventually overrun us. I guess between 50 and 75 hard-core NVA."

"If I can get a chopper in can you get them to it?"

"Hell no! Not now! I can't even lift my head. They're within 50 or 75 meters and it looks like they can shoot. Sarge, they're dug in. I don't think they will leave that cover. Why should they? The problem is neither can we. We have no defense here. We need to get where we can set up a line of defense."

"Ok, Doc, you are sure there are that many?"

"Can't you hear this shit? Yes, I'm sure at least 50 and probably more."

"Ok, Doc, I just know of one thing to do. We will have to call in artillery on you. Give me your grids and make damn sure they are accurate." Corporal Crooky was in charge, so I let him give me the grids. The rounds were still flying as I double-checked them and then got back on the net.

I gave him the grids. "What are you calling in?"

"105's - 81's are too inaccurate. But, at 50 meters, damn! It's a big chance."

"Yeah, and I think our only one. What do you want me to do?"

"I will fire a spotter-round, Willie Peter, adjust from that. When you are comfortable, I will order a 'fire for effect'."

BOOM!

"Holy shit! What was that?!"

"We hit a booby trap! The spotter-round is on the way. Give me a reading."

"FIRE IN THE HOLE!!!"

We all hugged the fresh earth. The spotter-round hit maybe 50 meters past the gooks.

"Sarge, that's damn close - 50 meters long. If they drop 100, it will be right on top of us. I think fire for effect and hope for no short rounds."

"Ok, here it comes - first barrage."

We grasped tight to the earth, hoping the rounds were long and that the grave mounds would protect us. The earth shook and trembled. Damn those were close but right on target.

"Okay, Doc, the last barrage is coming. When I yell 'Shot out!' grab the wounded and get the fuck out of there. Run to that tree line east of you and set in, in case they pursue."

"Okay. Guys get low and then get ready. When I yell 'Shot out!' someone grab Baker. I'll get Thomas. Let's get them out of here. Run east to that tree line."

"Okay!"

The rounds came thundering in.

"Okay! SHOT OUT!" I yelled at the top of my lungs. "SHOT OUT! RUN FOR IT!" I grabbed Thomas and threw him over my shoulder and took off. I had my head down running hard when the final rounds hit. We kept running. There were some AK rounds fired and some of the guys turned and returned fire, but nothing like it would have been had we not called in the artillery.

A Marine grabbed Thomas from me, taking his turn. I gladly let him, I was exhausted.

We reached the high ground and though far from ideal, it was still a place we could defend. We set up a perimeter with a rear watch and I looked after the wounded again. They were doing okay. Now at least I could get IV's going in them.

I called in an emergency med and a routine. Although out-numbered, we had a good piece of ground.

The NVA didn't follow us. The chopper was on the way when Crooky called me.

"Doc, Doc Gray wants to talk to you."

I said, "Hey, Squidly, what's up?"

"I have a chopper on the way here, too." I had forgotten about the booby trap while I was talking to Sarge.

"What ya' got?"

"One emergency and one routine!"

Uh-oh.

"What's the routine?"

He said, "Doc... Lt. Tommy's dead. Booby trap got him in the abdomen. I think it was his spleen but not sure. I tried to save him, but he just died - internal wounds." I heard the pain in Doc Gray's voice. We both liked Tommy a lot; and he loved his Corpsmen.

"I know you did, Gray. Damn! Thanks for telling me."

I turned away and walked to the edge of the tree line and allowed myself to cry for a few seconds. Damn! Tommy was gone. I was so afraid this would happen. It turned out the point man wanted to take a different route but Tommy told him to go the way we had been before. He did and someone in front of Tommy tripped a booby trap. Tommy had that damn Air Force flak jacket on.

I thought two main thoughts:

1. If Tommy would have lived, in 30 years the world would have been a better place because of him.

2. I wasn't with him. I knew Gray did all there was to do. But the fact remained, I wasn't with him. This would stay with me for years. But let me make this clear: It wasn't that Doc Gray did anything wrong or didn't do enough. Tommy would have died on me, too. It was that I wasn't there with him. I would learn a lesson here. Some deaths affect you in a way you don't expect. There was no blame for anyone, not even me. Yet this one I took personally. He was dead.

I would miss him very deeply and would never forget him - the bright red apple in a row of oranges.

Chapter 19
The Plan

It was December 24, 1968 - Christmas Eve. There would be no Christmas dinner, unless you consider a C-rat meal of "ham and mother fuckers" a Christmas dinner. I thought it funny - a few weeks ago for the Marine Corps birthday; they flew us out steaks, mashed potatoes, pasty gravy, something green and bread. I guess that was a more important day than Christmas in the "Corps". It was just as well, I guess. When we had eaten the steak dinner with the rich meat and gravy, most of us immediately threw it up - including myself. We just weren't used to real food. We had been on Go Noi a month now, and we were used to rice, green bananas, that cucumber looking squash and occasionally a C-rat meal. That, washed down with river water chemically cleaned with Halazone tablets was the normal meal.

Today we had C-rats and I chose ham and limas (affectionately known as "ham and mothers").

The word was there would be a "cease fire" in effect for the holiday. No ambushes, no patrols and the enemy was supposed to honor it! (Yeah, right! I'll hang a wreath!)

We had been on Go Noi a month now and had seen a few fire fights and booby traps since we lost Tommy, but basically routine for Go Noi. Sarge was Platoon Commander again and we were in "People's Village". We were set up in the southwest corner of the ville in a nice dry hootch right on the edge of the latest perimeter. I asked Sarge, "Do you really think they will honor a cease fire?"

"Hell no! They don't play by the rules. I think I will send out an ambush tonight."

"Okay, I'll go out on it."

Stuckey had the ambush that night and I sort of wanted to spend Christmas with him anyway. He was a Corporal now and squad leader. He was a good one, but he still walked point a lot. He didn't have to as squad leader. He could designate a point man, but he did it. That was just Stuckey. It seemed like a few weeks ago he was a PFC; then meritoriously promoted to Lance Corporal, and now Corporal. I had found out I was also promoted meritoriously to Hospitalman Petty Officer Third Class. Tommy had put me in for it and some medal as well. The rank brought a nice pay raise and, being married, I could use that.

Stuckey's squad was ready to go right before dark and I went along. I enjoyed Stuckey's sense of humor and he was the fastest beer drinker in the company. We had a contest when we were at the "Bridge" and it was amazing. Everyone, including myself, cut open a beer can and the can that hit the ground first won. Stuckey's can hit seconds before anyone else's. I don't know how he could possibly drink a beer that fast! You couldn't pour it out as fast as he drank it. I asked him and he said back in Nebraska on the farm they had contests all the time and he learned a method of "sucking it out". Ahh, the American farmer's ingenuity! No wonder we had such great crops! He also knew how to set up a squad-size ambush.

We went about 600 meters and set in right smack dab on the bank of the river. I took my usual 0100 to 0300 watch, and was on the radio when mortars started falling on the Platoon back at the ville. I took a chance and, since I had the hand set in my hand anyway, I called Sarge. "Papa Sierra, this is Alpha-2 Bravo. How's the weather?"

"Raining rockets and mortars! Merry friggin' Christmas!"

"Anyone hit?"

187

"Nope, not that I know of."

"Doc Gray okay?"

"Yep, right beside me watching the fireworks."

"I had better get off this thing then. Merry Christmas!"

"Merry Christmas, Doc!" I heard followed by that familiar bass roar of a laugh. Everybody was awake now listening to the battle of what was now to be known as "Christmas Ville".

Stuckey, the eyes and ears of the Platoon, was doing his job. He spotted muzzle flashes out across the river in the elephant grass. He called it in to Sarge and gave him the coordinates. Sarge called it in and within 30 minutes, "Spooky" (also called "Puff the Magic Dragon") was here.

"Spooky" was a gun ship. It was a converted airplane made into a flying arsenal. It was equipped with mini guns that fired 7.62 rounds so fast that even with every seventh round being a tracer round, it produced a solid red line from the plane to the ground, twisting and turning like a long thin red tornado. It would cover every square inch of a football field in seconds. It was awesome to watch and we were doing just that. Stuckey was on the net, and the rest of us were watching the show. I was closest to the river, but we all had a very good view.

It was amazing. "Spooky" kept circling, dropping flares so he could see below and continued to pour out rounds. The sound was almost like the purr of a cat - it was continuous and scary. The mortar fire stopped but "Spooky" didn't. We were laughing and joking; glad we went out on this particular ambush, when suddenly I saw "Spooky's" rounds getting closer. They were at the edge of the river, and now into the water not 30 feet from us.

"Check Fire! Check fire!" I yelled. Stuckey relayed it.

"Damn Stuckey! It was hitting right here by us!"

Stuckey called in, "Be advised the rounds were danger - close to our pos. Do they know we are out here?"

Sarge called in, "Roger that, Stuck! They see you. They spotted a group of NVA approaching your pos and took them out."

Keep in mind the football field thing and you can maybe see why I got excited.

"Spooky" soon opened up again and it continued for hours. It was a Christmas Eve I would not soon forget.

At first light of day we moved back to what we would now refer to as Christmas Ville. Sarge had caught a small piece of shrapnel in the shoulder but nothing serious.

Two days later we were on a patrol on the eastern edge of Go Noi, not far from the foothills when we saw three NVA soldiers dash into a tree line. We did what we were supposed to do, we called it in. We got the order we always got: Send a squad in online.

We sat back on the rice paddy waiting for the inevitable to happen. Sarge requested artillery on the ville, but to no avail. "Peep it out first. See if you can slip up on them."

Yeah, right. The three men were a decoy. They were waiting right now to ambush us. They knew our rules, our limitations. This was routine and what happened when you played "war" with rules. It made no sense. It was utterly stupid. Fighting a war with rules made by politicians! Ridiculous!

The squad got close to the ville and all hell broke loose. Surprise, surprise! We set up the two M-60's on the flanks and charged - right up the middle, shooting from the hip, shoulder, whatever seemed appropriate.

189

What mattered now was fire power. They had position. We had to overwhelm them.

I ran to the wounded as the Platoon took the ville. Three men hit. None would die. This is what pissed me off. Now, if we called, they would let us call in artillery or air strikes. Problem is, now we have a squad pinned down and we couldn't call in arty. Dangerous close - no fire mission. Frustrating!

We had a Marine named Whitney. He was a good Marine and everyone liked him. I was treating the wounded when I heard Sarge call out, "Whitney, get up there on top of that bunker and knock that machine gun out."

It was giving us a fit. Every time I tried to move to another casualty or better pos, the damn thing would open up. It wasn't just concentrating on me, it was indiscriminate.

Whitney charged firing on full automatic. The rest of the Platoon "put out rounds" to cover him. He ran to the side and turned and jumped right on top of the bunker housing the machine gun.

I looked up every so often but was concentrating on my casualties. I saw Whitney pull the pin on a grenade and toss in under him, inside the bunker. A few seconds later, it came back out and exploded nearby, but not inside the bunker where we wanted it.

"Whitney, knock out that damn gun!" He pulled the pin to yet another grenade and tossed it once again inside the bunker he was on top of. This time it came back out, only following it were also two chi com (Chinese Communist) grenades.

Sarge was yelling at the top of his lungs now, "Whitney! God damn it! Pull the pin, let the spoon fly, THEN lob that grenade inside the bunker!" I had to smile. It's amazing what adrenalin can do to you, both good and bad. Whitney knew how to do this; it was just the excitement of the moment, a little over anxious.

I looked up and this time he did it right. The gun was knocked out. It was nearly dark and we had to mop this up quickly. I got the wounded ready to med evac. The Platoon took the ville with minimal resistance. They ran. I called the chopper in - three priority med evacs. We had to change plans and set in a nearby ville for the night. We sure didn't want to stay here. They knew it too well, and so we moved a ways and set up a Platoon perimeter.

No ambush tonight. We didn't have enough time to get one set up right. We felt good about the fire fight. We only lost the three initial Marines and they would all be okay.

The next morning Sarge was in a good mood. We had a long patrol after we went and checked out the battlefield of the evening before. He called Whitney over and had him give a class on how to "knock out a machine gun bunker". It was fun for all, including Whitney - a good-natured black Marine and a good man. He took some ribbing, but after all, he had the balls to stick it out until the job was done. Nearly every man there understood his mistake - not holding the grenade long enough after letting the spoon fly. We had all done something similar in the heat of fire, all of us - even, I am sure, Sarge.

We saddled up and went back to the ville of the last battle. There was a lot of blood trails, it was a large force. We were lucky not to take more casualties than we did. The bodies were all gone - so were the weapons.

We continued on our patrol. We soon came to a nice little creek and crossed it. It was maybe five-feet deep and 40-feet wide and murky, but not bad. It had a little current probably due to the fact that it was very close to the foothills. We walked down the side of the stream a ways. As Sarge had taught me, I was aware of everything around me. I was also thinking, "What would I do in case of an ambush?" "Where would I go if we got hit here?" I kept looking around. We wouldn't get hit here. Booby traps were possible anywhere, but no ambush here. There were some trees along the bank. It was relatively flat, with high ground all around. There were rice paddies scattered to the east, and high ground all around them. You could even see the edge of the foot hills. From here you could observe all the way to the foot hills to the east. You also had great vision to the west. You couldn't see too far upstream or downstream, but you could put fire teams on both ends. I was getting excited. A plan was coming together.

"Sarge, mark this on your map so I can talk to you later. I have an idea." He slowly looked around. From anywhere else, this would look like the worse possible place to set up an ambush. But from here, it looked great. It would have to be a different type of ambush: Move in under cover of night, stay low all day, maybe slide down the creek bank and bathe quietly. But you couldn't make much noise. It would travel on the water. The beauty of it, and what I was excited about, is you could set in here for several days, and never be seen as long as you stayed put. You, in turn, had great vision all around. You could set here, spot the enemy and call in artillery and air strikes one after the other and they would never guess what the hell was going on. It didn't look like a place a squad or Platoon of Marines would set in. That is what made it perfect. I was excited.

Our patrol was over and I couldn't wait to tell Sarge my plan. "Sarge, remember that place I told you to mark? Listen to me a minute...I have an idea. It's different, but it will work." Sarge had already figured it out but listened patiently.

"Doc, we are going to try this. I have to get it okayed through the Skipper, but I am going to."

That was fine with me. He was the best. I envisioned us watching all these trails and calling in artillery and air strikes and the confusion of the enemy. I was also looking forward to no patrols or ambushes. This WAS our "patrols and ambushes", only from a stationary position. It would work - I was sure of it. The one draw back was if we were spotted it would be next to impossible to defend. No high ground - just a "swag" were we could lay low, kick ass and take names.

Sarge got it approved with the Skipper. The next morning two-hours before daylight, we slipped into the position. It had soft high grass (comfortable to lie on), a built in water supply, and a place to take a bath. You couldn't really swim there, but close to it. You could sure as hell get wet.

Day broke and a few guys slid down the bank and swam - well sort of. The water was flowing and we had all the drinking water we could want. It was less than an hour after daybreak when we spotted the first gooks on the move. They were moving into a tree line not far from Whitney's place where we had the fire fight. Sarge called in 105's from Liberty Bridge. He made an adjustment and it was right on top of them. This was great. We stayed right there. Weren't about to move. They had no clue what the hell had happened. They didn't know who had spotted them or from where - maybe it was just a coincidence. Within an hour it happened again. A larger unit this time - maybe company- sized. Sarge called in air strikes this time, 500 lb. bombs. This was so cool. We were kicking ass and not taking casualties. This went on for three days. The fourth day, we called in artillery on some gooks and Sarge called the Skipper. Soon the order came back...
"Saddle up, go check it out and get a body count."

"Noooooo!" Well, that was it. Once we left here, the jig was up. They would know what we had been doing. Playtime was over. We would have to go and be Marines again.

We gathered our gear and went to the ville we had just hit. Of course we were hit, but we took it without too much trouble. There were a lot of bodies and we took a count - 47 dead. Others were dragged away.

Sarge called it in. Then came the next order...."Well done, men! Go back to your pos and continue what you were doing..."

"What?!" No, that was stupid as hell! It was all over!" They knew where we were. They knew we couldn't defend that place. Sarge tried to talk the Skipper into letting us go back to the Christmas Ville.

"No, you are doling great! Keep it up!"

Sarge said, "Skipper, they know where we are now. They will come after us. We can't defend that place once they are on to us. We are done dealing."

"Nonsense! They don't know where you came from. Go back the long way and set back in the same place."

Nonsense is right! Damn!

We went back and set in. The excitement was gone now. I noticed by the time we got back to the spot, I was out of wind and dizzy.

"What the hell?" Something was wrong. It was a short hump and I was gasping for air. Sweating profusely. I slept well all night. The next morning when I woke up, I could hardly move. I didn't remember standing watch and wasn't sure if I did. I had the shits bad, but that wasn't too unusual. I looked at my stool and it was dark black. Uh oh!

We all had the shits, but this was different. Two other men were sick as well. I always used Halazone so couldn't figure it out. I had lost a LOT of weight, but over two months. I didn't think the problem was the weight loss. I couldn't think clearly.

I lay back down and dozed off. My buddy Steve came by and was playing with me. He saw I was asleep and patted me on the tummy. I jumped up like a shot and threatened to kick his ass. Well, I tried to jump up.

"Damn, Doc! I was just playing with you! Are you in a bad mood?"

I guess I was, but didn't know why. I lay back down and Sarge came over.

"Doc you ok?"

"Yes, just relaxing, this rain feels so good."

"Doc, it isn't raining. Look the sun is shinning bright."

"Yes, it is, damn it! I feel it hitting both arms! Look at the water!"

"Doc, it isn't raining."

I heard Sarge talking on the net. A "Cowboy" was flying over and kept coming back shooting rockets. "Cowboy" was a spotter plane, and in this case he saved our asses. He was cruising by and spotted a company of NVA moving down the river bank, no doubt to kick our ass. He kept hitting them with rockets. I was barely aware, barely heard the action. I was in fact, delirious.

Sarge got permission to move out and we did quickly. I didn't remember it. I remember waking up in the Christmas Ville and talking to someone. The next thing I remember was going through downtown DaNang in a jeep ambulance. I don't know how I got there. I don't know how I got back to the Christmas Ville but someone must have carried me.

I remember looking up, asking where I was.

"DaNang Doc. Just take it easy. You'll be okay. We're taking you to First Hospital.

I remember seeing the only words I could read - Shell Oil, Texaco, American - and thinking, "That's what this is all about! That's why I am here! Fucking oil companies!" As delirious as I was, I was right about that. Damn politicians.

After me and three others were med evaced, the Company sent a patrol back to our ambush site. Right up stream from us, they found 67 bodies sunk in the water. We had been drinking that water for four days. They were probably there from the battle where Whitney knocked out the machine gun, but who knows for sure. The one thing I did know was my ass was kicked. That one-celled wonder, the Amoeba, was a bad son of a bitch.

I sat on the shitter the next day staring at the walls. It was a two-holer right outside of my ward. The ward was a Quonset hut. I was now a patient. I had IV's in both arms, and had to take them with me outside to the crapper. I sat there. I had counted that day and this was my 50th trip to the crapper. I thought, "I have learned a lot of things in Vietnam just wish one of them wasn't how to piss through my ass!" I wondered if my dick would work anymore! Hell I never used it. I pissed through my ass and sex was out of the question!

I was very weak. I had lost a lot of blood. I had been in the hospital three days now and was supposed to get the "Silver Stallion" in the morning. It was an anal scope to see what damage the ameobiases did to my intestines. I guess I should be happy to be in the rear, but I wasn't. I was on the verge of depression. What the hell was wrong with me?

I thought about this a long time and couldn't come up with an answer. Did I miss the fighting? No. Did I miss drinking pissy water, eating crappy food, being filthy? No. Had I begun to like killing people? No. What was it? I was in this state of mind when I realized my mind was wandering. Where are they now? Were they hitting the shit? Who was walking point? Then, it dawned on me. I missed the Marines. **MY** Marines. I had received a letter from my best friend back in the world. We were very close through grade school, high school and college. While I was reading it, I realized, it wasn't the same anymore. I didn't KNOW if he would come after me if I lay in a rice paddy wounded. I wasn't positive he would lay down a line of fire to protect me while I ran to treat a wounded Marine. But, I knew 150 men who would, and I missed them. Yet it was more than that. I hated the fighting, the dying, the smell and the hell, but I had never felt more alive. In the bush every blade of grass had a meaning, a purpose. If it wasn't moving the way it should, I would spot it. I missed the adrenalin rush. There was nothing like it. It was an unbelievable high when you were being shot at, bullets kicking dirt up in your face, buzzing past your ears, hitting the tree next to your head. There, danger lurked everywhere and you had to be aware. I missed the awareness. I was probably much more aware than anyone on the ward now, but it was not like it was in the bush. There, your senses are taut - hearing everything - smelling things most people wouldn't notice.

I missed Sarge, Stuckey, Steve, Burke, Tommy. I missed the respect I got not for what I had done, but just because I was a bush Doc. They cared about me, I mean really cared about me. They would lay down their life for me. They had done it. I had done it. As I realized this, I knew my life would never be the same.

I wasn't depressed, I was lonely.

I would never look at my old best friend Ralph back in Missouri and feel close to him again. I wouldn't respect someone unless I had a reason to. I would never take life for granted again. Life was a precious thing as fragile as a lotus blossom. It needed to be appreciated.

We had a saying in the bush, "For those who have fought for it, life has a flavor the protected will never know." I knew now that was true. Who could possibly appreciate life more than those who experienced death daily?

I got off the wooden seat and walked back to the ward dragging two IV stands. I was still very weak. I needed to get strong again. I needed to go where I belonged - to the bush.

I got back to my rack, and a visitor was waiting. Mike! Damn it was good to see him! Mike was my best friend in Casual Company. He was one of the original 18 of us. I grabbed him, shook his hand and then we embraced. And I was happy again.

One question came to my mind first, "Mike, have you heard from any of the other 'Casuals'?"

Yes, he had. Mike had come in on a med evac with a badly wounded patient from his Platoon and was taking a breather. He had checked around. Mike looked at me and I knew it wasn't good news.

"Buddy, it is down to three. I got into personnel and checked the records of all our friends. That's how I found you. It is down to three: You, me, and Joe Redding."

"I know Joe is okay. I saw him four or five weeks ago. He is with my sister Company. We treated a triple amputee together! That bastard is crazy!" I smiled at the memory of Joe telling the engineer he would have his ass up running a mine detector in no time.

"Mike, are you sure that's it? Just the three of us?"

"I'm sure. We are the only ones left in-country. Five, maybe six, are dead - the rest seriously hurt, amputees or shot up real bad."

"Damn, Mike!" I lowered my head.

Mike was with 2/7. We weren't in the same area. Somehow I was glad he wasn't where Joe and I were.

"Okay," Mike said," tonight we are going to celebrate!"

"I can't Mike…I am a patient."

He said, "Sure you can! I will talk to the senior Corpsman. He'll let you go have a drink with me."

I smiled. If anyone could talk him into it, it was Mike. He did. We had a few drinks at the EM club at First Med Battalion. Then, we had a few more. We were sitting half snockered on a bunker at First Med when Mile pulled out a joint. I had never smoked pot in my life, but this was a good chance. We smoked it and then another. I was flying. So were the choppers. First Med was where most of our casualties went when we med evaced them. They kept coming. Some one was in the shit.

Curiosity got the best of me and I urged Mike to go with me to the Operating Room area. There we could find out what happened.

"Come, on! Let's just go see what unit it is."

"Okay."

We walked down and it was a mad house. I had never seen it from this end. I had PJ's on, but still looked like a bush Corpsman.

I heard someone say, "Another chopper coming in from 1/5."

Now I HAD to know. I looked for familiar faces among the wounded but saw none. I saw a Marine going by on a gurney.

"Hey, buddy; I'm a Doc with Alpha 1/5. What unit are you with?"

"Bravo 1/5, Doc. We really hit the shit on Go Noi. Daisy chain wiped out half my Platoon."

"Damn! Sorry man! Do you know Doc Redding?"

"Oh yeah, he was with my unit, got fucked up real bad." Now I had to know more.

I looked all around, asked around, nothing. We went from tent to tent - no Joe.

Finally I had to get to my rack. I was stoned and high.

"Mike, can you find out something in the morning and come tell me?"

"I think I can find out at personnel."

I stumbled to my rack and slept very little. Damn! Casual Company! We should have been called "Casualty" Company.

Mike came in around 0830. "I found him. Somehow he got sent to some 'doggie' unit on the other side of DaNang."

"Okay, let's go."

I went and talked to the Corpsman in charge, "I am going off the compound for a while. A friend of mine got fucked up bad last night and we are going to see him."

"I can't let you do that. You can't leave the compound! Hell, you shouldn't leave the ward! You were on IV's yesterday!"

I said, "Well, do what you have to do, but I am going."

We took off. We hitchhiked and caught a convoy. I was actually AWOL but didn't think they would have anyone out looking for me.

We reached the Army hospital and went in.

Joe wasn't hard to find. It seems they didn't get many Marines in here; there was some sort of mix up. I saw an Army Nurse, an honest to God round-eyed woman. I tried not to stare.

"Ma'am, can you tell me where Doc Redding is?"

"Do you mean the Navy Corpsman?"

"Yes, sorry."

The Navy Nurses didn't pull duty on the shore - hospital ships in the bay, yes; but shore duty, no.

"Yes, he is right over there. He is pretty bad but we think he will make it."

"What's wrong?"

"Oh, you don't know?"

"No, Ma'am. Diagnosis please?"

"Triple amputation, both legs and right arm."

Damn! I quickly recalled just five weeks ago. Joe and I together had treated an almost identically injured Marine. He made it, too.

We went to his bed. Joe was awake but woozy. He recognized us. We talked a while, somewhat in a daze.

"Joe, you take care now. I went AWOL to come see you, and I have to get back to the ward."

Mike and I kept our composure on the ward. That is, until we walked outside the hospital. We looked at each other and both had tears in our eyes. Mike said, "Bear, do you remember in Field Med School, when they told us two out of ten would finish their tour? I said to you, 'Well, it won't be you, and it won't be me!' You were too fat and I didn't know what end of a gun the bullet came out of!"

"Yes, I remember."

"God Damn, Bear! Who would have thunk it?"

We both broke down in tears.

Out of the 18 of us, according to their figures at Field Med School, three of us would make it. We had been in country a little over two month - now, we were two.

Chapter 20
<u>Dear Field Med Instructor</u>

Teach me, Instructor,
I need to know more!
Is being a Doc different since I'm now in the Corps?
Marine boot camp is over,
And next comes your class.
Vietnam will come quickly.
Please teach me fast!

Triage and cut-downs, chest wounds and such!
Teach me, Instructor; I need to learn much!
You say battle dressings will be my "best friend".
Tourniquets, hemostats…and it all starts again.

Traches, amputations, and of course CPR,
White phosphorous, AK wounds…
I'm with you so far.
Give me your wisdom!
Help me prepare!
For when the wounded start falling
YOU won't be there.

My tour is long over.
Do you mind if I share
Some thoughts, so the next Doc is better prepared?
Teach me the Marine bleeding as I fight for his life
Will whisper, "If I die, Doc, please write my wife."

Teach me, Instructor, when the firefight is done,
To ignore that the Corporal had a daughter and son.
Or when the booby trap smoke clears
And the chopper's called in,
That the Marine in the poncho
Is my very best friend!

You taught me to save lives,

But it's not over yet…..

Teach me, Instructor……

How to forget…..

Doc Hutch
Alpha 1/5

June 1968, I reported to the U.S. Marine Corps Training Center at Camp Pendleton, California.

I had my orders to the FMF, First Marine Division, RVN (Republic of Vietnam). I finally had to leave Bethesda Naval Hospital and found myself in a whole new world.

It was hard leaving Bethesda. I had been there 30 months: Three schools, and the first 18-months of our marriage. I loved the D.C. area. There was so much to do and to see - so many good memories. Now, everything had changed. Linda was in Missouri staying with her parents until she got a job and her own apartment. I was 3,000 miles away, basically in a whole new branch of service. I had worn the Navy uniform for nearly three years. Now I would be wearing the Marine Corps Green.

I had brought very little with me: One Navy uniform, personal items, writing stationary, and some pictures. My sea bag was less than half full. I left all my Navy uniforms behind. I would no longer need them.

I reported in and found that the next class had already started. There were several others in the same situation. I found this wasn't unusual. They dubbed us the "Casual Company". We were simply to kill time until the next class was ready to begin. We soon grew to 18 in number. We did things like trim grass, pick up trash, and basically kill time. They weren't real hard on us - just some stupid watches like back in Navy boot camp. We had all been in at least a year and most of us had been doing duties a little more important than watching a trash can. The 18 Corpsmen got very close. We laughed, played, made crude jokes about the FMF Corpsmen already in school, and drank a lot of beer. Those of us who didn't have a watch that night would usually find our way into Oceanside. We would hit the bars, strip joints, restaurants, and generally have a good time. We were quite a group. We had a gambler, a drunk, a bum, a few city boys, several country boys and three of the 18 of us were from Missouri. Mac was from Columbia. Jake was from St. Louis. And I was from the southern part of the state, around the Ozarks. We were "Casuals" for four weeks. We got very close, I guess, because we were the ones out of place. We weren't assigned to a unit; we were simply "Casuals".

Soon the four weeks were over. We had a class now of around 75. As the barracks began to fill, we "Casuals" stuck together. Mac was appointed Company Adjutant. He in turn saw to it that the 18 of us pretty much bunked in the same area, had the best details, and we were usually off the same weekends. We had a "click" and, though I hate to admit it, we were sometimes assholes about it. The 18 of us stuck together. That would continue throughout the schooling.

There were two parts to becoming an 8404 (FMF Corpsman):

Part one was eight- weeks of Marine boot camp;

Part two was eight weeks of Field Medical Technician School.

Then would come Vietnam.

Tomorrow morning we would begin Marine Boot Camp. There were rumors flying that we would have Sgt. Stacker. This was not a good thing. He was known as the toughest D.I. on base. He loved to run his recruits and he ran with them. He had no tolerance for quitters and was a diehard Marine. He was also a good D.I. - just tough.

We were asleep in the barracks at 0400 the next morning (probably whoever had the watch was, too), when a "CRASH" rang through the barracks. It was a "shit can" being kicked from one end to the other.

"All right, Sleeping Beauties! Get your scumbag asses out of the rack and come to attention. We are going to get a few things straight right fucking NOW!! First of all, you are RECRUITS, you got that? You are fucking 'BOOTS'!! I don't care if you have been in service for 20 fucking years - you are boots and you sure as hell had better act like boots! You know nothing! You are SHIT, pond scum, afterbirth! You are the lowest fucking thing on earth! You haven't been in the MILITARY! You've been in the fucking NAVY! NOW you are in the military! And let me tell you assholes, you are in for a rude fucking awakening! 'TEN HUT'!!!"

Well, hell, this wasn't going to be much fun at all.

Sgt. Stacker was about six-feet tall and maybe 180 pounds. There wasn't an inch of fat on him. Most of us were soft from hospital duty or school, but Sarge had a remedy for that......running our asses off.

He lined us up outside and we were appointed a marching spot. That would be our spot for the next 16 weeks. That's how we would run, go to classrooms, the mess hall and everything else we did as a unit.

"Company............forward....   Double time....MARCH!" Off we went on our first five-mile run. Stacker was tough and he was an asshole, but his reputation was he was also a very good D.I.

My position was about two-thirds of the way back in the column on the left, right where Stacker would often run.

"Come on, you lard asses! Move it!!!!!!"

I weighed in at 252 pounds - the heaviest I had ever been in my life or for that matter would ever be.

I played basketball at Bethesda and walked some; but other than that. I was out of shape. I was, however, determined. I would NOT be the first one to drop out on a run. Word had it the first one who slacked off or dropped out was hassled for the whole 16 weeks. It wasn't going to be me. After three miles I realized obviously, everyone else felt the same way. We finished the five-mile run and no one had quit. We were huffing and puffing like a bunch of beagles in heat, but no one had quit. This pissed Stacker off. He ran us another three miles. Again, no one quit. The last three-mile run ended in front of the chow hall.

"Alright, you pussies! Chow time! Go to your troughs, you fucking pigs!"

We fell out for breakfast. It was SOS, eggs and coffee. A far cry from Navy chow, but breakfast nonetheless.

Afterwards we mustered and it all began.

"You call that a shoe shine, you Squidly piece of shit?" And so on. Guys who wouldn't or couldn't do push ups were stomped, kicked, threatened, cursed and treated like what we were, the lowest thing on earth.

Now when regular Marines go through this shit, they are really boots. I had been in the service nearly three years and the others close to that or longer. It was a real blow to the ego.

There was another difference between us and the true Marine boot camp. Around 1800 it went like this:

"Okay, Lard Asses! Have your sorry butts out here at 0400 and we will run, and you pussies better really run or I'll kick your sorry asses to Camp Lejune! Dismissed!!"

Then, "Hey, Doc, you want to go to town later and knock down a few beers?"

Now I personally had a problem with going to town and having a few beers with someone who has spent the last 14 hours calling me "Shit Head". Maybe it was just the way I was brought up in the Ozarks, but this wasn't the guy I wanted for a drinking buddy. The Casuals usually all went together - at least the ones who didn't have to guard a shitter all night.

Daytime was a bitch. We were treated like boots and the training came along as well. Simulated booby trapped trails, crawling under wire under fire, climbing the sides of ships on ropes, jumping into and out of helicopters.

The last week would be Bivouac. We would go into the rattlesnake infested mountains of the desert and play John Wayne. Stacker's favorite saying was heard many times everyday. "Damn, Doc, do that in 'Nam and Charlie will put a round right between your running lights."

It was about two weeks into this that I realized we were actually being trained to be Marines. We were trained to set up and set off ambushes, to use a compass, and not just to call in choppers but to call in artillery and air strikes. We were being trained to walk point, spot booby traps, and shoot to kill. At the rifle range I was right at home. Mac was pathetic. Stacker came up behind me while I was shooting my target to qualify and said, "Damn, we have a zinger here! Where did you learn to shoot?"

I said, "In the Ozarks! We shoot assholes that make us run five miles a day." No sense of humor at all. "Well, get your head down! You're going to catch a round right between the running lights."

It was about six-weeks into our training when Sarge talked to us one night at the strip bar about him going over (to 'Nam).   He would be right behind us. We were in a club and he sat down at our table and said, "You know, you guys think I'm a hard ass, but I am just trying to save your lives.   I have had Docs tell me if I was hit in 'Nam that they wouldn't patch me up.   Do you think they were serious?"

I said, "I'd patch you up, Sarge.   Right after you gave me 100 push ups!   Then I'd say, 'Want some Morphine asshole?   Another 50!'"   We all had a good laugh, but I could tell he was really worried about that.

In a year, I would be out of the bush at 1st Med Bat.   Mac would be the Chief of Medicines Clerk.   He would tell me that Stacker went to our sister Battalion, 3/5.   In less than a month he was dead.   No, no one refused to treat him.   He took a round "right between the running lights".

Our last week of boot camp was here.   Soon we would be treated like Corpsmen again.   But first, the mountains.

It was hot and snaky.   We learned a lot.   I found myself really hating this aspect of Field Med School.   I tried to learn it, but I was not the gung ho one.   We had a Casual we nicknamed "Ricky Recon".   He was really into this shit - a regular Chesty Puller (the great Marine hero), but it wasn't me.

We set up night ambushes, walked into them and took turns setting them off.   We ran up and down those mountains like a bunch of goats.   After the week was up, Sarge congratulated us.   We had made it through the Marine part of it.

Part two was medicine, and I was far less concerned with that.   Medicine came naturally to me.   I learned it easily and I retained it well.

It turned out to be the best course I had ever taken. It was short (eight weeks), but very intense. I now knew more about first aid than I thought was even there to know. We covered everything: Tracheas, amputations, triage, Willie Peter, gunshot wounds, literally every wound man has managed to find a way to inflict on another man. We watched films. We simulated wounds and treated them. We made homemade trache kits, casts, and braces. It was amazing.

I began to notice one thing right away that bothered me a lot. In fact, it scared the hell out of me. It was a strategy to help keep us from cracking up. They called it "Attitude Checks".

The Instructor would yell out in the middle of a class, "Attitude Check!!"

We were to respond with, "Fuck it!!"

Now, I wondered, why would they want us to have a "fuck it" attitude? Why would they train us to have an "I-don't-give-a-shit" attitude? There had to be a reason. It began to become apparent. At first we were given stats.

"You will serve six-months in the bush, and then be sent to the rear according to your specialties for your last six-months before you go home. Those of you, who make it six-months, will most likely make it back home. The reason you spend the FIRST six-months in the bush is a simple one: There will be an ungodly amount of pressure on you, and it is better if you have to handle that pressure the first six-months than the six-months before you would go back to the 'world'. It will also give you a little time to adjust from being a 'bush Corpsman'."

Ok, let's go back to that little "those-of-you-who-make-it" thingy.

Someone asked, "Chief, give us some percentages here. What are our chances?"

Chief calmly said, "Two out of ten of you will finish your tour – twenty percent. The rest will either be killed or wounded bad enough to be shipped stateside."

Mac looked at me right then and said, "Damn! Well, if it's two out of ten, it won't be me, and it won't be you. You're too fat and I don't know what end of a gun the bullet is supposed to come out of!" We laughed, but it wasn't funny. Out of 18 "Casuals" meant, by their own figures, at best three of us would finish our tour. James Cravens was a good prospect. He could bench press 300 pounds. There was "Ricky Recon", Andy, Peterman - all possibilities.

I thought my best chance was to be assigned to First Med as a NP (Neuro-Psychiatric) tech - or an orthopedic tech. Mac could talk his way out of about anything, and his best chance was to do just that. Neither of us did.

We were down to our last week of Field Medical Technician School. We were to have another camp out, but this time as Doc's. Sgt Stacker, of course, was still our D.I. But he just marched us to classes, made us run and stuff like that. He had nothing to do with the medical end of it, just our constant reminder that we were Marines now. The last week was very well organized. We had simulated-wounded brought to us, we tagged and treated them, and had to explain what we did and why. It was very intense. They were dead serious about us knowing what we were doing. They also told us it would be a little different over there. The bodies and ammo would be real. We had one main objective: Do whatever it took to keep that Marine alive long enough to get him to a surgeon.

Soon, it was all over but the graduation and we had a weekend off. About half of us "Casuals" decided we were going to Tijuana Mexico and raise some hell. It was our last weekend together and we were going to "tie one on". We rented a car, filled it up with 8404's and gas and headed to TJ - Mac, Joe Redding, Andy, Pete, Ricky, Bumper, Jake and myself. I was married but the rest were single. I planned to do a lot of drinking and wasn't interested in a hooker, but Joe was. "I am going to Vietnam in a few days. I am single, so I am going to get both drunk and laid!"

We crossed the border with little trouble, parked the car, hoping it would be there when we came back, and started hitting the bars. Tequila was the drink of the day, and some beer. I did the beer thing after tasting a few watered down Margueritas.

After a few drinks we decided to go to the infamous "Donkey Show". Enough said about that.

As soon we went in to this "classier" bar, we ran into a fellow "student". He was an E-6 HM1 petty officer. He was also a Preventative Medicine tech. We were all acting stupid (and not much acting was involved). This bar was nicer than the others. After the Donkey Show, I think we were ready for some civilized entertainment. This was a strip joint and the girls were young, pretty and butt naked. They danced nude inside this "rail" for a while, then would come outside with the crowd and solicit "johns". They would take these guys to a back room and offer them more personal services.

While out mingling with the crowd, they would wear something skimpy to "flaunt their wares". I wasn't interested - Joe was.

What I was interested in, though, was our HM1 Petty Officer 1st Class Preventative Med tech. Those gals dancing inside the short rail would get close to the rail and for the sum of a quarter, they would allow, in medical terms, the guys watching to "suckle the maiden's breasts". Now, our HM1 was innovative. He was paying them a dollar and they would plop a leg up on the rail while he performed cunnilingus on them -

211

ALL of them. Now I am not a prude and certainly not against oral sex. I believe what a man and a woman want to do in the bedroom is fine and dandy as long as there is no bloodletting involved, and they BOTH want to participate. But, this was a PREVENTATIVE MEDICINE TECH!!

He was going down on all the local whores who had just been sleeping with who-knows-how-many different guys in the last few hours! This amazed me and I must say made me more careful about what I drank.

Joe found a girl to his liking. She was attractive and it was around 0200 so that didn't mean a lot. We had to get back to base for graduation the next morning. She wanted $15. Joe had $7, so the rest of us chipped in. Off they went.

We had a few more watered down drinks and Joe was still gone. Finally about 0400, we decided he had either been kidnapped or killed and we all left the bar to go find a cop. We headed around the corner, passed an alley and here came Joe, walking down the alley with a big smile on his face.

"Where have you been, we thought you were kidnapped?"

"She liked me!" He laughed, as did the rest of us, somewhat relieved. I guess he got our $15 worth.

At graduation, we were inside a large auditorium. Parents and wives were there.

The Chief opened up with a statement that continued to bother me, "I won't ask these guys for an "Attitude Check". Sure, a little inside joke, but I wasn't buying the "lightness" of it. It was for a purpose. Everyone laughed, except probably me, and the ceremony began.

We went up on stage to receive our certificates. All the instructors were there, and I have to admit, they were excellent. After they spoke, it was Sgt. Stacker's turn. What I thought was going to be a "hoot" turned

212

out to be a very moving speech. He began with the first day, the first five-mile run, then the additional three because no one would quit. He apologized to us for taking it easy on us. He said he had been easier on us than any other company he had D.I.'d in two years; and the reason was we had more heart than any unit he had ever seen. Probably said the same thing every graduation, but I felt he was sincere.

We left the Hall and went back to our barracks. It was time to get orders. I had a big surprise. I had orders for twelve days of leave before flying from Travis to 'Nam. The problem was I knew I didn't have twelve days. I just took 30 days 16 weeks ago before reporting here. I went to personnel and told them I didn't have twelve days coming. They told me to go ahead and take it, it was on my orders and I had the check.

This meant the other 17 "Casuals" would go over twelve days before me. We all got together for a photo shoot. I had a Kodak M14-8mm movie camera, which I would also carry in 'Nam. I had Mac take the movie of the other 17 of us. I wish I would have thought more about this. He was my best friend and should have been in it, not taking it.

Then we all went to the airport - I headed to St Louis - the rest to Okinawa. I had not expected to see my beautiful wife for a year. Somehow, we were granted a wonderful, undeserved twelve days of leave. We went to Hannibal, Missouri, and did the Mark Twain tour. It was an incredible 12 days, but always on my mind was, "Will I ever see her again?"

We lived the time we had together to the fullest despite knowing there were bad times ahead. This "goodbye" was the hardest. I thought I had said my last one when I left to go to Field Med. But this time, I wasn't looking into those blue eyes thinking, "I have three months of training - anything can happen - the war could end - I could flunk out of school!" This "goodbye" was different in the fact that in three days I would be wearing Marine Corps cammies in a friggin' war zone. At Lambert Field, I tried to be strong. I saw the tears in her blue eyes - the very eyes that drew me to that rundown coffee shop every morning to see her.

And I made a promise: "Linda, I will make it back. I give you my word, and I don't break my word. I will be back." (I said this long before "Awwwnold" would be famous for that line.) We kissed one more time as I headed down the ramp, now dressed in Marine Corps Green.

I was on my way to Travis Air Force to catch my flight. There were two big things I was unaware of. In the video which I had left with my wife of our "Casual" group on graduation day, I would be the only one on it still alive and well in Vietnam in 60 days. Mac, the one who took the video would be the only other "Casual" left.

The second thing was that on Oct. 23, 1968, when I set foot on enemy soil - just 12 days after graduation - four of the 18 were already gone. Two were dead. Jim, who could bench press 300 lbs., lost his right arm, and Pete was hit three times in the stomach by a machine gun.

I learned a lot in Field Med School. Now I would really learn what it meant to be a Field Medical Tech. in The U.S. Marine Corps.

Now I would truly earn the right to be called "Doc".

Chapter 21
Back To the Bush

I sat across from the Chief at the 1/5 BAS reporting in so I could return to my Platoon.

Chief said, "You are doing a good job out there, but I want you to be more careful. I have three citations here written up on you from your Company. You are taking too many unnecessary chances."

I replied honestly, "Chief, I'm not taking unnecessary chances. I would guess necessity would depend on whether you were the one wounded or not. But you know I don't care about medals - I just want my six months in and then to go to DaNang."

"You just got a meritorious promotion to HM3rd Class and I have another here recommending you to be promoted again, to HM2. I appreciate the job you are doing; I just don't want to lose you."

"I wouldn't want that myself, but I have another bigger problem I would like to talk to you about."

"You're changing the subject, but what?"

"Chief, it's those damn 'gook sores'. I need something more to treat them more effectively. We have Tetracycline, but that's doesn't always work. I need some Emycin, and ProPen VK. If I can keep the 'gook' sores under control with antibiotics, then I can keep the more experienced Marines in the field, which, in turn, will cut down on casualties."

"Bear, you know the regulations: no penicillin or erythromycin in the bush. You don't have medical records out there, so you don't know who is allergic to what. By just allowing Tetracycline, when you med evac someone, the MD's know what they have been treated with."

"I don't have their medical records, Chief, but most of my Marines can talk and I can ask them if they are allergic to anything. The way I see it, the benefit far outweighs the danger. If I can treat infections out there, make them wash and use Phisohex surgical soap regularly, then I can keep the veterans in the field instead of having new guys out there screwing up. I think fewer men will die if we keep the unnecessary med evacs down."

"Point taken, Bear, but we have regulations. You can't expect me to violate regulations on a theory."

With this statement, the Chief got up, dropped his set of keys to the med locker on the desk, and walked out of the office. This was a career man I could respect. He put the good of the men above regulations. He was probably not over 30-years old, and already a Chief Petty Officer. He was knowledgeable and very bright. As I stocked up on meds, including ProPen VK and Erythromycin, I thought, "Alpha 1/5 is very lucky to have that man as BAS Chief, and if I get sick or hit, I would want him working on me." I still resented "lifers", but there were two big exceptions, Sarge and the Chief.

It was good to be at the BAS, but I missed my Platoon. I thought about them all the time. I was issued a new set of jungle utilities (28-inch waist now) and boots. I kept my old flack jacket and helmet. I didn't want to be too shiny when I was choppered out in the morning. I didn't know where they were, and Chief wasn't exactly sure either. I would soon find out. I was still very weak. I had lost a lot of blood. Chief gave me iron tabs, potassium and a multivitamin to take daily.

That evening I had two beers, a steak, and potato; then saddled up and had the driver take me to the Alpha Co. tent. I would go to the chow hall in the morning, load up on milk, then catch the supply chopper to my Company. As I lay on my cot that night, wondering where the company was, I thought about Chi Com. It had been over a month since I had seen her. I wondered if she was even still alive, or if she would remember me when we went back there. What kind of life will she have? I didn't recall seeing her mother, and was sure her dad was in China, if still living. It was a sad thought and I put it out of my mind.

Many things ran through my mind as I spent my last night on a cot for a while. I knew my wife was worried sick about me. I wrote often and had even called over a HAM radio in DaNang. Then there was the other 16 "Casuals". Four or five were dead, the rest screwed up bad. I thought of the Platoon waiting for me to come back to them. It would be great to see them, and I hoped they were all still there. Gray had been alone I guess for the ten days I was gone. He was a good Corpsman and I was glad to have him as a partner. I tried to get back in the right frame of mind to function properly in the bush, and, in doing so, fell asleep.

I went to the chow hall at 0530 and had milk, eggs, bacon and bread. It would be a while before I had decent chow again.

Around 0900, the chopper came in. I loaded up along with three other guys from the Company I didn't know, and we were off.

I watched the terrain as we flew and saw we were headed SE of Go Noi. The chopper was descending and as the ramp lowered on the Ch-47, I was searching the Marines waiting for supplies and mail. I saw Sarge right away. He had heard I was coming.

He shook my hand, "Damn, Doc! I'm going to have to load you down with blooper rounds so you don't blow away!" I was down to 172 pounds, and didn't look great. I looked much better when I was 190 and healthy.

It was good to see Sarge. It lifted my spirits, and soon I would see others as well - Stuckey, Gray, Mac, Phil, Steve, and many, many others.

217

We were south of Go Noi, had just been resupplied and were about to move out to a new pos, close to the ridge that bordered the An Hoa Basin. It was a hairy area. No friendly villes - no Chi Com.

We packed up a three-day supply of rations and moved out. Second Platoon had point. We would lead the Company to the new position. They would fall out and we would continue to a platoon-size patrol and ambush. We were almost to the area where we would split up and I both saw and heard excitement ahead. There was a commotion, though not an ambush or booby trap. I looked and saw what the big attraction was. Everyone was pointing and watching with awe and respect. It was a dog. It was a black dog. It was of average size. It had no back legs. He would hike up his hind quarters and walk on both front legs. Not only would he walk, but he walked very well. Perfect balance! This poor dog had no doubt hit a booby trap and had both rear legs blown off. It survived - not just to exist. It functioned! He was the family's watch dog and as we approached the ville, he did his job: He alerted them we were coming.

He came out to meet us - to check us out. This dog had earned the respect and admiration of an entire company of combat-hardened Marines. I got out my M-14 movie camera and took a video of it which I will always keep. This plain simple black dog had heart. He would go on with his life and he would make the best of it. He would have made a good Marine.

The next day we went on a platoon-sized patrol. We were crossing a huge rice paddy when we were hit from a large ville. It was about 100 meters away. We were close to a large burm, so we ran to it and returned fire. I was capping away along with everyone else when I heard the radioman, Phil, call me.

"Doc, are you all right?"

I said, "Yes, why?"

"They just called a 'Zulu' in on you, said you were killed in action."

"Give me that net."

I got on the net and informed the Company CP I was not dead and as far as I knew, no one else was either. I was not happy hearing of my demise.

When a Doc gets killed, the morale goes way down. The Marines, as I have said so many times, take care of their Docs. They pride themselves in that and deserve to. The morale also goes down because they know if they are wounded, we will do our best to keep them alive. This did not start my second day back in the bush off very well. I was pissed and was also wondering if perhaps it was a warning- an omen. Was this the day Mike would be the only remaining "Casual"?

The Company Skipper was planning an attack as we hid behind the burm.

At this point I was still recalling hearing of my demise.

When the word came to "lay low" Phantom's were coming with 500 lb bombs my pulse went up. We were within 100 meters, very close for bombs. "Mercy, Sarge"

The jets were soon there and the ville was fast becoming a pile of rubble. I think maybe hearing I was killed had a bad effect on me. I felt a deep hatred and fear- and anger.

When the F-14's had dropped their loads, we assaulted the ville online, shooting anything that moved, fragging all bunkers. There was some resistance, but not a lot. We got inside the tree line and set up a perimeter. Sarge was on the net and he didn't look happy.

"Skipper wants a body count."

"What?"

"He wants a body count. He wants us to dig up these bodies and bunkers and get a solid body count."

I said, "Sarge, just make one up! Hell, tell HIM to make one up! Who the hell cares? These guys don't need to be digging bodies out of these bunkers."

"He wants it done, Doc. We are up for the Presidential Unit Citation and this could clinch it." The order stood.

I said, "Well, I'll have nothing to do with it!" and walked away. I knew it would have an effect on these young men. We often assaulted a ville when fired upon, "Shoot anything that moves; frag all bunkers." It didn't take a genius to figure that the civilians would run and hide in their bunkers, but we didn't see them. We didn't dig them out. They were the enemy. They booby trapped trails, fed and clothed the enemy, and spied for them. This was war. In war, you killed the enemy. You took ground and destroyed it. Along with that, "civilians" got killed. But, going into these bunkers and digging out women and children was stupid. These men would never forget this day, and it pissed me off. They wouldn't remember the NVA we dug out; that memory would soon pass away as a part of war. But they would remember the women and children.

I walked away, steaming, and sat down by a small pond. Soon a Marine came by, walked out into the pond, and like he had sonar or something, bent over and pulled out a SKS Chinese Rifle. "Well," I thought, "Maybe I could find one, too!" so I waded in and started looking. I was wading around in the mud when a mamasan walked up to me. She spotted somehow that I was a "Bacse" (doctor). This always amazed me. I sure as hell didn't look like a "Bacse", but she knew I was. She pointed to a large chunk of shrapnel in her cheek and said, "Bacse, Bacse, you fix?"

I hated her.

I hated that these guys would have horrible nightmares for the rest of their lives because of her and the others that catered to the NVA. I pointed my M-16 at her chest, flipped it to full automatic, when it hit me.

It was almost like a voice. It was very strong.

It said, "John, what has happened to you? Where is 'Gentle John'? Where is your compassion? What has happened to your concern for the abused and neglected? Where is that protector?"

I didn't know.

I had really changed. I didn't like that change. I had always prided myself on the fact that I would always defend a woman in need. I had all my life been a rescuer.

I put the M-16 down and removed the shrapnel. I sutured her cheek, and gave her a shot of Pro Pen so it wouldn't get infected.

I didn't like any of this. I didn't like my reaction and I didn't like the fact that these men would remember this day for the rest of their lives - all for a medal.

It was here that I began a defense mechanism. There was a song out by my favorite duo, Simon and Garfunkel:

"I've built walls...a fortress deep and mighty
That none may penetrate.
Hiding in my room...deep within my womb...
I touch no one...and no one touches me.
I am A ROCK!! I am an island!!
And a rock feels no pain.
And an island never cries!
I have no need of friendship...friendship causes pain.
It's laughter and it's loving I disdain.
I am a rock!!
I am an island.
And a rock feels no pain....
And an island never cries...."

Chapter 22
The Old Man and the Well

It is natural to have "favorites" in the "bush", or anywhere else for that matter. I certainly had mine. My favorite ville was the Dog Bone, mostly because of Chi Com and those big brown eyes and innocent smile. I had a favorite squad to go out with, a favorite gun team, and a favorite fire team. This day was looking good to me. We were going to pass through the Dog Bone, get supplies and mail, and then move on to our night pos.

Pop's fire team had point. They were my favorite fire team. I think the reasons vary. First, Pop was the old man in the Company. He was 25 - two years my senior. He and the other two members of his team were all married, so I identified with them. We were more settled, family oriented. Pop hadn't been a Marine long, but was a good one. He joined the Corps just last year. He wasn't a 25-year old Lance Corporal because he was a shit bird. He was a 25-year old Lance Corporal because he had just joined the Corps.

He was 5'10" tall, probably 185 pounds, redheaded, with big mustache and a ready smile. He was barrel-chested and a pleasure to be around. His fire team consisted of himself, Wagster and McDuffy. Wagster and McDuffy were great guys as well and very good Marines. A few days ago, Wagster had come to me with a major problem. He had received a "Dear John" letter.

Even though I was a Neuro-Psych Tech, these were so hard to deal with. Back in the world you could say, "Well, Rob, remember how you got her in the first place? Maybe you need to "court her" like you did the first time. Try being more affectionate and considerate. Spend more time with your family. Give up your "night out with the guys", and let her know how much she means to you." All good advice, but hardly appropriate here.

I talked to him about staying focused, trying to get his wife to go into detail as to why she wanted to break up their marriage. Things like this were one of the most devastating casualties of combat. I can stop the bleeding of a brachial artery. I could replenish lost body fluids, deaden the pain and stop the bleeding of a gunshot wound. But I could not mend a broken heart. A lot of Marines and soldiers received these letters.

These wives were under tremendous pressure and financial stress. Some of them gave up. Most of them did not. They had married a Marine, and through both good and bad times, they were committed. Those who stuck it out deserve a true "salute". It took courage, faith and determination.

The Dog Bone was just ahead as we approached from the northern trail. I saw a group of children watching and waiting for us. It was a big time for many of them, a chance to get a "treat", or some real food.

As we got closer I saw a little four-year old girl watching us. Chi Com was watching each Marine that came into view. She still looked out of place. She still was an outcast. She still looked bright, acutely aware, quiet and shy. I kept my eyes on her as we filed into the ville. Would she remember me? I had only seen her once, and that was weeks ago.

Our eyes met, and a smile came to that face and those big brown eyes. "Bacse!"

I smiled back, "C'mere, Chi Com! I think I have something for you." I had put a "shit disc" and a can of peaches in my medical bag when I learned we were coming here today.

She said very little. She gave her "thanks" with a smile and those eyes. She took the disc and peaches

223

and happily took off. I saw her look back again and smile.

I may not appear to be "Gentle John" any longer to many people, but Chi Com had found a way to touch a hardening heart. From the look in her eyes, I think she knew it.

We got supplies and moved out. We were about four miles NE of An Hoa, and would be moving SW. We humped a click or two, and began setting up a perimeter on an old abandoned ville. The hootches were all gone. You could see where bunkers had been torn out and filled in. The hill was mostly barren, but at the western edge was an old rock well. Pop's fire team was to set in beside it which they did. The Platoon CP was in the middle of the old ville. There wasn't a lot of cover anywhere, but the elevation of the old ville made it defendable.

We were setting in, when Pop called out, "Gooks in the tree line". Sarge looked at me and slowly started walking that way. Without making a big fuss, he let other fire teams know we were going to move that way, get into position, and open up on the tree line.

We didn't make it to the well. It disappeared. The explosion was horrendous. I was knocked down along with anyone else within 50 meters. The well, Pop's fire team, weapons and all were blown to bits. The Platoon opened up on the tree line and I ran to treat the wounded. There was nothing to treat. They were simply gone. We gathered pieces of flesh in a C-rat box, and sent them on the chopper the next day. Pop, Wagster, and McDuffy - all good men - and there wasn't enough left of them to fill a C-rat meal box! There was nothing left to testify that three good men had served their country and paid the ultimate price. Nothing but three young widows - one of which I wondered if she would even care. The other two dedicated faithful wives and mothers would have to find a way to go on without the love of their lives. God help them.

That night, as I stood my watch, many things went through my mind. When I was relieved and wrapped up in my poncho liner, I closed my eyes.

"I have no need of friendship...
Friendship causes pain.
It's laughter and it's loving I disdain.
I am a rock!!!
I am an island....
And a rock feels no pain.
And an island never cries... "

Stuckey was on point. We reached Henderson Hill, the old deserted CAP unit base and set in. We were to have an afternoon patrol then a night ambush. The patrol was a short one. About 200 meters from the "hill", Delta 1/5, our sister Company, was overrun a few days ago. We were to look it over and figure out why they were overrun. They had been set in on a hill, good field of fire, and a good perimeter. The signs were there. They had been hit by rockets and mortars, then a human wave assault. They were overrun and took heavy casualties. It was obvious there had been one hell of a battle here a few days ago. I kept thinking, "If that would have been us, would we have been overrun?" There is no way of knowing for sure, but I didn't think so. It looked defendable, even against a human wave assault if you had claymore mines set out and guns in the right positions. I guess I had a lot of faith in Sarge, but I didn't think they would have gotten to us.

We set in at Henderson Hill and I had the ambush that night - Stuckey's squad. We were going to set up along the road to An Hoa and try to ambush some "sappers" trying to booby trap the road. We put three fire teams on the road: The squad CP, the middle one, and one fire team covering our rear.

I took the usual 0100 to 0300 watch. This was more than a nightly routine to me. You get superstitious in the bush. It is stupid, and you know better, but you still do. Everyone has their own little things. Mine was no less stupid than anyone else's. I took my wedding ring off each night before dark and read the inscription, then put it back on. If I had treated wounded that day, his blood was still on my hands. From my first casualty my first day in the bush, I did this. I would never wash a Marine's blood off my hands. Wipe them on my utilities, yes, wash them, no. Not until it wore off or wiped off. Each night I checked my wallet to see if the medallion for the patron saint of protection or some silly crap my Dad had given me was still there. I thought it was silly, but I checked every night to make sure I had it.

I always took the same watch, but there was more to that than superstition. Between 0100 and 0300 was the most likely time to have contact and I wanted to be on watch if it happened. I knew I wouldn't fall asleep for one thing. Sarge had taught me something else. After my watch was over, I would usually lay there with my head in my helmet for a pillow, and watch the sky. I would look for the "Morning Star". When I saw it, I figured we most likely wouldn't have contact that night. The gooks would be back on their way to the mountains by then, and unless we were hit going back to the Platoon, we wouldn't have any more contact after the "Morning Star" appeared.

This night was like most nights. This ambush like most ambushes. We stood our watches, and tried to keep from get eaten alive by these giant mosquitoes. I lay there thinking once again, "If we could only TRAIN these damn things, we wouldn't need helicopters!" These things were huge. They could carry med evacs, supplies, and they were always around, so they could get them to you fast; and if one got shot down, "Good riddance!"

I was now three months into the bush and worried about my sanity, or lack of it.

We left at first light and returned to Henderson Hill. This is when I would usually sleep. It wasn't unusual for me to get by on one or two-hours sleep a day - not unusual at all.

"Saddle up, we're moving out!"

It was around 1000 and I had just dosed off. We had great news. Well, for us it was great news. For the rear echelon guys it would probably be terrifying. There was an old abandoned German fort a mile outside An Hoa. We were headed there for two or three days. It had walls, a barbed-wire perimeter, and four towers. It was just the right size for a Platoon. Best of all, the resettlement village "Duc Duc" was nearby. We would be passing through the edge of An Hoa and also Duc Duc. There you could buy beer (well, Vietnamese beer) and Manila rum. There were also sicalo girls (Vietnamese prostitutes).

We were all excited. It was, however, time to have a "talk" with my Marines.

"Ok, you guys! I have APC's for your hangovers, but some of these whores have things running through their veins yet to be named. Keep your pants on. If you "have" to screw one of these germ factories, you had better make damned sure you have a good 'rubber'! Personally I think anybody who would screw a gook, is too lazy to masturbate."

It fell on deaf ears no doubt, but at least I had warned them. After a few hours of humping, we were passing through Duc Duc. It was indeed a luxury for us. They had Cokes. I bought a fifth of Manila rum and three Cokes. I took the top off the rum and smelled it.

"Hey, Stuckey! You want a bottle of rum?" I could tell from the sweet smell it would make me sick.

"Hell yes, Doc! Thanks! You don't want it?"

"No, not after I smelled it. I'm going to buy a couple quarts of Tiger Piss (Vietnamese beer)."

I stuffed them in my back pack and was in a very good mood.

Blaine was walking point. I smiled as I thought of what had happened to him a few weeks ago not far from here.

Tommy was still with us. We had a platoon-sized ambush going out, and for some reason, Sarge wasn't going with us. I think he was in An Hoa re-enlisting. Tommy was the man. We went to a trail intersection and turned west to find a good ambush site. Gray and I were both on this ambush. We were walking along this ridge, looking for a good place to set in (and there were many), when I heard Tommy talking to the point man.

The next thing I knew, we had left the ridge and were heading straight into this small little isolated village that sat all my itself in the middle of a little rice paddy. The ridge we were on made a sharp turn to the north making a perfect L. We were heading to this little ville which was 50 meters from the trail and 50 meters from where the trail turned north, leaving us set up in a ville right in the middle of what could become a perfect L-shaped ambush, with us being the ones getting ambushed. Blaine was on point as I ran up to Tommy.

"Have you lost your mind? We can't set in there! We'll be surrounded by high ground on three sides. Plus, there would be no place to escape to. We would be setting ourselves right into a trap."

"But, Doc, we would have a good field of fire from there."

"And what would we ambush? Water buffalo!! There won't be any gooks out there in that rice paddy! They'll be up on those trails shooting the shit out of us!"

Well, he was the Platoon Commander and we set in that little ville. It was a nice ville, as villes go, and the Platoon CP set up right in the middle in a family hootch. It had a hammock. I staked my claim on that hammock determined to get some benefit out of this. I threw my gear on it. I may be killed that night, but I was going to die dry and comfortable.

I called for my usual watch. It didn't make it that far. Around 2300, AK-47's opened up all around us. I bailed out of that hammock like a whore in church and landed right on Gray. Sweet Jesus! The rounds were flying! I got as low as possible and waited for the inevitable call for "Corpsman up!" After about ten minutes, which seemed like ten hours, it let up. I stared at Tommy with daggers in my eyes. He knew he had screwed up. We were so lucky. They didn't hit anyone. The tendency is at night to overshoot and that is what they must have done. The next morning, Blain came up to me. He showed me his helmet. There was a neat hole going straight in the front and right straight out the back.

I said, "And tell me, Blaine...where was your head during all this?"

"Doc, I was on watch sitting on a stump with my helmet beside me. That whole damned tree line opened up in front of me 50 meters away, and I dove off that stump. My helmet was between my legs. I just lay there holding on to my M-16 and rounds were hitting all around us. This morning, I started to put my helmet on and saw this hole through it."

I laughed. He was lucky. In fact we all were. We screwed up in the worst way, got caught and were lucky to be alive - perhaps Blaine more than any of us.

A few days later, we were moving through a rice paddy, spaced about 15 meters apart, and a sniper opened up on us. I saw a Marine knocked off the paddy dike and took off towards him, thinking it probably wouldn't matter - looked like a head shot. I got to him, and a stunned Blaine looked up at me.

I said, "Where are you hit?"

"Am I hit?" He was trying to get up. "I don't know what happened, Doc?"

"Lie down and let me check you out."

There was no blood, but we all saw that round knock him off the paddy dike. He was staring at me, and I was looking right at the bullet hole in the front of his helmet from a few nights ago.

I said, "Take off your helmet."

I couldn't believe my eyes. Another round had entered the right side of his helmet, apparently spinning the helmet around, and exited out the other side. Not a drop of blood. No Purple Heart - just a dazed Marine. Now he had two bullet holes through his helmet. One going through the front and coming out the rear, the other coming in the right side going out the left side - only the second time his head WAS in the helmet. It made a perfect cross.

I said, "Blaine, I am writing up a chit for you to take to the Top Sergeant the next time we are near the rear for you to send this home as a souvenir. It won't do you any good. No one will believe this shit. I saw it and I don't believe it. But I am giving you one anyway."

He was stunned and I was amazed.

Blaine, if you are reading this, show your friends and family this part, because I am here to verify you are one lucky bastard! I watched now as Blaine turned the Platoon into the old German compound. He was wearing a shiny new helmet.

Chapter 23
Nothing Is As It Seems

We moved into the tiny compound with great enthusiasm. It was heaven compared to what we were used to. There were four towers, each with a roof. There were tents with plywood floors. That would be where I lay my poncho liner tonight. It felt safe to be in the old fort. We would still run patrols and ambushes from here, but, at least while in the fort, all we had to worry about was possible incoming rockets and mortars. The gooks didn't want the old fort. They couldn't keep it. There was nothing of value here. No Ammo, supplies, no chow hall - nothing but an empty compound. But we loved it. We didn't make it permanent either, because it couldn't be defended against a large assault. It was too small.

We had concertina wire and claymore mines - and felt pretty damn nice to me.

Tonight we had no ambush. There were watch assignments, but I didn't take one. I would have if needed, but we were semi-in-the-rear. There was enemy territory between us and An Hoa, and a neutral German hospital, but we were as close to the rear as we had been in a long time.

Of course, with mountains all around us, the gooks knew we were here, so we couldn't take ambushes or patrols lightly. Tonight, however, we had beer or rum. No girls were allowed inside the fort. They didn't interest me anyway, other than I would probably be zapping some asses with 1.2 million units of ProPen in a few days. The beer, however, did interest me. I was still weak from that amoeba. Beer had nutrients, right?

I lay back and re-read some old mail, and then reflected on the last three months.

Yes, I could see I had changed a lot. I was much harder now in many ways - some good - some not so good. It was necessary.

I thought about Sarge. He had spent a lot of time with me. My mentor, my friend.

I thought of the well. Damn, that was bad. They had our number that day, knew where we were going to set in and were ready for us. If they would have waited a few more minutes they would have gotten me, Sarge, and a few others. The engineers had estimated it was an eighty pound box mine. All powder. The shrapnel came from the rock in the well itself. It was a devastating explosion.

How many times should I have been killed in the last three months? I tried, and honestly couldn't count them - many, many times, and many different ways. How many AK rounds had come within inches of my head or chest? The "bouncing Betty" I stepped on! Box mines! Booby traps! Incoming rockets and mortars! The dud round that hit between the head of Sarge and me on Go Noi! Go Noi itself! So far, not even a Purple Heart! Damn amoeba almost killed me! I had been hit by "friendly fire" once, but just a scratch.

Gray was working out very well. I liked him and trusted him to treat me if I was hit badly. I had made him promise me one thing: If I was a multiple amputee, he would overdose me with morphine. I expected I would be killed and I accepted that. I did not, however, want to go through life with no arms or legs. One arm, or one leg, I guess I could live with, or without, depending on your point of view.

Tommy was dead.
My favorite fire team - gone.
Casual's gone forever.
The list was mounting.
"And a Rock feels no pain...."

232

I reached over and took got out the bottle of "Tiger Piss". It was party time at the fort. One sip and I realized how the name came to be. It sure wasn't brewed with Rocky Mountain Spring Water.

It was nearly dark now - the posts were set out. The towers occupied. Stuckey was in the hootch with me. We were getting very close. "Getting close" was becoming an issue with me. It was too late as far as Stuckey was concerned. We were already there.
He took a drink of the Manila rum. It was 80 proof and sweet as an Ozark Mountain maiden.

I finished my first quart of "Tiger Piss" and went out into the compound. I climbed a tower and "shot the shit" with a few guys. I smelled pot, but didn't say anything. Finally I was offered a joint. I didn't take it. If we were in An Hoa, maybe - but not here. We could still be hit here. Not likely, but possible. I said, "No, thanks. Pretty safe here, but take it easy on that shit. We could still be hit." I went to all four towers and talked a while at each one. I really liked these guys. Even the ones I didn't "like", I could tolerate and respect.

Booze and drugs (other than what Gray and I prescribed) were not allowed in the bush. I know it wasn't like that in some units, or so I have heard. But in Alpha 1/5, you waited until we were in the rear for pot, booze or anything else.

I got back to the tent, and Stuckey was shit-faced. I mean he was drunker than the proverbial skunk. He was stumbling around, laughing and was downright funny. He was a very nice guy, always there when needed, but right now he looked like a three-legged man in an ass kicking contest. He was snockered.

Stuckey said, "Sarge better not come around here fucking with me tonight!"

233

Sarge never fucked with anyone who did their job, which Stuckey did, and I told him that, laughing with him.

"Well he had better not start tonight, I'll kick his ass!" Then I knew he was really screwed up. He had nothing but respect for Sarge. We all did...down to the last man.

Well, in the door of the hootch walks Sarge. He was just checking the Platoon, making sure everything was okay.

Stuckey said, "Sarge, what are you doing here? We're just having some fun!"

Sarge knew he was buzzed and said, "Be careful your fun doesn't bite you in the ass."

"Yeah, well I am man enough to handle it. I'm the meanest bastard in this Platoon!"

Sarge looked at me and grinned. He walked away. This man was a leader. He knew Stuckey was a good man and a good Marine. He also knew if he stayed, there would be trouble tonight. The thing is, Stuckey thought the world of Sarge. It was that Manila rum, and I was already regretting giving it to him or anyone else for that matter.

As he went out the door he turned around and gave me a look that said, "Take care of him."

Well, I would spend the night taking care of him. Stuckey was soon puking up his socks. He lay on the floor moaning, "Doc, I'm dying!" And I wasn't sure he wasn't right. I felt so bad about giving him that rum. He would have been fine with the beer, but that sweet rum screwed him up bad. He was so sick - throwing up that rum and writhing in pain. He was funny, though, and I drank my other quart of beer and laughed along with him.

"Doc I'm dying!" went on much of the night. I gave him some Probanthine, a gastric sedative and it helped a little. I didn't have any pain killers that wouldn't hurt his stomach except for plain Darvon, so I gave him one of those and a five-mg. of Librium. It was a long night. I was glad I only had two quarts of Tiger Piss. It turned out I had to be alert after all.

Sarge came in the next morning, grinning. "Stuckey, did you want to kick my ass last night?"

Stuckey said, "I'm sorry Sarge! I think I had a little too much rum."

Sarge laughed, "Yeah, I think I would have had to hold you up to hit you."

Stuckey laughed. All was well.

Later, Sarge asked me, "Was Stuckey really pissed at me about something?"

"No, Sarge, he was just feeling his oats and his rum last night."

We had a patrol going out that day. I remember one patrol we were on when Sarge had a lesson for me:

We went into a small ville, looked around, and basically found nothing but rice. We were ready to leave, but it didn't look like we were leaving.

"Doc, nothing is as it seems in the bush. How many people do you think live in this ville?"

I guessed, "Maybe 75 or 80".

"How many hundred pounds of rice do you think they have stored in those bins? It's for the gooks, Doc. They are VC, supplying the enemy. Destroy it! Have everyone piss in the bins, throw some smoke grenades in there and ruin it. There is enough rice here to feed an entire regiment of NVA for a year!" Nothing is as it seems in the bush.

Today it was a squad-size patrol into the foothills, just outside our new "home for a few days". Britt's squad had the patrol with Jake's gun team. We were walking along this ridge and I was paying close attention to the map, looking for possible ambush sites, trails, and places we could get hit from. We topped this ridge, and I looked starboard, (right) and there was a beautiful site. There were mountains around, foothills here, and nestled in between was possibly the most beautiful lake I had ever seen - crystal clear with rock ledges all around. It was a very clear deep lake. It looked like a poster for Adolph Coors. We slowly moved down to it to check it out. We didn't call it in yet, not until we had "peeped" it out.

I was getting visions of a bath, then maybe skinny dipping with semi-clean utilities to get into afterwards. We were all drooling looking at the beautiful lake thinking the same thing. We just didn't know if it was secure or not, so we checked it out. There were many trails to and from the lake, going in all directions, but no apparent movement now. How could something this beautiful be in this stinking hot country?

Britt said, "What do you think?"

I said, "Damn, call in and say we are checking out some trails (which we were), and we can post a watch on that big rock and take turns swimming for a few minutes."

I was excited. We all were. Britt called it in.

I loved to swim, was raised on the Big St. Francois River in the Ozarks, and was a pretty good diver as well. I used to swim all the way across the river under water. This was making me homesick. It almost looked like a rock quarry where we used to swim, and was as clear as an Ozark Mountain spring-fed stream.

Steve had told them we would check back in 20 minutes. Utilities were flying off dirty hot bodies. One fire team took first watch, but they were mostly watching the beautiful water. Duncan was ready first. He stood on the rock butt naked and dove in. There was no danger of hitting a rock. You could see deep into the

236

clear water. You couldn't see, though, what was under and attached to those rocks, and had let loose and went after Duncan as soon as he hit the water.

"Duncan, get your ass out of there right now!!!" I screamed. He looked at me confused, thinking I was kidding. I wasn't.

As soon as he hit the water, tens of thousands of leeches went after him.

"Duncan, get your ass out, NOW!!!!!"

He swam to shore and was getting out, still wondering if we were fucking with him when he saw them. He was covered with at least 100 leeches. I began squirting "bug juice" on him, trying to get them to drop off. Others were throwing salt on him, both of which would work, but there were so damn many. He had them on every part of his body. He started to scream.

"No, man shut up! We will get them off you."

They started dropping off and the squad started stomping them. If it wasn't so sad it would have been hilarious.

"Nothing is as it seems in the bush..." This beautiful place was infested with blood suckers and filth. It seemed everything in this country wanted your blood, one way or another.

We got Duncan cleaned off and talked it over. We decided to try to "decoy" some of them away, go to different areas, and at least each of us take a short fast dip. We all got a few leeches, but nothing like Duncan had. Sometimes pleasure is worth shedding a little blood.

We had a platoon-size ambush that night, so both Gray and I went. We went outside the compound and down the road towards the "Bridge" and then took off west. We weren't far from where Tommy had us set in on that ville and where Blaine had taken a round through his helmet. We were going to try to ambush some gooks along the trail, and this time, with Sarge running things, I figured at least we would be set in right. From the ridge, we could also see tube flashes pretty good if they hit An Hoa with rockets and mortars. So we had a pretty good chance to "get some".

We moved almost silently down the ridge, and found a junction where three trails came together and set in. Looked like a good ambush site, and the Platoon CP set up out on the perimeter as a fire team on the ridge.

I took the 0100 to 0300 watch, and was doing a radio check to the skipper when An Hoa started getting hit by rockets and mortars. We could hear them flying over our heads and into the compound, maybe a little over a mile away. The combat base was getting hammered, but we weren't.

Sarge was searching for muzzle flashes as we all were. He was on the radio, then came over and nudged me. He didn't explain what we were doing, but he wanted me to go with him. He wanted me to think. There was a finger going north, the direction the rockets and mortars were coming from, and soon the two of us were slipping down that finger. It all just seemed to fall in place. Sarge was slightly in front, maybe three or four meters covering the port side. Without him saying a word, I knew my duty was to check out the starboard side. We were almost side by side now, moving silently. No helmets. No flak jackets. Just our M-16's and a few M-26 hand grenades. It was just the two of us - something like a two-man killer team; but probably more accurately described as a two-man recon team. I was honored he chose me to go with him. It told me he trusted me and my instincts. It meant he trusted me with his life. That he knew I wouldn't screw up or do something stupid that would get us both killed. To me, it meant I was trusted by the best Marine I knew, and I was honored.

We made very little, if any, noise slipping down the ridge. We had covered maybe 400 meters and An Hoa was still getting hammered. We needed to find out from where, and stop it. That was our unspoken mission. We kept low because of being silhouetted from the valley below us. We could now hear the mortar tubes, but they were too far for us to knock out. Sarge signaled me to turn, and we would go back and call in artillery on the Mortar tubes when we got back to the Platoon.

We were slowly making our way back up the ridge when I heard it coming - a B-40 rocket. Sarge and I dove at the same time, almost side by side. I knew it was coming, and it was aimed at US. It was maybe two seconds, which seemed like two minutes, when it hit. "Thump!!" Right between our heads! I felt my ass pucker as I waited for it to go off. I knew it should have already, but was still waiting. It was a dud round!

That made the SECOND time within a month that a dud round - one a mortar and this one a rocket - that had hit between our heads and not gone off!

We got up and moved much quicker now back to the Platoon. They knew where we were so we needed to get out of there. We got back to the Platoon, and as Sarge picked up the net he said, "Mercy, Doc!"

I could only say, "Mercy, Sarge!"

The feeling of this near miss was incredible. It gave you a feeling of vulnerability and invincibility at the same exact moment - one spark away from both of us being blown into tiny fragments of rice fertilizer. Yet, once again, we escaped unscathed - a little more aware of our mortality, but in one piece.

We didn't laugh this time - either of us. Sarge called in artillery on the pos - 105 rounds. We never spoke of that incident again for over 30 years.

The next day, Gray had the patrol. I stayed back at the compound. We had one more night there, then were going to work our way up the road trying to catch gooks setting up ambushes or booby traps. Then we were going to the "Bridge". This sounded too good to be true.

That night I had two more hot quarts of Tiger Piss and so did Stuckey. We had a nice buzz, but it was a lot more pleasant than the previous Manila rum incident.

Early the next morning, we were going to "sweep" the road before the convoys came through. This was to make sure the convoy wasn't ambushed and also to find them booby trapping the road. What we did was line up on both sides of the road and cover both sides. We did trip a couple of booby traps, but no one was killed.

We sat in for the evening, to continue the sweep the next day all the way to the Bridge, and a tall "splib" dude went off the trail to take a dump. "Splib" was the common term for Afro-Americans. "Chucks" was the term used for white guys. As far as I could tell, neither was derogatory.

We all used them a lot, like, "You know what Peters did?"

"I don't know Peters."

"Yes you do. He's that skinny "splib" dude in Brock's squad."

Well, this splib dude went into the bush and I soon heard an explosion. I ran right there and he was lying on his back.

"Doc, they got me man."

I checked him out and he had some shrapnel in his leg. I was convinced he lay down, stuck his leg up in the air, and threw a grenade. He was hoping to catch a piece of shrapnel, get out of the bush for a while and get a Purple Heart. He did just that. I patched him up, no big deal at all. And we waited for the convoy to go by and we would put him on it. He wanted morphine, but I didn't give him any.

The convoy came by, and my last words to him were, "You and I both know what you did, and you have to live with it."

He didn't say a word, confirming to me I was right.

I told Sarge about it, and what I thought happened. His attitude was, "If he is that kind of a Marine, good riddance!"

The next day, we swept the rest of the way to the "Bridge". We found out it was to be a short stay. Alpha was going back to Go Noi Island, where we would be for a while - back to the hatred, elephant grass, fire fights and hell that was Go Noi. The last time we went, we had a new "boot Louey". This time would be no different in that respect. Our brand new, straight-off-the-press Second Lieutenant Platoon Commander was waiting for us at the Bridge.

We went to the north compound again, which was fine with me, and there waiting for us, was Second Lt. Robin Montgomery. He was a chubby little rascal, but not soft. He was maybe 5'9" and 185 pounds. I did my "analyzing" and this was not another "Tommy".

He had "love handles" and blue eyes with blonde hair. He had an air of confidence about him that I hoped was deserved. He was totally "green", knowing nothing about the "bush".

I shook his hand, and did a quick check. I felt this was a man who was trustworthy. I was right.

I felt this was a man who would listen at least with an open mind to Sarge. I was right.

I felt this man could be a leader. I was right.

I felt this was a man who wasn't afraid to die for his country or fellow Marines. That was a gross underestimation!

I was afraid to get close to another Platoon Commander. I had three months or less left in the bush, if my luck held out.

This new Platoon Commander would soon be tested well on Go Noi Island. I would be watching, hoping to see a true leader surface. We needed a leader so Sarge could return to being Platoon Sergeant.

We needed a leader that would look out for his men - a man with courage and conviction. I had no fucking idea I had just shaken the hand of a true hero - a man who would be written up for the Congressional Medal of Honor, and deserved to be. He would receive the Navy Cross.

I would never try to get "close" to him in the "bush"…"*A rock feels no pain…*"

He would, however, have my respect and admiration. Thirty years later, he would be my friend. It would be an honor.

Chapter 24
<u>Elephant Grass and Army Pilots</u>

Go Noi is the same as it always has been. We are on a company-size move which right now is no movement at all. Third Platoon has point and right now they are up ahead of us fighting it out with the NVA to see who will occupy a worthless clump of banana trees and elephant grass.

I am sitting on a trail that most of the Company has already gone down. We are tail-end Charlie. Right now, I'm glad we are. I look around at the terrain and can hardly see beyond the seven-foot elephant grass. It is also high ground. All along these trails, if you can find them, are spider holes - tiny holes in the ground alongside a trail where an NVA soldier will sit with a slab of grass over the hole. When Marines come by, he will pop up and cap a round or two...Then, back inside his hole. Sometimes you can find them - sometimes you can't. I have been watching our new Platoon Commander for a few days and I have a good feeling about him. He has a lot to learn, but given the time, he will do that. I can tell Sarge likes him, and that means a lot to me. He has respect for him, not just the rank, but the man.

I see him just ahead of me now, and want to go up to him and say, "Damn, Lieutenant! Get your head down!" But I don't. He is eager for battle, trying to get things figured out. I am already under the impression this guy has balls that wouldn't fit inside a five-gallon bucket. Third Platoon wins the battle of the hour, and we begin to move again. We are on Go Noi, west of the "Christmas Ville" - right in the very heart of Go Noi.

We are moving again and make it to the pos where the Company will set up for the night. Second

Platoon will go on and set up by ourselves a short way
from here.

We pull away from the Company and, after
about 500 meters, we are to turn north to the old French
railroad. We make it to the turn, and a 6'6" Marine
named Owens hits a booby trap.

As I run to the shouts for "Corpsman up!" we are
ambushed. It is an ugly place, elephant grass, dead trees
and a lot of cover for both the NVA and us. They,
however, know this area better. It is their home. I get
to Owens and he is hit badly. I drag him a few meters to
safety and begin treating him.

"Emergency med evac!"

The booby-trapped grenade has shredded his
lower leg. This is where I wish I had an x-ray. I put a
tourniquet on just below his right knee to stop the
bleeding while I decide what to do with him. I get an
IV started and give him a morphine syrette. This is
going to hurt; I am going to try to save the leg. The fire
fight has slowed some and it is getting dark. Both the
tibia and fibula are shattered - not just broken, shattered.
I go in and clamp off and tie off bleeders. I had
checked his lower leg and there is a blood flow there. I
need something to stabilize this leg, so I send a Marine
off to get me something strong and flat. There are no
hootches with SP cardboard here so I will have to use
something else. I look and probe the wound and am
reminded of HM2 Brown, and what seems like years
ago. I get an idea. "Owens, where are you from?"

"Philly, Doc! Why?"

"Do you know anyone in Maryland?"

"No, but it's not too far from home to the
border."

"Well, when you get sent back to the world, tell
them you have family in Maryland and you want to be
sent to Bethesda Naval Hospital. When you get there, I

want you to ask for Capt. Green, and tell him 'Bear' sent you to him as a referral."

Capt Green would get a charge out of that and he would also know I am okay. If that was my leg, that is the man I would want in charge of the grafting that would have to be done. He said he would and I felt better already about saving the leg.

We couldn't find much for a splint and I had no doubt the Marine I sent did everything he could to find something. He came back with a couple of stiff pieces of bark. Right idea, but too dirty. I had two Marines give me their entrenching tools. I opened them up and screwed down the handle. With one on top and the other on bottom, I had two firm flat surfaces. I had the bleeders clamped and tied, and made a note to order more gear for my field surgical kit.

I applied the last battle dressings, drawing the leg tight, immobilizing it. Then I put the two entrenching tools on and tied it all together with more battle dressings. Owens was doing okay. He would make it and I believed he would still be 6'6". He had asked me if he would lose his leg and I told him I thought it could be saved. I truly did. I repeated to him what to say once he got through First Med and sent back and he had it.

The chopper came in and it was almost dark. As he descended, the gooks opened up on him and he came in anyway. Soon there were two "Huey gun ships" circling overhead firing into the tree line to our front.

It was quite a show. The Hueys would dive and shoot rockets and their mini guns as the NVA shot back at them. You could see tracers flying everywhere - our red ones going into the tree line and their green one returning fire. As they dove, it looked like they were going to dive right into the ground then they would pull up. Then here comes a "cowboy". This was the observer plane also equipped with rockets. He got in on the battle, diving almost to the tree line and then pulling up and doing a victory roll. It was a sight to behold. The chopper took off with Owens and I held my breath as it lifted off. The gun ships and "cowboy" stayed and worked the tree line. It was dark now and we were basically screwed. We had to stay here and dig in. I mean really "dig in", as in digging fox holes, which was rare indeed for us.

Gray and I were going to dig our own and share it. Vision was bad. The foliage so dense you couldn't see 15 feet from your fox hole. We made the hole narrow and a little over waist deep, lowering the odds they could lob a grenade into it. It was going to be a long night. I thought this was the night we could possibly be overrun. We simply didn't have time to set in where we wanted to or get ready for the night because of the booby trap and ambush.

I sat with Sarge and talked about the Huey gun ships and "Cowboy". They were impressive. He said these were Army pilots, and did one heck of a job. Our Marine pilots did a great job as well, but sometimes these Army pilots were younger guys like us, who got a chance to fly a helicopter and after a few months were commissioned. Many of the Marine pilots were Naval Academy graduates who took the Marine Corps option. Normally you don't hear Marines say any thing good about the Army, but these pilots were exceptions. They had our respect. Tonight, they quite possibly saved our asses.

They flew right into the jaws of death and defied it. I loved the "victory rolls". It was so cool. They were basically saying, "Missed me, ass holes! Try again!" It was a long night.

Every so often an NVA would throw a grenade at us, trying to draw fire. We would do the same when we heard movement. Lob a grenade and hope they would open up with their AK's so we could tell exactly where they were, and then wipe them out with a more accurate grenade toss. They knew basically where we were, but would love to know exactly where our holes were.

I lay back for a while and thought about Owens. I'm glad I didn't know what was going on in DaNang that very moment. I found out later that the surgeon at First Med took his leg. I would be pissed when I found out. I believed with all my heart then and still do that I had saved that leg. I was sure a good surgeon like Dr. Decker or Dr. Brown would have Owens walking again. They didn't get a chance. It is my feeling an overworked surgeon at First Med took the easy way out and Owens's leg as well. I would find this out in a few weeks and all I could do was be pissed.

The next morning we moved out toward the old French railroad. We took some sniper fire, but, all in all, we reached the railroad with much less resistance than I had expected. The Company, on the other hand, was in the shit. We could hear them fighting it out about a mile east of us. On the radio we heard they had prevailed and had taken both prisoners and weapons. I had another problem. My ass was kicked after the long two-day hump. I was still weak from that damn amoeba. I was still not replenished from the blood loss and dehydration. I could tell heat exhaustion was very close. It was very upsetting. I had humped right along when I was 232 pounds and now that I was no longer carrying all that extra weight, I was having a hard time. I popped salt tabs and drank all the pissy water I could handle. We were walking along the old railroad, now just an elevated trail. I was walking behind Frank, who was attached to us from Weapons Platoon and the 3.5 rocket man. I didn't know him well but I didn't like the way he walked. He seemed reckless.

As we were walking along the trail, I was watching up ahead, and saw everyone was pointing when they came to a certain spot - booby trap no doubt, or a potential one. Each man turned and pointed to the man behind him, including the man in front of Frank. It was a stick which looked suspicious and I could already see it from where I was. Not only did Frank not turn and point it out to me, he stepped right on the damned thing. I responded faster than I could think. I grabbed my M-16 by the barrel and rapped Frank up beside the helmet with the stock, knocking him down.

I said, "If you ever do that again, I will put a round right through your head so fast you'll be in hell before God knows you are dead!"

He said, "What?"

"You were shown that was a potential booby trap and you not only didn't pass the word back, you stepped right on it. Get your shit together or I will kill you myself."

He got up and went on. I was so pissed. We were lucky it wasn't a booby trap.

We met up with the Company where the old rail road used to cross the river. We got down off the railroad and met under what was left of the old bridge. Seemed it was hard to keep a bridge up over here.

They had eight prisoners and several AK-47 and AK-50's. We were waiting for a chopper to come in and pick them up so some of us took the opportunity to fire the AK's. I got my hands on an AK-50 and adjusted the stock. I picked out a target by the river and fired first on semi then full automatic. That was one sweet weapon. It had a great feel and though slower than the M-16, it was heavier and more accurate. I really liked that weapon and hated to give it up, but, of course, I had to. The sound would draw fire from our troops if used in the bush. They had a very distinct sound. It was an eerie feeling liking the enemy's weapon better than your own.

The M-16 had taken a lot of criticism it didn't deserve. We all had heard about how they would jam, but if you treated it the way you were supposed to, it wouldn't happen. It had to be cleaned after each fire fight. That weapon was your life and had to be a priority.

We were together as a Company again. I hadn't heard what the next move would be, but being on Go Noi, it was sure to be interesting.

Chapter 25
<u>The Change</u>

Time was flying by, yet also seemed to stand still.
It was February 1, 1969. I had been here since
Oct. 23rd. If I could make it through Feb. and March,
then the first two weeks in April I would be going on
R&R (rest and recreation) to Hawaii to meet my wife on
April 18th. By then I should have one or two weeks left
in the bush and I could go to DaNang. Still so far
away...so much can happen.

I recalled that night before I came out to be with
my Company for the first time. Stape had told me about
the young Platoon Sergeant. He was right about that.
Oh, we were still a Platoon of mostly 18 and 19-year
olds, and we certainly had screw ups. But, all in all, I
felt we were a strong fighting unit. The same could be
said for the entire company. Now, with Lt. Rob, we
had three strong, good Platoon Commanders. We were
a fighting unit indeed.

If rumors were true, we, as a Company, had
more kills than any other Company and would soon
receive the PUC (Presidential Unit Citation). I really
didn't care about medals or ribbons or much else other
than getting out of here.

Early on I had tried to adopt an attitude of, "This
is 365 days out of your life. Nothing you do matters.
When it is over, you go home. Then you forget." I
doubted it was as simple as all that, but sometimes still
tried to convince myself that come Oct. 23, 1969, I
would never think about this place again.

Sarge continued to amaze me. He was truly a
great "Papa Sierra". He expected a lot - he got a lot.

Rob was coming along very well. He was
learning fast. I had no intention whatsoever of getting

close to him. I was friendly to him, but that was about it.
I had respect for him and was glad he was with us.

The reason for the big "change", though, at least
in the Platoon was Sarge. All in all I was proud of our
unit. I had never been so close to a bunch of guys in my
life, even though I recently was trying not to be. I liked
them and I worried about them.

We were on yet another move on Go Noi.
Second Platoon had tail-end Charlie. There was another
change here on Go Noi. I had noticed it and was
somewhat grateful for it, but didn't know what was
causing it. This trip, we weren't having near as many
fire fights. We were hitting booby traps, and took a few
sniper rounds. That wasn't unusual at all, but our
actually fighting it out and assaulting online into a hot
tree line wasn't happening.

The Company was on the move and the rear fire
team sent up word that they had spotted movement
behind us. Sarge and Rob talked it over and, as we
passed through the next ville, two fire teams dropped off
and stayed behind - one on either side of the trail.

We had gone perhaps 200 meters when we heard
a few M-16 rounds, a few AK's and Charlie squad
called in that they had taken prisoners. We held up and
they brought them to us. The Company CP sent us our
"Chu Hoi" (NVA or Viet Cong, who had surrendered to
our side and now served as an interpreter and advisor).
Our grinning potential serial killer interpreter was with
another unit.

"Chu Hoi" was interrogating them. He
threatened them and seemed serious about it. Some of
these guys were real rough on prisoners. These
prisoners were hardcore NVA with uniforms, packs and
a radio. We soon learned why.

They were assigned to follow our Company,
anticipate where we were heading, and radio ahead so

their Company could set booby traps for us. They were under orders not to make contact with us: No ambushes, no fire fights - just tail us and try to guess where we were going.

I guess that was a compliment to us. We had a "reputation". They still wanted to wipe us out; they just didn't want to lose too many people doing it.

We choppered the prisoners out and were underway again. We had lost some time interrogating the prisoners and were the last to arrive at our new night pos. We set up a platoon-size ambush and a squad leader, Collins, came up to the Platoon CP.

"Sarge, I need to order a claymore mine. Oswell left his back where we were interrogating the gooks."

Sarge said, "What? Send his ass over here."

Oswell came over and Sarge talked to him. "Where is your claymore?"

"I left it behind, Sarge."

"Why did you leave it behind? Was it too heavy? Did you forget it? Did you feel the need to supply the gooks with another way to kill us?" Sarge was pissed.

Oswell had screwed up bad. It was a weapon easily booby trapped with a pressure devise that could wipe out a whole squad.

Oswell really had no answer.

"Oswell, you go back and get it, and you bring it back and show it to me. I mean YOU! No one is going with you. Don't come back here with out it."

He looked terrified. I would be too. This was Go Noi where no place was safe let alone tromping through the jungle alone in the dark. He took off and I thought about this. Gray had the ambush that night, so I was set in with Sarge.

I didn't think he did it to punish him. There are unwritten laws in the bush - principles. One of them is:

You don't provide the enemy with means to kill you or fellow Marines.

It was dark, and we saw a pencil flare go up. Green. Oswell came into the perimeter. He was scared but he had the claymore. The claymore is an anti-personnel mine that is concave in shape. It has an outer plate and when blown with the electronic "clicker", it disperses hundreds of jagged .45 caliber pellets. It is a wicked weapon and one you don't want used against you.

He showed it to Sarge and Sarge nodded. Enough said. He had made his point; and he was not going to "rag" him further.

I asked him later that night. "Did you think he would make it back?"

He smiled. "Well, I knew we would either be rid of a shit bird, or would possibly have a Marine return. Shit birds are expendable out here. They get good men killed. Good Marines are a valuable commodity. Let's hope Oswell will be a good Marine now that he has learned a very valuable lesson."

I had felt the same way about Oswell. A few weeks ago, we were crossing a paddy dike and took sniper rounds. I had heard "Corpsman up!" from ahead in the column. I took off, and the rounds were flying. Dirt was hitting me in the face and helmet from incoming fire. I was running low and dove when I was to the "call". It was Oswell. I saw him and he was lying on his back looking up.

"Are you hit?"

"Yes, Doc! Got me in the thigh."

He had a scratch on his leg barely tearing his utilities. A round had grazed him, but he was barely bleeding and certainly in no danger.

I said, "That is where you are hit? You had me come up here for THAT?" I was pissed. I told him, "As far as you are concerned, I don't make house calls. You just used yours up! If you get hit again, deal with it until I get to you!" He damned near got me killed for a "scratch".

This wouldn't be the end of my woes with Oswell. In a few weeks, he would get hit again. This time he would be shot through the leg. Doc Gray went to treat him, was cutting off his utilities and found he had shit his pants.

"Oswell, what did you do?"

"I was scared, Doc."

"Well, I'm scared too, but I'm not shitting in my pants. Show a little class! Damn!"

I liked Doc Gray more everyday.

Oswell was med evaced, never to be seen again by us. He was lucky to be alive and we were lucky he didn't get good men killed.

Sarge was going to An Hoa. He had re-enlisted. He would leave February 8; get two weeks leave back home in Texas with his wife and son; then return to us as an E-6, a Staff Sergeant.

I have mentioned probably too many times I have little respect for "lifers". Sarge wasn't a "lifer". He was a Career man, a Servant and dedicated Marine - one who was committed to protect those who lacked the ability or the means to protect themselves.

He went in the next day on the resupply chopper. It was February 2.

We were on a Company move slowly working our way south towards the edge of Go Noi. Rumors, as usual, were flying. You never really knew what to believe until an order came. We were always rumored to be going to the "Bridge". In all my time in the bush, we spent less than 12 days there.

We were reasonably sure they had dreamed up another operation for us. We were moving closer and closer to the edge Go Noi. Something was up.

February 4, we were near the foothills heading further south, when our resupply chopper came in.

The ramp dropped and out came Sarge.

I saw him walking to the Platoon CP and said, "What are you doing here? You are going home in four days!"

Sarge said, "I know, Doc, but we are going on a short operation in a bad area and I am needed here."

That was Sarge.

The order finally came down. We were moving south, going through the Dog Bone where we would get supplied, then come back north. I don't know if we were "faking them out" or what, but I was glad we were going to pass through the Dog Bone first. I hadn't seen Chi Com for a while. I had received another package from home and had a little of that wonderful "Oberle" sausage left. I could imagine those eyes when she bit into something that tasty.

That night, we had an ambush and it was my turn. It had been a long hump and my ass was pretty much kicked, still weak from that amoeba. I had put a little weight back on and actually looked pretty good now, around 185 pounds. But I was still struggling to keep up on long humps. I never mentioned it to anyone, not even Gray or my buddy Stuckey. It was a personal problem. It would take me a while to get my strength back.

The ambush was at the edge of the foothills, which can be very hairy. But this one went the way I liked them to go - no contact. We rejoined the Company the next morning and passed through the Dog Bone.

As we approached the ville, I once again found myself looking for Chi Com. We were deep into the ville before I saw her. She was watching, solemn faced and serious. I watched her watching us as we filed in. She wasn't coming up to the Marines like the rest of the kids. She stayed back, alone, observing. By the time she saw me, I was actually smiling. This time she smiled immediately, and slowly walked my way. She didn't call my name this time, but she was expecting something. I don't think she was disappointed. I said, "Here, Chi Com, #1! Chop, chop!", as I handed her a sliver of Oberle and a can of pears. I didn't get to see her bite into it. She took it and she was quickly on her way, turning again and smiling a "thank you". We set in, and to my surprise, she came to our hootch.

"Bacse want nook?" (Vietnamese for water.)

I said, "Thank you Chi Com!" and handed her three canteens.

She was gone a while. When she came back, she handed me the canteens and said, "Bacse #1! Nook #1!"

It was. She had gone to a well somewhere and brought water that was actually clear, cool and sweet. For the first time since I had been in the bush, I didn't add Halazone tablets. It was delicious. Chi Com had become a ray of sunshine in a dark world to me.

We moved through the Dog Bone and were going to set up yet another ambush tonight not far away. Stuckey had point, and he spotted a 500-lb. bomb, a dud we had dropped there in some other battle. We had to call the engineers to blow it. This would give our position away, but you can't leave a 500-lb. bomb there to be used as a booby trap or booby traps later. The engineer came up and blew it. It could be heard for miles, but that couldn't be helped.

Now we were on the defensive instead of the offensive. The gooks knew exactly where we were. Such was war in the An Hoa Basin.

Chapter 26
<u>Losing Control</u>

We were set in on the outskirts of the Dog Bone. It was a good site, with the exception being the enemy knew where we were.

We sent out two 3-man LP's, but no ambush. We are inside the hootch right before dark shooting the breeze, when Sarge said, "Doc, do you have any pictures?"

"Yes, I have my wedding picture," as I went for my wallet. It was wrapped in plastic for water proofing and it took me a while to get the picture out. I handed it to Sarge and he sat there a few minutes looking at it. I could see something was on his mind. It was my wedding picture from when I was stationed in Bethesda, Maryland, and I was married in my Navy uniform. He held the picture staring at it intensely for a few minutes, making me wonder what caught his attention. Soon, I found out.

"Doc, what the hell are you doing in a Navy uniform?" This surprised me.

"I AM in the Navy, Sarge, remember? Doc? Navy Corpsman?"

He sat there staring at the picture a minute then handed it back to me. "I'm, sorry, Doc - you are a Marine, not a squid! I can't think of you as in the Navy. You are a Marine."

It was the biggest compliment he could have given me. He had truly forgotten I was a Navy Corpsman. He thought of me as a Marine who happened to treat casualties. Perhaps he had just realized that a few months ago he had asked a "squid" to make sure the ambushes were set in right. I don't know for sure.

I took my usual watch and was on it when I heard a "freight train" coming in. It was a B-40 rocket. "Incoming!!!!!!!!!!"

I had been half expecting it, seeing as the whole NVA knew where we were. But it still sent shivers up my spine. I hit the deck and was hugging tight along with the rest of the CP. You can't fight these things - you just try not to get your head blown off until maybe someone spots a flash or movement. Then you can retaliate. No more came.

The next day we got supplied yet again and another mail call. We were also ordered to stay there another night. Now I was really nervous. They for sure saw where we were; and, yes, it would have been great to get supplies and then move out after dark where they wouldn't know our new position or perimeter. But that wasn't going to happen.

I could almost envision them carrying rockets, mortars, and 357 recoilless rifles in to hit us with tonight. I wasn't looking forward to this. Sarge felt the same way, but we had orders. Mail had come two days in a row, so I took advantage of this and settled back to read it.

That night we were still set in. It was around 2300. Sarge said, "Doc, we're moving out. We're going about 500 meters south of here to this little village and set in for the night."

I was thrilled, but didn't know how this had come about. We saddled up and made the night move with minimal noise.

This was one night move I was happy about, though none are safe. We moved into the village and the Platoon CP set up in a small family hootch. The residents were already sleeping inside their bunkers but came out when we came in. We sent them back into their bunker, motioning that they were okay. We were there to "Bac Bac" VC.

It was during my watch by the time we settled in, so I took the net. Sarge was still awake, so I asked him, "We were ordered to move this time of night?"

"No, we just did it. That ville is going to get hit tonight, so I talked to the Lieutenant." (Always the Marine, he referred to all officers by rank) "I told him what I thought, and he said, 'We are moving out.'"

Lt. Rob had just gained even more respect from me. He went against orders to protect his Platoon. It would have been stupid to stay there, but we were supposed to. I thought we finally had an officer for a Platoon Commander who was a leader.

It wasn't long before it paid off. Rockets, mortars, recoilless rifles, all opened up on the ville we had just vacated. It was getting hit hard. I didn't know if a human wave assault was to follow and, thank God, we weren't there to find out. Now we had avoided a lot of casualties but had another problem. That is to explain why we weren't there. A story started coming, then acted out and worked in. We told the skipper we had an ambush out, it spotted movement, and was setting in to retaliate. Then we supposedly moved the rest of the Platoon to a better ambush site because of the movement the squad out on ambush had spotted. We did call in 105-rounds from An Hoa on the muzzle and mortar tube flashes. We safely sat back and watched the war.

The civilians had come up briefly again when the action started. They went back to their bunkers. After the incoming had stopped, I lay down and went to sleep after my nightly rituals.

I awoke around day break, and knew something was wrong, out of place, not as it should be. I looked around, and then I saw it. My wedding ring was gone. I had checked it last night before going to sleep. I had it then. The family where we were staying was down in the bunker. I had heard movement during the night, someone going to take a leak or whatever. We weren't worried about them. But I knew someone had stolen my ring from my finger. I had lost so much weight, it was very loose, but I had checked it before going to sleep. I didn't lose it. It was stolen. I called the family out. I was pissed. I felt a rage boiling up in me I had never felt before. My pulse was throbbing, head pounding, and I felt the power of reasoning give way to pure unadulterated hostility. I knew they couldn't understand me, I also knew from their eyes they knew what I was talking about.

"No combeit!" was the comment I got in return, meaning "I don't understand." They may not have understood the words, but they understood the reason. I grabbed papasan and slugged him. Never had I laid a hand on a civilian before this day. I called for our interpreter. "Tell them I want my ring back. If I don't get it, I will destroy this fucking village single-handedly!"

I had never lost control of my temper in my life. Now I had totally lost it. I could only think, "I come here against my will to help these people, giving a year of my life and possibly the rest of it, and they steal the only thing I have of value!" I grabbed another papasan and threw him across the hootch, and then hit another. I heard, "Get some, Doc!" in the background, but I just couldn't stop, or think. I grabbed papasan and was ready to hit him with my best right cross, when an 8-year old boy handed the ring to Sarge.

"Doc, lighten up. I got it. It's okay." Sarge quickly gave me the ring and got the boy away. He had never seen me like that; hell **I** had never seen me like that. I had boxed for three years. I played football, basketball, wrestled, all kinds of contact sports, but had

261

never lost control before. It was a strange feeling for me, something foreign to my very nature. I hated violence, especially a larger man against a smaller one, or a man physically or mentally abusing a woman. I think it was a warning to me, and I took it as one. I would never forget that day, and was thankful no one was seriously hurt.

For the next eight years, I would be torn by nightmares, hatred and anxiety. But not once would I lose my temper again. Never again would I allow myself to lose control.

Later that morning we went back to the ville we were supposed to be in last night. It had been heavily hammered. I could only imagine the effort and time it took to hump all those rockets and mortars down from the north. They blew it all up in a ville where we had escaped unharmed.

Yes, I thought Rob was working out rather nicely.

I felt we were the strongest we had ever been as a Platoon: Lt. Rob, an eager and wise Platoon Commander; Sarge, the ever-efficient Platoon Sergeant. Tomorrow we were to start the new operation. We were going north towards Go Noi, then turn west toward the road. There were a lot of gooks in that area and a lot of booby traps. We were going back to the north end of booby trap alley. None of us were happy about that. You can't fight booby traps; you can only count the wounded. I would much rather face the NVA head on. We had had a lot of fire fights. I don't think we ever really lost one, not when it was all over.

I hated booby traps. So did Sarge. That morning he told the Skipper, "This is a bad idea, but if you are going to send us in there, you had better have med evac choppers in the air, because we are sure as hell going to need them." Sarge - always thinking ahead. Duty! Honor! Country!

Sarge was supposed to be in An Hoa. On February 8 – two days from now - he had a flight scheduled to take him back to the world for two weeks with his family. He would return as a Staff Sergeant. I would miss him, but was happy for him. No one deserved a break more than he.

He had two days to get to DaNang and catch his flight. Still, as we woke for this short operation, he gave the command to his troops.

"Saddle up! And for God's sake, watch where you step!"

This was February 6, 1969.

Chapter 27
<u>February 6, 1969</u>

Second Platoon had point as we approached two large villes ahead.

I was thinking about my latest conversation with Sarge a few minutes ago. He would be back in two weeks. I would be out of the bush, hopefully, the first part of May. We had planned to meet for an in-country R&R at China beach in July. I would be at First Med Bat.

It may seem a little strange. Our relationship had been based so much on a student/mentor thing: How to fight, tactics, avoiding disasters, creating others, how to survive and help others survive.

How would it be to just kick back with the ol' Sarge and just relax, have a few beers, take a swim in the ocean, go to a club, and talk about the states? I was looking forward to it. We got along great, appreciated the same jokes, and had a good healthy bond. I was sure we would keep in touch after all this hell was over. He would be the namesake for my first born.

I never dreamed of knowing all he had taught me. Actually, I hadn't wanted to until it became necessary. Most everything I had learned, one way or the other, came from him. I was fairly confident now in my abilities in the bush, in day-to-day operations - all except for booby traps. I still hated them and now we were south of Go Noi in a very heavily booby trapped area. We weren't all that far from Liberty Bridge, but that was deceptive. This was a bad area.

Sarge had advised that we should pick up some "locals" to escort us through this area. They knew where the booby traps were and, hopefully, would keep us off those trails.

We were nearing the two villes now, one larger than the other - but both big and both "unfriendly". The terrain was mostly high ground. Hills. A lot of cover. Danger loomed ahead on every twist and turn - each and every trail a potential disaster. I wondered if the Skipper had taken Sarge seriously when he told him that if we were going in here, we had better keep choppers in the air because we would have med evacs.

Brock's squad had point. We had five gooks with us, civilians, hoping they would keep us away from the dangerous trails.

We were heading into an elevated area, another ville close by. The point man stopped. I wasn't sure why. Had they spotted something? Had the civilians said to change our course? Did the "locals" show fear here? I didn't know the reason, but I wasn't comfortable stopping here - too exposed.

I heard Sarge coming up from behind me.

"Excuse me, Doc," he said as he went around me. "I'm going to go get the point man un-fucked."

I smiled at his description of our situation.

Sarge was going around the column, and went up about three men ahead of me, then put his right hand on a Marine's shoulder as he was going around him.

The explosion was massive. The earth seemed to spew hell-fire and brimstone. Sarge went flying into the air. It was a booby trapped 105-round, one of our artillery shells.

I found myself running towards him, somehow not believing this was happening. This couldn't be. "Oh, no! Not Sarge! No! NO! **NO!**"

Normally when someone was hit, I felt an adrenalin rush; it sharpened my senses; brought back volumes that I had learned and studied both at Field Med School, and other places.

He hit the ground with a dull thud.

Now, as I dove beside him, I didn't feel that adrenalin rush. I felt numb. I felt like my breath had been knocked out of me. Shocked.

Something was wrong about this picture. This couldn't be happening. This was Sarge, the best Marine I knew.

Both legs were gone all the way to the hip. The right arm was shredded as well.

Finally I began to think. Adrenalin, he needs adrenalin. He needs an IV. He needs battle dressings.

The reality began to sink in, "Get your shit together, Bear! Sarge is down!"
I started mumbling things, not sure what, but the intention was to get him pumped up, or pissed off. Anything to get the adrenalin flowing. I was applying battle dressings as I did this, though the heat from the artillery round had cauterized the wounds fairly well with the exception of the dangling arm. It could not be saved. Perhaps Sarge could.

I had to get an IV going fast. It wasn't surprising that the veins had collapsed in his only limb, his left arm.

Cut down.

No choice. Had to do it. Emergency med-evac had already been called in. It was supposedly on the way. I popped a Ringers Lactate out of my web belt and got it going. Had to run it fast. He was awake - alert.

I mumbled something about, "You aren't going to get another Purple Heart for this pussy wound!" Still trying to keep him pissed.

Sarge said, "Doc, don't you be worrying about me! I have a son at home to raise, and BY GOD, I will raise him."

I looked at him. I could see the determination on his face - the acceptance, yet the courage and the will to live. Such strength and courage this man has!

266

I could hear the reaction of the Platoon in the background - the sound of a unit that had lost a true leader. Lamar, a wiry tough little Marine from St. Louis, grabbed his M-16 by the barrel and heaved it as far as he could. "Fuck it! I QUIT! I'm not doing this shit anymore!" He walked over, picked up his M-16 and threw it again. "I fucking QUIT!!"

I yelled out, "Where is that chopper? I want it right fucking NOW!"

I tried to think it was someone else lying there - anyone else! Sergeant "No Name"! Anyone...but not Sgt. Vince Rios!

I suddenly realized how much I depended on his skills - listened to everything he said; took the good natured ribbing from him, because always there was a lesson. He was my teacher, my mentor, my friend and my security.

How would I possibly make it through my six months without his wisdom?

The chopper came in. I checked his vital signs again. They were stable. I still didn't give him morphine. He could handle the pain and shock was still a danger.

Once again, Sarge amazed me. He was going to make it. He never lost consciousness. I was sure now he would live, but what kind of life? Was he doomed to be in a V.A. Hospital for the rest of his life?

No, if I had learned anything in this God-forsaken country, it was to not underestimate Sarge. He would make it, and my son would still bear his name.

Two Marines carried the poncho into the chopper. I walked up the ramp and talked to the crew.

"Is there a Corpsman on board?"

A Corporal said, "No, Doc, but I will do what I can."

I said, "Okay, I am running this IV fast. It will run out; he will need another. When this one gets low, simply pull this out here and insert it into this bottle. Then hang it up on the hook, I have it set right, I think."

"Okay, Doc, I got it."

"Corporal, I want this man to arrive in DaNang alive. Are you sure you can switch the bottles?"

"Show me once more".

I did, thanked him, and walked down the ramp.

The chopper went up. I was shaking. I felt somehow alone. My mentor was gone. I wondered how often I would recall the things he had taught me - tactics, awareness, the deception of the way things seemed here versus reality. How many times in the next two or three months would I wonder, "What would Sarge do if he was here?" The answer was: Constantly!

As we moved out all I could think of was how was he doing? I knew he would live, but what did that mean?

The name of this book is, The Names NOT on the Wall. The title indicates it is about those who lived through their service in Vietnam. For the next few paragraphs we will leave Vietnam.

On Oct. 27, this same year, I would be discharged from Travis Air Force Base in San Francisco. I had no idea, that less than an hour from me, Sgt. Vince Rios had already enrolled in the University of San Francisco, and was working on the first of his two Masters degrees.

As promised, he would raise his son. He would also raise three other children not yet born.

In 1981, I would find him and he would meet his namesake. We would forever be close friends. Despite the fact that we lived on opposite coasts, we would get together every few years.

On February 6, of each and every year, there is a party in San Francisco. At this party, Sarge celebrates his "second chance at life". He knew he should have died in the explosion, but he lived, and he would never take that lightly. There is no self pity here, nor does he want anyone else's.

He drives a car that has been altered to fit his needs, an old Oldsmobile we all call "Sherman". It is a normal car, other than the alterations.

On a visit in 1999, I said to him, "Sarge, you should get a van. It would be easier to get in and out of and I'm sure the V.A. would assist in paying for it."

He said, "Doc, I don't want a van. If I drove a van, people would think I was handicapped!"

He isn't. Inconvenienced maybe - but in no way handicapped.

He got his two Masters degrees, and has always had a good job, doing what he does best - serving others.

He has a list of awards and achievements and citations that to this day amaze me. But then again, he always did.

On February 6, I sometimes call him. The conversation goes something like this.

"Sarge, I know you are celebrating your 'day of second chances', and you know, as always, I support you. But I just can't celebrate it with you. I remember it as the worse day of my 23 years. I just wanted to call and let you know I am thinking about you and supporting you."

"Mercy, Doc! Thank you for calling. We are having a great time here, and I hope some day you will join me on this day."

I won't. I have and will continue to celebrate July 4th with him and other days, but I can't bring myself to celebrate that day.

Before we return to our journey in Vietnam, let me say I think the above is the best example I can think of that distinguishes a true hero from the rest of us. What kind of man can have that strength? Only a hero - a man dedicated to serving others - a Statesman.

The same man who on February 6, 1969, was supposed to be in An Hoa getting ready to fly home in two days, instead went back to the bush - and for one reason. His Platoon needed him.

This is the man I named my son after.

This is Sergeant Vince Rios.

Chapter 28
<u>How Do You Like Your Eggs?</u>

It had been a rough few days. There was a different attitude among the troops.

We all tried not to get close to people, at least in theory. But how could you keep from it? I was going to try harder. Gray and I were already close; and Stuckey and I would always be close. But other than that, for self-preservation's sake, I would try to stay to myself more.

We were heading into the much-needed compound of Liberty Bridge. We once again got the north compound, which was fine by me. I needed some time alone.

We got set in and had been there less than an hour when I grabbed my dirty towel and headed to the river for a swim/bath.

I was walking to the river alone on the road and saw a jeep coming up the road, after just crossing the ferry. It stopped, and I looked up.

It was Stuckey. "Hey, Doc! Let's go to DaNang and see Sarge."

He had stolen a Jeep!

"Stuckey, what are you doing? Are you crazy?"

"Come on, Doc! We are going to go see Sarge."

"Who's going?"

"Lt. Monty, Mac, you, me and whoever else we can get in here."

Now, this is our Platoon Commander, squad leader, right guide, and whoever else - going to DaNang in a stolen Jeep.

DaNang was 18 miles away and it was not secure until you got to Marble Mountain. No convoy, just a Jeep going through the boonies unprotected. That, however, wasn't what I was worried about.

271

If we were going to get hit, I would have been with perhaps the best fighting unit ever assembled in a stolen Jeep. I just didn't want to go.

"I'll pass, Stuck. You guys go ahead. When you get back, I'll buy you a beer."

I could tell he was puzzled that I didn't want to go. I walked on down to the river, wondering myself why I had refused the invitation.

I think I was in a grieving process. If I could have done anything to help him, I would have. Maybe I just didn't want to see him this way at this point. I'm not sure. I was confident he would make it. If he made it to DaNang, and we knew he did, then he made it. I didn't feel that was where I belonged at this time.

As it turned out, I believe I did the right thing. Rob and Sarge had a long talk about his future. Lt. Rob had told him, "You aren't finished yet. Your country needs you. Society needs your leadership. Don't you even think about giving up. There is work for you to do."

Lt. Rob was right. That was what Sarge needed to hear. Sarge was a dedicated Marine, and coming from his Platoon Commander - well, it was a positive step.

I waded out into the swift river and took a bar of soap and scrubbed my dirty utilities. Then stripped down and scrubbed my dirty self. I was alone and I was happy about that. I had been holding it in for four days - now I could let it out. I cried - a hard, heaving, all-out bawling session with myself. I had looked ahead ("Always have your bases covered, Doc. Leave yourself an out."), and if anyone had come up on me, I would have had "soap in my eyes".

Damn! Sarge is gone. He was just gone. A replacement? Impossible. Oh, we would get a body, someone to fill a billet. But he wouldn't be able to replace him. There was no replacement. I would not get close to the next Platoon Sergeant, no matter who it was.

I was thankful we had Monty for a Platoon Commander - that would help. Still it would never be the same. With Monty and Sarge, I felt we may be the best fighting unit in the country.

I composed myself and went back to the tent. I lay there a while thinking and dozed off.

Soon, I heard a Jeep pull up. They were back. Sarge was doing as good as could possibly be expected, which was no surprise.

That night we had a few beers and talked a lot. Everyone missed Sarge. He had touched all our lives.

The next morning we were going to chow. I approached the line and was asked to come on in with several guys. I got in line by Stuckey, the Jeep thief, and began looking forward to real food.

A Marine named Johnson was behind me. He was a good-natured Marine whom everyone seemed to like and was currently engaged in a game of "grab ass" while in line.

I was looking forward to the hot fresh food and of course, milk. The cook asked Stuckey, "How do you like your eggs?"

"Scrambled, please – medium."

Then he asked me, the same question to which I replied, "Over easy, please."

Then he interrupted the game of "grab ass" and asked Johnson, "Lance Corporal, how do you like your eggs?"

Johnson turned and looked at him with a blank stare. "Well, I like 'em!"

I laughed so hard I couldn't talk.

It was like asking "Freddy the Freeloader" which caviar he preferred.

All Johnson could think of when asked the now unfamiliar question was, "I like 'em!"

That night we were having a party. The right guide was going home tomorrow. It was a big deal. We got beer from the Seabees and ice from the chow hall and filled up an ammo box. I remembered when Mac had been promoted to right guide and Stuckey became squad leader of that squad. I had thought we just lost the best point man in the country; but no, he still walked point and he was still the best. It seemed he was always on point. Such was his heart, that of a giver.

The beer was flowing and the inevitable beer drinking contest began and Stuckey always won. A good time was being had by all.

Mac was lit, as most of us were - only maybe a bit more. He decided he wanted to fire the 105-Howitzer. There was no one around who really knew how to man the gun. Finally after ample brew, he got down behind the big gun, screamed into the breech, "BOOM!!" and went to his tent and passed out.

We were all happy for him. It was a big deal, which shows you how rare it was. He was the first Marine in our Platoon I saw rotate out without a Purple Heart. Think about that: A Platoon has 50 or so men. I had been in the bush four months, and had never seen a single man go home who hadn't been hit at least once!

It was a good time, giving all of us hope when it was badly needed.

Later that night we were inside the tent where Mac lay passed out. I hadn't laughed this much in ages and was keyed up. It may have also been an outlet for losing Sarge. I don't know for sure. We had a candle burning inside the tent for light. It was so nice to have light after dark.

I decided to "mess" with Mac.

274

I knelt down beside him and whispered, "Hey, Mac, let's me, you and Stuckey go out on a three-man killer team tonight."

He barely moved.

I nudged him, "Hey Mac, come on! You, Stuckey and I are going out on a three-man killer team."

He said, "Oh, okay, Doc. Damn, you sure know how to fuck up a party!" and started to sit up. He cleared his head a little and looked at me then remembered where he was and why we had a party.

He said with a laugh, "Fuck you, Doc! I'm not going on any damn killer team; I'm going home tomorrow! Whoopee!!"

We all had a good laugh, then he went back to sleep.

I guess we were a bit noisy because soon he woke up with a start and said, "PUT that damn LIGHT OUT!" and slammed his hand down into the lit wick and hot wax. Then, "Owwww, damn that burns!" I treated the burn and it was a second degree. I bandaged his hand, gave him some Furacin gauze to take with him to change the bandage, and the next morning we said our goodbyes. It was a happy, yet sad moment.

Later that afternoon, after another warm meal, we decided to chose up teams and play a football game. Now, the bragging started.

"Choose me! I was an All-State fullback at Iowa!"

"Hell, there ain't any schools in Iowa! I was an All-American tight-end at Tennessee!" On and on it went. I thought I was maybe the only one there who didn't get at least 14 college scholarships for football. I had played football in high school, but this was ridiculous.

"I was an All-State quarterback at Nebraska!" I looked at who said that. There stood 5'6" Tom Edwards, who right after getting out of the river may weigh 130 pounds.

We finally overcome the bragging and got our teams lined up. I was still the biggest even at 190 pounds, so I played tackle, which was one position I had played in high school. Tom was our self-proclaimed quarterback.

It was the first play of the game, and Tom called a play: "Lamar go long, I will hit you on a long pass. Just keep going - everyone else just block and give me some time." We had a play - not much of one it sounded like, but a play.

It was first down - in fact, the first down of the game. The ball was snapped, and Lamar took off. He was covered the first 25 or 30 yards, but like he was told, kept going. We blocked. And then we blocked. I was blocking and looking and Lamar was still running.

I thought, "Well, we blew that! Nobody can throw a football that far." The coverage had stopped and Lamar was still running. Lamar was wide open, the defense thinking the same as the rest of us. The play was over.

Tom dodged a tackler and stepped up and released the ball. It looked like it was launched from Cape Canaveral. It just kept sailing right into the waiting hands of Lamar. He caught it and looked as shocked as the rest of us. Then turned and ran it in for a touch down.

From that day on, I would listen when Tom told me something. I had never seen anything like it. In a few months Tom would be sent to "Land Mine Warfare Tech School." When he came back, he would one day be on a patrol and spot a "blooper round" (the M-79 round that has to go so far and spin so many times before it would detonate) by the trail. And detonate it did - right in Tom's face. He would go through life blind.

It was things like this that bothered me the most - stupid, careless things that resulted in loss of life or limb or eyes. What a terrible waste.

That night we were informed we would move out the next day. I lay there and thought of Mac, now on his way home.

I thought about last night when I was messing with him. Then I recalled the candle incident. He woke up and saw a light and quickly reacted by splattering hot wax everywhere. I thought about how things would be for him. I realized it wasn't over for Mac or me...or anyone leaving here. How long would it be before we would wake up wondering why there was a light on? Or why someone was making noise? Or jump at the sound of a flushing toilet? Strange things to us. Not acceptable. You had to be swift, silent, and deadly to survive here. This is the first time I realized it wasn't a 13-month tour - or, in a Corpsman's case, a 12-month tour.

Sarge had told me early on, "Doc there's two ways to leave this place. If you have your shit together, are a little lucky and pay attention, you can leave intact. If you don't, you will leave tacked in."

I knew now my thoughts that, "It was 365 days out of my life, and nothing I do matters; in 365 days, I go home and forget about it," was horseshit. Now I knew it wouldn't end just because I got on that great "Freedom Bird" home.

Mac left intact, but it wasn't over for him, nor would it be for any of us. It was just beginning.

Chapter 29
<u>Brave Little Soldier</u>

The morning we were to move out, a chopper dropped in a surprise for us. We had a new "Papa Sierra". His name was Staff Sgt. Woody - a true lifer as far as I was concerned. I was polite as I shook his hand and introduced myself, but was "checking him out".

He was much older than Sarge. He would never replace him, though. I decided to listen to him, and then do what I thought was best.

We left Liberty Bridge and were headed east to the mountains, then were to go north to Go Noi. It was a long hot hump and, once again, I was reminded of my bout with that amoeba. I had no idea how long it would take before I had all my strength back, but all I could do is keep going.

We never made it to the foothills. Our orders were already changed and we were to go south and set in somewhere near the Dog Bone. I made a mental note that when we stopped at a check point, I would dig into my pack and find something special for Chi Com. I smiled even now as I thought of her. I felt sorry for her, but she was such a cute little shit. She was special.

It was a seven-hour hump to the Dog Bone and we made it with little trouble other than the expected leeches, mosquitoes, creek crossing and treading the rice paddies. No ambushes - no booby traps. We would take all of these moves we could get. It was almost "Tet", and we all were well aware of what happened in the 1968 "Tet" offensive. It was almost dark when we moved into the ville. We were south and east of the main part of the Dog Bone. I didn't see Chi Com, but would make a point of getting over there tomorrow and giving her a "shit disc" and peaches with pound cake.

These were the favorite of most of us. Whenever I was fortunate enough to find peaches in my C-rat meal, I always saved it until I also got pound cake. Then I would mix them together and it was a real treat. Tomorrow I would give both to Chi Com, wishing I could see her face as she ate it.

I was also looking forward to a few more canteens full of that cool, sweet water she got me last time. Water without Halazone - now that was a treat.

Doc Gray had the ambush that night, and I made an effort to set in at a hootch close to the Platoon CP, but with just me and the radioman. He would be over with Lt. Rob most of the night, so I had both a bunkmate and privacy. Privacy was becoming more and more desirable to me.

Everything was different now. The absence of Sarge changed everything. I laid out my poncho and poncho liner, and then looked at the way we were set in. It was a good perimeter and everyone seemed to be set in, claymores out, positions all with a good field of fire. Yes, Rob was going to work out. I knew he missed Sarge as well. They had gotten close in a short time. There was a lot more pressure on him now; he didn't have Sarge to go to when he needed advice. Neither did I.

Around 2300, we were hit by four B-40 rockets and a little small arms fire. I dove behind the bunker, M-16 and medical bag in hand, hoping I wouldn't hear "Corpsman Up!"

The call didn't come. No one was hit. They had overshot us. I was lying back down, thinking it was over for now, and was going to try to sleep a few minutes before taking my watch.

I heard movement outside the hootch and someone say, "Where's Doc?"

"I'm here, man! What's wrong?"

279

"Doc, I have a wounded civilian here. She came walking into the lines calling 'Bacse!' Damn near opened up on her! Thought it was a trick!"

"Ok, bring her in here."

Berry walked in with a little girl in his arms. My heart sank.

It was Chi Com…and she was terrified.

"Berry, would you go down in that bunker for me and set up a light, candles or whatever, and I will bring her right down."

"Sure".

I looked into those dark brown beautiful bright eyes and saw something I hadn't seen before. Fear!

She had on a dirty white silk top, the usual attire for locals, and a black pair of shorts. The top was bloody.

I grabbed my poncho liner, main medical bag, and then Chi Com and followed Berry into the bunker. He had two candles going and I told him to throw a poncho or something over the entrance to the bunker so the light wouldn't draw fire.

I spread out the poncho and laid her on it.

For the first time since she was hit, I looked deep into those big brown eyes. She said nothing. She didn't cry, scream, nothing. She just stared at me, frightened and scared. Those eyes were so wide. They penetrated all the way to my soul. I saw trust there, and without saying a word her eyes told me, "Do what you have to do, Bacse. I will understand."

I took off her little white top so I could see the wound. Shrapnel had gone both in and up. She must have been lying down when the rocket penetrated her insecure world.

"It's okay, Chi Com. Lie still."

She couldn't understand anything other than the name I had given her four months ago, but she didn't move a muscle.

I got out a morphine syrette and mentally calculated how much to give her. It was a squeezable metal tube with syringe built in. I estimated she weighed about 30 pounds, so I injected about $1/5^{th}$ of the pain killer into her thigh. She was so brave - so innocent.

I got out my field surgical kit and went to work. I had to see where the shrapnel went, how large it was and figure how to treat this little child.

I was thinking as fast as I could - my brain flashing thoughts and options as the adrenalin pumped through my veins.

A horrible thought passed through my mind. "Would I now lose Chi Com as well as Sarge?"

No!!! I can't let that happen.

I felt a need to cry. This was ridiculous. I was a combat-hardened Marine, wasn't I? *"...A Rock feels no pain..."*

To save the life of a patient in the bush is always the first thing to consider. In her case, there was also a second thing to consider: Here was a four-year old girl who was a foreigner in her on village. If I sent her off on a chopper she may never find her mother again, assuming she had one here. She couldn't tell them in DaNang who she was or where she was from. She would most likely be mistreated anywhere else because of her heritage. I had to consider all these things and make a decision. Most important was her immediate welfare.

I decided to probe the wound and try to find the shrapnel. I don't recall this being mentioned in my "job description".

Tears were rolling down her broad cheeks as I probed the wound, and yet she kept nodding. She was telling me to go ahead and do what I had to do. I was suddenly overwhelmed that she trusted me. My God, why would she? We come into their villages to kill their fathers and brothers, destroy their crops, and search their bunkers and food bins!

The bleeding wasn't bad yet, but it would increase when I went in after the shrapnel, which was my decision. The wound was about an inch above her left nipple, one and a half inches long, and three-eighths and inch wide. I wasn't yet sure how deep.
I started an IV on her. All I had were 18-gauge needles. It would have to do. I got it going and was watching to see if the morphine had taken effect yet.

It was time to go in.

Chi Com was still laying there nodding her head with tears running down her cheeks. Not a whimper. I was about to cut into a VERY brave little girl. I remembered the first time I saw her, four months ago. How she had somehow caught my attention with her innocent smile; the quiet manner in which she approached me; the unexplainable bond. Was my guardian angel telling me this child was special and to take care of her?

I had more questions than answers.

I found the shrapnel; it had gone in and up. It had to come out.

"Chi, Com, this will hurt, baby. Hang on."

"Baby?!" I had never called her anything but "Chi Com", but she was a "baby" - a beautiful, precious innocent little "baby", in a place that was hell on earth.

She just nodded. Trust still in her big brown eyes. Somehow she had confidence that I would do what was best for her. Her courage amazed me. This little four-year old girl was a fighter. She had spirit - heart.

I went in and felt it. I looked again into those eyes to give me strength. They were looking right through me. I got a hold on it. I needed to do as little damage as possible as I removed the jagged metal from her chest. I cut a little to give me room to remove it without tearing her tender tissue.

She was crying now, but not shuddering.

"Hang on, baby. I got it!" I smiled.

I nodded back to try and let her know she would be okay.

The jagged edges were cutting new flesh as I removed it. I got it out, wiped it off and put it in her sweaty little hand. She smiled. The IV was going well, and I had to stop the bleeding. It was a bad place to put a pressure dressing.

I decided to take yet another chance. I would have to suture the wound, give her some anti-biotic that I hoped she wasn't allergic to, and then hope it didn't get infected. I didn't want to send her off on a chopper; she may never find her way back.

I got out my suture kit and she was still nodding her head. Yet another 18-gauge needle in that little chest, this time filled with Lidocaine.

As I sewed it up I looked into her future. I thought she would make it okay. The next time we were through here I would remove the sutures. But, where would this brave little soldier be in 20 years? What kind of life could she hope to have? There was something special about her. She was certainly bright. Her courage was amazing. Even with being raised in a village where she was an outcast, she kept her dignity. I felt nothing would rob her of that. Somehow, Chi Com would rise above this life and find a way to happiness.

Where was her mother? She wasn't waiting outside the hootch. Perhaps she was an outcast as well.

Was Chi com an orphan? I didn't know if her mother was even alive.

What I did know was this: This was a very special little girl. She had the heart of a warrior. I couldn't control her future, but I had kept her from going to Saigon or DaNang or somewhere they may send her with no one at all to look out for her. I felt someday this little girl would be taking care of herself. If she wanted to be a nurse or a doctor, she would be one. She had the heart to find a way.

I stopped the IV and took it out. The bleeding had stopped. I picked her up and carried her out of the bunker, and lay her down on my poncho liner. It was soft, and relatively clean. I wrapped her up in it then, reached over and closed those big eyes with my fingers. I lay down on the dirt beside her.

She opened her eyes and smiled.

Then, she reached over and closed my eyes with her fingers. We both smiled. I patted her on the head and told her goodnight.

I pulled my M-16 over where I lay in the dirt. She was asleep now, as I still watched her. I had no control over her future, but tonight, by God, she would be protected.

Florida, 2001

I had often thought of Chi Com. By that I mean daily. When I returned home, Linda and I thought about trying to adopt her. There was no possible way. The war was still on, and I only knew her by the name I had given her.

My daughter, Jamie, and her husband, Derek, had been trying to bring a baby into the world for six years. They decided to adopt, and chose the option of adopting from abroad - Kazakhstan. They found a baby boy, seven-months old, and a little girl, two-years old.

284

They came to make the announcement, and had pictures. The baby girl they would name Jaden looked so much like Chi Com I had to go into a room by myself for a few minutes to gather my thoughts.

It was an adoption that was meant to be. Jaden is four now, about the age of Chi Com when she was hit, where I operated on her in a third world hootch under barbaric circumstances. She is special, as was little Chi Com.

Chapter 30
<u>Tet 1969</u>

I did manage to doze off a time or two during the long night. Chi Com was doing as well as could be expected - better actually. Breathing was regular, bleeding stopped; the main concern now was an infection setting in. I thought about loading her up with an injection of Pro pen, but was afraid she could have a reaction, and then I would have to med-evac her in spite of all the efforts to keep her there.

I gave her an adult dose of Erythromycin that night and again in the morning. In the light, I examined my suture job; not bad for candlelight and a wide-awake patient. There wouldn't be much of a scar. She would not be ashamed; in fact, it wouldn't surprise me if she wasn't just a little proud of it.

I couldn't get over how she just laid there and took it, trying desperately to ignore the pain.

Squeezing morphine into her fragile little body was scary. There was no way of measuring it. It was all "guess-timation". Approximately 1/5 of a serrate! Geez! I guess they needed to add one more class at Field Med School.

Soon we were saddling up and the rumors were once again flying. We found out why we were pulled south instead of going on to Go Noi Island two days ago. S2 (Marine intelligence - and still an oxymoron) had received valuable information from some source that An Hoa was to be the "Hue City" of the 1969 Tet offensive.

Supposedly tens of thousands of NVA and VC were congregating and would get all hopped up on drugs and pull a human wave assault on the combat base of the Fifth Marines.

Alpha 1/5 was chosen to stop them.

Our emotions were mixed. These reports were so often pure bullshit, but who knew for sure. It did make sense. An Hoa was the home of three battalions. It had a small airport and a large ammo dump. It was also an easy target being surrounded on three-sides by mountains. I recalled what Bob had gone through at Hue City, or at least what I knew of it. Was An Hoa next?

Were we going to be overrun and would have to fight our way back to reclaim or own area? Most of us - me included - were looking forward to spending some time there. No one knew for sure, but they were pulling Alpha 1/5 inside the perimeter for what they thought was a good reason. It wasn't because they missed us or wanted to reward us.

They set us up in the south-eastern quadrant. It was closest to the mountains to the east and where they thought the human wave assault would take place. We were to turn them back.

Being "bush" Marines there were two things on the minds of most of us. There was a chow hall here and not too far away there were showers we could sneak into.

Secondly, we supposedly wouldn't be running patrols every day, or ambushes every night. Instead we would slip outside the perimeter after dark and set in.

Personally I was excited about it. Yes, we were to be used as the force to stop a human wave assault, but we would reap benefits as well. We would have the hot meals (C-rats were really getting old), and showers - access to showers! And probably we could get beer and soda occasionally. I could run over to the BAS and get supplies when I needed them instead of ordering them through Weird Warren. We were taken to our A/O (area of operations) and dumped there. We just sat there in the dirt and mud like so many hogs. There was no cover, no shade - nothing.

Things were different here in the rear - a lot of things. In the bush, race was of no real importance. It meant nothing to me as a bush Corpsman. I did a quick triage, and he who was in the most need was treated first. If we were under fire and I needed a Marine to lay down a line of fire to cover my ass, I could care less what color his skin was or of his heritage in general.

It was different in the rear. They had a "Black Shack". It was where blacks hung out who, for whatever reason, were trying to get out of the bush. The rest of us took it for what it was; they were cowards, looking for a way to get out of their sworn duty. We had many blacks, or as we called them, "splibs". These other brothers or "splibs" in the Platoon seemed to feel the same way. They stayed away from and wanted nothing to do with the "Black Shack". They were true Americans – fighting for freedom. And, by far, the majority of them were good men and good Marines. One of our best point men was a "splib". I can honestly say this: Race was never a factor when it came to my treating a casualty, nor was it one for any other Doc that I am aware of. It was never a factor when someone was covering me. In the bush, we were equals - brothers in arms.

It was very common in the bush to see a "chuck dude" and a "splib dude" sitting together shooting the bull, sharing pictures, thoughts and problems.

Here in the rear it was different. The blacks ran with the blacks. The whites ran with the whites. It was obvious there was tension between the races here - something foreign to us in the field. Two of my favorite Marines were of different races, (excluding, obviously, Sarge). Connors was black and Hernandez was Mexican or Hispanic. I would have laid my life on the line, and probably did, for either of these men, and was confident they would do the same for me.

I was raised in the Ozarks, as I stated earlier. We had no blacks in the town I grew up in, nor did we have Mexicans. You may think if you weren't familiar with a situation like that, that I would be automatically prejudiced. It wasn't like that at all. I wasn't around blacks or Hispanics until I went to Navy boot camp. I got along fine with all and judged each man on his merits whether or not I would be a friend. The reason for this is simple if you think about it. I was never taught to hate them.

I was very disturbed about the hatred here in the rear, "Black Shack", and congregations of white - both equally. I just didn't get it. Did we not have the same enemy? Were we not a stronger force united?

The sun was setting our first evening in our new "home". While it was still light enough to see fairly well, it all started. Incoming! Lots of incoming - 122-mm rockets, and 82-mm mortars, but they weren't hitting An Hoa, so to speak. They were hitting Alpha 1/5. It made sense when you thought about it. Were they afraid of the "dudes" in the "Black Shack"? No, they didn't want to fight anyway except among themselves and their comrades. No, they were concerned with the grunt unit that was up for the PUC and was currently out in the wide open with no place to hide. They had us by the short hairs and we were bombarded. All we could do was hug the red clay dirt and hope they got tired of dropping rockets and mortars on us. Gray and I were busy as long-tailed cats in a room full of rocking chairs, and just as nervous. We had many men hit, but none killed...yet. It was at this time, maybe because we had so many shrapnel wounds, maybe just because all we could do was lay there and think, that I became more aware of the "fear" I had been carrying since Chief Valdosta had gotten my attention in Hospital Corps School. In all my time in the field, I had never had a Marine die on me who was alive when I got to him. Yes, I had Marines and ones I considered friends die, but they were dead when they were first hit. They didn't die after I treated them, nor did they die in my arms. I was still haunted by that fear.

After dark and after it stopped raining rockets and mortars, we went out for our first time to do our new assignment. It was like setting up an ambush on the moon - barren, no trees, no bushes, nothing. The land had long ago been burned clear with a flame thrower and it apparently worked.

There were a few low places, and that is what we did: We crept around in the dark until we found something slightly resembling a hole to take cover in. We did have a good field of fire, but no cover. If the human wave attack did take place, we could fight it out for a while, blow our claymores, and run back to where we were set in, but the same problem remained. There was no cover there either - nothing. So basically, as I saw it, we would catch them coming across the ground and kill a bunch of them; but as far as keeping a few thousand NVA from getting to the perimeter? I didn't see that happening.

The first night on "An Hoa Security" was long, and scary. A little before it was light we packed up and headed back to our assigned position. Rob had very little rank as an officer, but asserted his personality. And before dark that night, they brought out a backhoe and dug a trench for us to jump into when we were hit. It was obvious to everyone we were the target of the attacks - at least at this point. It made sense at some time they would hit the air strip and ammo dump, maybe zero in on a few gun (105-Howitzer) positions as well.

The backhoe dug a nice trench about four-feet deep and long enough to give us a good spot to defend. For some unknown reason, it also dug a small trench perpendicular to the main trench. It was maybe 14-feet long and two-feet wide. Doc Gray and I took one look at it and claimed it as the "Docs' trench" - the "Bear's Den" – "Club Med"! You get the point; we had our own little squid cubby hole. It was just big enough for the two of us and, for some reason, the fact that it ran in a different direction than the main trench was appealing. We climbed down the end and set up our gear. From inside it looked like they started to dig a trench there and then changed their minds, which could well be what happened.

We were hit regularly - shortly after daylight every morning, again midday, and once more before nightfall. It was taking its toll. We yet had a man to die from this, but a LOT of shrapnel wounds.

Late one afternoon, after we had our evening meal and were waiting for our night ambush (if you could call it that), and our barrage of rockets, I was talking to Gray and Stuckey. A chopper was coming in to the airport and I suddenly heard a "whoosh". I knew someone had just fired a rocket at the chopper that was attempting to land.

I said, Doc, I think I'm going to stroll on over to the house."

He said, "Why?"

"We are about to get hit. I heard a rocket go past the chopper that was landing."
We did get hit.

Before we could get to our "hole", rockets and mortars were falling like a rainstorm from hell.

Now, earlier that day an amazing thing began happening. We were at the chow hall for lunch and Gray and I were sitting at the wooden table eating our sandwich and drinking cold Kool-Aid, when Gray said, "You know, Doc, if those gooks had their shit together, they would hit this chow hall during mealtime."

"WHOOOOOOSH! BOOM!"

A 122-mm rocket hit right outside the chow hall door and knocked us off our benches. We got up and ran to a nearby bunker. (Every area had bunkers, each branch of each unit except for us sitting out there - and we were the ones taking most of the rounds!) We stayed there a minute or two and I was afraid maybe the human wave attack would come now and we were away from our unit, so we grabbed our gear and took off to be with our Platoon.

Up ahead there was a group of Marines all bunched up together making their way back to their units and Gray yelled, "Hey you guys, you better get uncluster-fucked! They will drop a rocket in on you."

"WHOOOOOOSH! BOOM!" It landed right behind them and several were hit. We treated them and were once again running toward our unit when I heard a rocket coming in. I saw a bunker to my right, and headed for it. Gray said, "Doc, duck!!!!" Too late. I felt the force lift me up and throw me in the air like a toy GI Joe. I do not remember the explosion. I do remember flying through the air, trying to turn so I would land on my feet. I didn't. I hit the ground and rolled and got up running - a little dazed. We got to the Platoon and there was no human wave assault this time, but we had men down. We both got busy and as I was treating a Marine I said, "You'll be okay, man! But blame this one on Doc Gray...he's been calling in artillery on us all day."

So, now we were running the last few feet to our hole amid the explosions. Everyone else was headed to the "main" ditch. This was going to be a good one. There was even some small arms fire and I was happy to get to our "hole". We knelt there waiting, hoping no one would call "Corpsman up!" At this point I wondered why the hell we set up away from the rest of the Platoon; it would be much safer to get to them if we were in the same ditch.

We were as low in that hole as we could get and Gray says, "Doc, we have to get out of this hole."

I said, "Did you hear someone call for us?"

"No, but Doc, we have to get out of this hole."

I said, "Yeah, right, just as soon as I eat this watermelon."

He didn't laugh. "Doc, I'm serious we have to get out of here."

"Are you crazy? I'm not leaving this hole unless someone is hit."

Now, Gray was a very good Corpsman. I literally trusted him with my life. I had every confidence in letting him treat me, or anyone else; he was a good man in every way. But right now, I wished he would shut up.

"Doc, we have to get out of here, now."

I looked at him, and then remembered the incidents earlier that day.

"Are you having one of your premonitions?"

"We have to get out of here fast."

I was convinced. "Well, shit! Do you want to go first or do you want me to?"

Rockets and mortars were still dropping all over our area. He said, "You go first."

I waited just a moment for a lull in the attack but it didn't come.

"Ok, I'm going now," I said as I ran up the side of the trench with my medical bag and M-16 and turned on all I had as I ran the 30-meters to the main trench. I jumped in.

I had no sooner landed than in dove Gray, head first doing a belly flop on the bottom of the trench.

I said, "I can't believe you did a damn swan dive in here." He was scared and completely convinced we would have been killed had we stayed in that hole. I was watching the fireworks and capping a few rounds every so often as was everyone else.

"Corpsman up!!!" Oh, Shit. Someone was hit. I ran down the trench, jumping over Marines, gear and equipment asking, "Where?"

Someone cried out, "Here, Doc, Lt. Montgomery's hit."

Well, hell, my heart sank. We finally had a good Platoon Commander and he was already hit. I ran as hard as I could.

I yelled, "Rob? Rob?"

"Here, Doc."

I got to him and, as usual, he had his head up returning and directing fire. I swear this guy did not know the meaning of fear.

I said, "Are you, hit?"

"Yes, I'm hit."

I said, "WELL?"

"Well what?"

"Damn, Lieutenant! Where are you hit?"

He said, "I don't want to tell you, Doc."

"Damn it, Rob! Are you hit or not?"

"Yes".

"Then where in the hell are you hit?"

He looked at me, sighed, and finally gave in. "Doc, I'm hit in the left fat."

I said, "The left fat? Where in the hell is your left fat? Monty, don't play games with me here...where are you hit?"

"Damn it Doc! I got hit right in my left love handle."

I tried to hide my relief, "Damn, Rob - only you!"

I checked him out and sure enough, a piece of shrapnel had gone into his "left fat" - apparently when he was running to the trench.

I said, "Okay, Lieutenant, as soon as this is over, you are out of here. I want an x-ray."

"Awww, no, Doc! I'm okay! It's just my fat."

"Monty, you are out of here. It is most likely nothing, but it is headed towards your left kidney and I'm not taking any chances. I want an x-ray."

"I'm okay, Doc, "

"Rob, we are in An Hoa. The BAS is a mile away. I want an x-ray to make sure your kidney is okay. You will probably be back here in the morning."

When the attack was over, he was off to the BAS.

Gray and I went and looked at our "hole". A rocket had hit about a foot from it, but wouldn't have killed us or injured us seriously. That put an end to Doc Gray's prophetic career, and along with that the accusations that he was calling in artillery on us. In the future we would occasionally laugh about that day.

The next morning we were hit again, right on schedule. They were for sure concentrating their efforts on us. They were out to destroy Alpha Co. for whatever reason. That day a mortar round hit right by Doc Gray's head. It shook him up bad and gave him quite a concussion. I med-evaced him out.

Lt. Rob returned as predicted, but I was now once again the only Doc in the Platoon.

Chapter 31
<u>Year of the Monkey</u>

In the local religion, it was proclaimed the "year of the Monkey".

Who the hell cares? I had better things on my mind right now.

The chow hall was really not bad - cold milk, eggs to order, bacon, bread, cereal, and coffee for those few who liked it. Add a shower to that, which has been partially warmed by the sun, and there were times when I almost felt human again.

Feelings, though, can be deceptive. The recent good meals did refuel the body, but the body of a "grunt" often ran on adrenalin. I was heading back to the Platoon after a shower and a quick look at Robin's x-rays. (I just wanted to see for myself and I had read a lot of x-rays in orthopedics.) I was walking down the road by the chow hall when the rocket and mortar attack started. My walk quickly turned into a "run" as I tried to get to my Platoon. Doc Gray would be back soon, but for now, I was it.

As usual, I had my helmet, flak jacket, major medical bag and my M-16.

I heard the 122-mm rocket coming in and started to dive. It lifted me off the ground and hurled me through the air. I must have been thrown at least 30-feet, but I landed on my feet. I stumbled, caught my balance, was dazed again, but kept running. The Platoon was just ahead and getting hit.

Things slowed down a little as I got to them, but several were wounded. Rodney had a huge chunk of shrapnel sticking out of his cheek. I took it out, and called for a med evac.

I was treating another wounded Marine when SSgt. (Staff Sergeant) Woody came over. "Doc, are you okay?"

I said, "Yes, I'm okay. Get me a med evac jeep ambulance in here so I can get these guys to the BAS and I will be fine."

I was suturing a wound when SSgt. Woody came back. "Doc, are you okay?"

I said, "Yes, where's my damn ambulance?"

"It's on the way. Are you sure you are all right?"

As planned, I had deliberately not gotten close to our new Platoon Sergeant, and didn't intend to, but was wondering why he kept asking me if I was okay.

"Sarge, get me an ambulance in here, stat! Why do you keep asking me if I am okay?"

He said, "Well, I guess I just don't know how bad you are hit."

I said, "I'm not hit, but these guys are! Get me the damn ambulance!"

He said, "Doc, yes you are hit! How bad is it?"

I said, "I'm not hit! What are you talking about?"

"Doc Bear, you are hit! Your left arm is bleeding badly. Are you going to be okay?"

I looked down and saw the blood. Yep, looked like mine. It wasn't from a patient. Suddenly my left arm started burning like a swarm of fire ants had crawled into it.

I said, "I'm fine. Just help me get these guys out of here."

"You better go, too, Doc."

I was the only Corpsman. I said, "And are you going to take my place, too?" It wasn't fair and I apologized, "Sorry Sarge, just a little stressed here."

"Sarge said, "Its okay, Doc, but you need to get on that ambulance.""

"Thanks, Sarge but I'm okay." Damn it hurt.

I took off my flak jacket and my t-shirt and I had been hit in the left deltoid. Nothing major, the shrapnel tore on through, but left a nasty gash. It hurt like hell, but I was the only Corpsman and it had to be sown up. I couldn't leave them without a Corpsman. Sure it was the rear - it was An Hoa - but it was An Hoa under siege.

I got out my suture kit, popped 25-mg. of Demerol and recruited Brock to help me. I directed him to hold the flesh tightly together while I sutured it up with my right hand. I had him help me tie the knots as well. The adrenalin began to subside and it hurt like hell, and I wondered what life would be like without that adrenalin. That is, if I made it home.

I got it sutured and it looked pretty good for a one-handed job. I thanked Brock. I gave myself a shot of Pro Pen, put on some Betadine and bandaged it up.

A few days later I went to the BAS to get supplies and was greeted by a concerned Chief and several Corpsmen who had become friends. They had to look at the wound. "We heard your arm was half blown off and you refused to be med evaced."

Now that was grossly exaggerated. I had to laugh. "No, it just took a few sutures - I am fine." I was.

It was my second time to be hit in four months. My buddy Mac had been hit in the ankle, nothing serious; but when you look at the big picture, what had happened was: in four months, 18 out of 18 of us had Purple Hearts. Only two of us were left in country. Mercy, Sarge!

I was heading back to the Platoon to await our afternoon rocket and mortar attack, and decided to stop and see Gray in the psych unit. I didn't know why he was in a psych unit for a concussion but I don't decide these things. The little shit was anything BUT crazy. I stopped in the bunker/psych ward and talked to the Corpsman on duty.

"Are you a Neuro-Psych tech?"

"No, I'm just an 8404."

This pissed me off.

"Well, I'm a NP tech and my ass has been out in the bush for the last four months. How did you get this job?"

He said, "I just went where they told me to go."

I was really hot. The Navy had spent all that money sending me to NP school, at their own figures over $100,000 and then assigned someone who had no clue what to do with a psych patient to this "ward". I wasn't mad at the Corpsman. If I was him, I would have jumped at the chance as well. I was mad at the Navy! I couldn't wait to get out of this stupid green so and so.

I went to Gray's bed and said, "Gray, hey! It's Doc Bear - how ya' doin', buddy?"

Nothing.

"Gray, it's Bear! What's going on?"

Gray looked my way with a blank stare.

"Doc Bear! I know a Doc Bear! Best damn Corpsman to ever set foot in this country. More balls than anybody I ever seen."

My chest swelled a bit. I was feeling pretty good about myself. We talked a while, but he wasn't really with it. Bits and pieces made sense but a lot of it was gibberish. I diagnosed "concussion". Nothing was wrong with his mind. It was that damn round next to his ear. But what did I know, I was a bush Corpsman. This other guy was the psych Corpsman. I only studied this shit for two years.

I left and went back to yet another night of sitting and waiting for Charlie to launch the big human wave assault. It was better than the bush in a lot of ways, but given a choice, put my ass back out there where we can fight back. I hated laying there and "taking it". We even had restrictions: We couldn't return fire, not even the 105's, until 0800. Now tell me that isn't crazy as hell. And the public wondered why we didn't go in and win this stupid war. Let a good Marine General take control of this thing, put no restrictions on him or his troops and see what happens. It would be over in a year or less. Politicians can't fight wars. They don't have the right mentality. It takes a warrior's mentality.

I had been in a lot of fire fights, and we never really lost a one. Pinned down for a few minutes, yes, but we always took the high ground, or where ever we need to go. Yes, we had our asses kicked by booby traps a few times, but that can be overcome if you know you will get to kick their ass as well. Sweep us from Saigon to Hanoi, including Jane Fonda's traitorous ass, and we would win this war. It may look like a parking lot, but we would win. We had the men to do it. We had the leaders to do it. They just needed to have their hands untied. You can't win a war with a bunch of mealy-mouthed politicians who are afraid to offend someone, running the show. Yet, they didn't want to let go of all that oil in the South China Sea. Of all the cluster-fucks I have seen, the one in Washington was the biggest. There you have it in a nutshell. The truth - like it or not.

I went back up to see Doc Gray again the next day.

"Doc, it's Doc Bear! How are you feeling today?"

He lay there in bed staring at the ceiling.

"Gray, it's me; Doc Bear...how are you?"

He slowly turned his head towards me.

"Doc Bear! I know Doc Bear! He don't know shit!"

I left there somewhat deflated. And maybe hoping he was psychotic after all. "Damn squid!"

Actually in a year and a few months, Gray would name his son after Sarge and me, Vincent John, so I guess he did have at least some respect for "The Bear".

I go on back to the Platoon and we are getting ready to go out on a patrol. I am excited about this. At least we will have a chance to "get some".

There is a huge steep mountain right outside the An Hoa perimeter. It is called Noi Song Soi. We are going to climb it and take a look. We do and it is a steep rascal.

Once again I am reminded of that "one-celled wonder" (amoeba). My butt is kicked by the time we reach the top.

The view was breath-taking. ("Doc, nothing is as it seems in the bush.") We were looking for places the gooks were using to launch their rockets and mortars. It could well have been from here. It was well worn and you could see every single part of the compound.

As we were observing from this vantage point, we spotted movement. I went over where I could see what was going on and there was a column of soldiers on a trail far below us. I looked at Rob and he was excited. We set up the M-60, got online and were about to open up on them, when I heard something I didn't want to hear: "Maybe they are ARVN's (Army of the Republic of Vietnam)."

ARVN"s never did anything that I had seen, but as I watched I was convinced that's what we had spotted. They were holding hands, laughing, and joking. Made you want to open up on them any way. Is THIS worth dying for? Helping a bunch of so-called soldiers who do nothing but goof off? Was this worth losing Sarge, Pop, and all the others?

Lt. Rob called it in and it was confirmed - ARVN patrol, if you could call it one, in the area.

Somehow I felt cheated. I was ready for some real action instead of staying here getting our butts kicked by incoming. Just waiting there while they dumped their load of artillery on you was the "pits". I wanted to be able to at least fight back - use tactics. Either out smart them or out fight them and prevail. I was ready to go back to the bush, hot chow or not.

I knew when the time came I would be ready to go to the rear, but this wasn't "the rear". This was the Tet offensive and that "Year of the Monkey" crap was a pain in the ass.

That night we loaded up and went out on our routine night position. It had been two weeks now. Sarge was hit February 6. I was hit February 25. We had been sitting in here at night, and then enduring the attacks for over two weeks. We were the "sacrificial lambs", out here to absorb the initial attack and try to stop it. But if it was a human wave attack, we couldn't. We had our trench back where we stayed during the day, but here all we had were small indentations in the earth. During a human wave assault we would have two options: We could stay here and fight it out until we all died; or we could do all the damage we could then retreat to our trenches and finish the fight. No one, not even us, thought we could hold off 4,000-5,000 hopped up NVA and keep them from getting into the An Hoa perimeter.

We could kill a pile of them, and An Hoa would know they were coming. That was our purpose.

Tonight looked to be like the other night. But "Nothing is as it seems in the bush."

"...*And a rock feels no pain...*"

302

Chapter 32
<u>The Deadliest Weapon in the World</u>

We slipped into the night, once again approaching our designated site to repel the expected human wave assault. It was pitch black tonight, the only light coming from flashes that the occasional 105's put out as they fired their missions.

We slipped into the shallow fighting hole which was no more than a natural indentation in the clay earth. This was our home for the night, our mission, once again, to wait for Charlie to make his move.

Tonight felt eerie, and it seemed it wasn't just me that felt that way. Rob ordered "two-men-up, one-man-down watch". That meant all night two men from each fire team would be awake and alert, where normally we had one man from each fire team on watch while the other two slept.

I sat there next to Rob and Sgt. Woody and, for my own satisfaction, looked to make sure all the claymores were out. I liked the claymores; they could save many lives on our side, obviously by taking the lives of the enemy.

In Marine boot camp we were taught, "The deadliest weapon in the world is a Marine and his rifle." This may very well be true; but a claymore mine at close range will ruin your whole weekend.

It was now 2400, midnight. Then 122-mm rockets and 82-mm mortars began raining on the An Hoa fire base. The southeast perimeter, where we stay during the day, was getting hammered hard. They had moved some 105-Howitzers in behind us, which were good for long range, but useless in a human wave assault. That was what we were here to stop, or at least try to stop.

The phrase "Things are never as they seem," once again came to mind. I honestly believe being aware of that was one reason I was still alive. The attack on An Hoa went on, it was the biggest yet. They were dropping that entire ordinance on us for a reason. I didn't expect a human wave assault on our position, at least not right now. They knew we were set in here, why would they challenge us? Why not pick a position less fortified? Still, as the explosions continued, I did expect something big. They had carried all those rockets and mortars from Hanoi, they did have a plan. "What would Sarge do?"

The incoming was still heavy. This was the times my mind raced back, recalled all that happened the last four and a half months. My adrenalin was pumping, something was up, and though I wasn't expecting it, I still watched for silhouettes in the night.

My mind drifted as I watched. I smiled at my first encounter with Stuckey and the big orange mail bag the sniper was shooting at. I was so green then. I recalled so many wounded I had treated. I couldn't think of a type of wound I HADN'T treated - also all the foot problems, dysentery, gook sores, malaria, so, so much. I remembered those who had made the ultimate sacrifice…"*And a rock feels no pain…an island never cries…*"

WHOOMMMMMMMMM!!!!!!!!!!!!!!

The shock waves filled the air. The sheer force of the explosion shook the earth and made me do a 360-degree turn. What? What the hell?! Something big just went off. Huge. It came from An Hoa, but it sure wasn't a rocket or mortar.

WHOOMMMMMMMMMMMMMMMM!!!!!!!!!!!!

Multiple explosions now! Different from the rest! Many of them! The sky behind us was red. An Hoa was lit up like a Christmas tree.

The ammo dump! They got to the ammo dump! The rocket and mortar attack on the southeast quadrant was diversionary. They had hit the west side of the compound with small arms and B-40 rockets, and laid ladders over the concertina wire as the Sappers rushed in and blew the ammo dump. Rounds were flying everywhere - hot rounds - OUR rounds! There were 105- rounds that could explode at any moment from the heat, tossed into the air like tiny firecrackers and scattered over the An Hoa Base by the big explosion.

We heard the panic on the net. The "pogues" in the rear were getting a taste of "war" at last. Many were killed. We heard a report that the Alpha Company First Sergeant had taken a direct hit in the chest. An Hoa was chaos.

I was watching the red sky behind us when my old phrase dawned on me. "Nothing is as it seems in the bush." If the human wave attack was to come, it would come now. And if it was to come where we were, this would be the moment I would launch it. The attention had been diverted to the ammo dump, away from us. The compound behind us was fighting its own war. Sappers were killed in the wire trying to escape. Satchel charges were still being dropped. Any Sappers that came through that wire would die there. There was no way out.

Bob had told me a little about Hue City in the Tet offensive a year ago. The NVA were so hyped up on drugs they were twice as hard to kill. They believed it was an honor to die during this celebration. They even left their dead behind, something they normally did their best to hide.

I kept my eyes front, on the area east of us. The battle of An Hoa was their battle. Our duty was to stop an assault if it came and if it was going to come, I felt it would be now.

It never came.

We waited and watched, but the battle was over, at least this leg of it. They had succeeded in destroying tons of bombs and artillery rounds.

We pulled back inside the compound at first light and were immediately sent out on a patrol to the area the Sappers had come from. We found very little. The concertina wire had been cut and ladders thrown over it. The Sappers took their satchel charges in and blew the ammo dump. It was as simple as that. Fifteen Sappers had given their lives to get that job done. They had made a grand exit. An Hoa was a mess. Even now, we could hear "hot" rounds going off. It was a scary thing, our own artillery rounds exploding within our perimeter.

Rumors were flying again. It was over. That was the big plan and they were finished. I didn't think so. I hoped I was wrong, but I didn't think they had yet accomplished their mission for the Tet offensive of 1969. Battalion apparently didn't either.

That night we went back out to our so-called ambush site. Everyone seemed a little jumpy, myself included. No one knew what to expect, but most of us didn't think it was over.

Shortly after 2400, the rockets and mortars fell on An Hoa - nothing like last night, but several rockets and a barrage of mortars. We were taking turns looking to An Hoa to our rear and of course our assigned area to our front. That soon changed. To our left, north of us about five miles, we both saw and heard Liberty Bridge come alive. The diversionary attack on An Hoa was over. The real attack, the Battle of Liberty Bridge, was on.

The Marines of Delta 1/5 happened to have "Bridge security" and they were fighting for both the "Bridge" and their lives. It was being hit hard. We could both see and hear the flashes. There went the

106's, the anti-personnel rounds called "Bee Hives". They were small "darts" shot out of the big guns like a shotgun and used for human wave assaults. We also heard the weapons of the enemy: 82-mm mortars, 57-recoilless rifles, rockets, satchel charges and small arms fire. The expected human wave attack was on; it was just going on five miles from where they expected it.

Soon the word came down: Liberty Bridge had been overrun. It had fallen. The NVA had the forward BAS of the 5th Marines. Last year it was the 5TH Marines they hit as well - Hue City and Khe Sahn. Of course, they hit many other bases as well - not just the 5th Marines, but the main force once again was the Fighting Fifth.

Sitting five or six miles away from your rear area while you know they are fighting for their lives is a strange feeling - a new one for me. I had felt many new emotions in the last four and a half months in country, but this one I hated most of all. I felt guilty that my unit was under attack and there wasn't a damn thing I could do about it. Guilt was a big part of this war. You either felt guilty for reacting in a way during the heat of combat that is foreign to your nature, or you felt guilty that you couldn't do enough. Sometimes you got pissed off in a fire fight and later, after you won the battle, you would even feel guilty about that. There was also the "guilt" feeling of not being where you thought you could help. That was happening now. There was a reason for it.

Thousands of miles away was a country that no longer supported its fighting forces. Marines and soldiers who were fighting for the freedom and rights that our forefathers founded were looked down on in the very country we were defending. In ALL former wars, these Marines and soldiers would be welcomed home as warriors, heroes, and the patriots that they were, but not in this war. We were doing our duty – fulfilling (despite our personal, moral and political convictions) our oaths. We had never lost a fire fight - a major battle. These men were as dedicated to winning this war as all the great warriors of our predecessors. These Marines were every bit as dedicated as those who went up Iwo Jima Hill, Guadalcanal, the Chosin Reservoir, or Omaha Beach. They put their lives on the line everyday and were willing to die for a country that rejected them and limited them to a war run by politicians. We weren't dedicated to the politicians, nor were we dedicated to the protesters who violated us. We were dedicated to the principles this country was founded on: Freedom for all - honor. The guarantee our Founding Fathers gave us of "Life, liberty and the pursuit of happiness."

Many Marines and, yes, Army soldiers as well, would go home after laying their lives on the line, sacrificing limbs and futures for their country. But how would they be received? They would be spat upon at airports - shunned by the very people they fought for, to preserve their rights and freedom to voice an opinion. Never in history had a gallant warrior of a nation been so badly treated. Many would live with this rejection for the rest of their lives. What a shame. What a travesty. The gallant are scorned - the cowards are honored.

The battle of Liberty Bridge was still raging, with NVA soldiers who were supported by their country and families fighting courageously. The Mess Sergeant of Liberty Bridge was right now defending his chow hall. The Corpsmen of the forward BAS were protecting the wounded with their lives and risking all they have to save a wounded Marine.

The Marines of Delta 1/5 were fighting hand to hand, out numbered and out- gunned, but they would not give up the "Bridge". They would fight to the death, and many of them did. Those who survived, who turned the NVA away and buried them, would someday go home to a country that didn't care - a country who would wonder why these gallant men had problems dealing with the war. The Marines of 1/5 won the battle of Liberty Bridge. What 105's, 106's, mortars, claymore mines, concertina wire and hand-grenades couldn't stop, the most dangerous weapon in the world overcame. The Marine and his rifle reclaimed the "Bridge" and they did it one bunker, one foxhole, one tent at a time. Only we would know.

This novel is about "The Names NOT on the Wall" - the men who fought and survived - the men who would return home, but never would their families or friends hear of the honor, the dedication, the sheer determination of these fighting men. These heroes would be forced to feel ashamed for doing the duty to which they were assigned. Many years after this battle would end a Wall would go up to honor, much too late, those who died for their country. Our nation should be ashamed for the way it treated those who fought and sacrificed. To all of you who did your duty, I, for one, salute you.

Chapter 33
<u>What did He Say?</u>

First thing the next morning we were sent to Liberty Bridge to help secure it, and clean up the mess. As we walked through the gate there was a bulldozer burying hundreds of dead NVA and Viet Cong soldiers. Many Marines had died as well, but they had won the battle. They had been highly out numbered, but they prevailed. The kill ratio was staggering. It was estimated that for every Marine that died, 15 NVA soldiers gave their all. This was the Battle of Liberty Bridge. This was war, and it was such a waste.

We were there for one day. The next morning found us working our way north, heading to Go Noi Island. S2 thought the Tet offensive was over and we could go back to war.

Marines really did have helicopters. They had a lot of them. The fact that we never were transported from one place to another on them unless it was to a hospital was a matter of tactics, not shortage of choppers. We "humped" everywhere we went. I could see the advantage and wondered why the Army operated the way they did. Sure, I would rather ride than walk, but I would also prefer the NVA didn't know where we were. If we choppered in 150 Marines to an area, I somehow think the element of surprise would be theirs.

So, I didn't complain as we walked.

Go Noi Island hadn't changed. Other than the railroad being converted into bunkers, it probably hadn't changed for centuries. We were in a different area of Go Noi: Different villages, same hatred; elephant grass and spider holes; banana trees and small rice paddies.

The point man is down. It is First Platoon's problem and we wait in the elephant grass while the

Corpsman does his job and the Platoon eliminates the sniper.

We are moving again. It is March now, and next month, April 18th, I am supposed to meet my wife in Hawaii on R&R. By the end of April, possibly first of May, I should be out of the bush. I was what they called a "short-timer" now. "I'm so short I can't start a long conversation" was one of the many sayings short-timers used to make the others envious. Right now, I had other concerns. This was Go Noi. Anyone could be a "short-timer" here and not in a pleasant way. Death was always a step away. So much cover - so many hiding places - such deep hatred.

We moved into a new ville and I am acutely aware of the surroundings. "Beware the banana trees." The enemy has been here recently. The leaves have been harvested to chew on and to use as mattresses. The sap is still dripping from some of them.

We move on through and leave the village and are hit. Snipers. We hit the deck, set up the M-60 and the "blooper" starts working the next tree line. "The most dangerous weapon in the world" advances and the snipers flee. These young Marines do this so well. So very young, yet so good at their job. I know most of them well now. Many I will never forget. There are the ones who amaze me and also the ones that make me wonder why they are still alive. Some I doubt if they will live another month. Two are dead within ten minutes. Sniper rounds to the chest. No chance to save them, a clean deadly shot. Life isn't worth much here.

We set in for the night, send out an ambush and it is an uneventful night. We had no element of surprise. Snipers followed us all day and an ambush was merely a routine, we weren't going to catch them unaware.

The next morning we saddle up once again and are on our way. I have altered my routine very little, but it is always the same. Cammie t-shirt, then flack jacket, then bandoleers of battle dressings. Over these go my two claymore mine medical bags. I have up-graded my load some - experience influencing what I will use and need most. I always carry two pairs of socks in my pack now, and change and rinse them out often. I wish I could get my men to do this more often. It would save a lot of pain and sores, but many of them just can't grasp the importance of dry socks. I find myself preaching a lot about foot care.

My "pharmacy" had changed a lot as well. I still carried a variety of medications, but tried to only hump what I may use.

I carried my morphine syrettes in a plastic waterproof cigarette case. Not so much to keep them dry, but to keep them clean and from puncturing the soft metal squeezable tubes.

Morphine was something I struggled with. We had free access to it, was never questioned about it, so some Corpsmen used it liberally. (For their patients - I am not talking about personal use.) I could possibly use it more often than I did. There is so much to consider when you treat a wounded man in the bush. Most wounds extend from some type of trauma. Booby traps for example. A man is walking along, in perfect health. Suddenly a grenade explodes and he is in danger of losing a leg, or arm, or life.

In treating these wounds, you have to consider so many things. One major consideration is shock. Here is the problem in a nut shell. If you give morphine to a patient and he is put on that chopper, and then goes into shock, he may die. There is no one there to treat him for shock. He won't be treated until he arrives in DaNang and is unloaded. There they could treat shock, assuming he is still alive. I admittedly have withheld giving morphine a lot of times where in the states, or if medical personnel were around, I would have given it. It certainly wasn't because I didn't care if they were in pain, it was because shock was a possibility, and I thought he could stand a little pain rather than take a chance on killing him. So many things to consider as a bush Corpsman. Many times I wished I could have consulted an M.D. It was impossible, so you made decisions - hopefully good ones.

Malaria tabs, salt tabs and Halazone I carried in huge quantities. For pain killers I humped APC's, Darvon compound 65's, Demerol 25-mgms tabs, and morphine syrettes.

Lidocaine injection was a must. Antibiotics, anti-histamines and topical anesthetics and anti-acids were also necessary. Everyone had dysentery, so Kaopectate was given a lot, but only in extreme cases.

My map was also in a waterproof cigarette case in my side pocket. Compass was snapped on my web belt. My surgical kit was small but efficient. I also carried a bottle of Betadine surgical scrub, which was heavy, but since everything was "dirty", it gave the patient at least a better chance of not getting infected.

I had learned all the sterile techniques in Corps School, Orthopedics and Field Med School. But that was all out the crapper here. It was impossible to keep things sterile! Hell, I was lucky to get a shower once every two months myself. I did a cut-down with a K-bar.

I used the same scalpel on several patients. This was the "bush". Our job, bottom line, was to keep that man alive for two hours. This was meatball medicine in its rawest form. We had no gloves, no autoclave, and no sterile blades. The battle dressings were sterile, and that's about it. Maybe you could keep a few needles from getting contaminated.

The reason this worked is relatively simple. The MD's at First Med knew what we were dealing with.

They used antibiotics liberally. They knew infection was not just a risk, but a probability. Because of this, staff infections were rare.

When I was a stateside Corpsman at Bethesda Naval Hospital, I was in charge of a "dirty orthopedic ward". I was amazed how few serious infections we had there. Now I knew why: Antibiotics were part of the routine at First Med Bat.

I still had my "doggie" pack and I was thankful for it. I was used to it and relied on it. I loved the quick release snap that freed me to get to the wounded. You did what you had to do to save a life here. Each Doc had to figure out for himself what worked best for him. I had my routine and I was comfortable with it.

I wasn't comfortable with the hatred I felt growing inside me. I had never hated anyone before I came here. Now I hated many things. I hated death most of all - then destruction and decay. I hated the enemy - all of them.

I also hated the Chu Hois. The success of this program was highly questionable. It allowed the enemy to "surrender" and "come to our side". It seemed to me the only time they did this was when their only alternative was to be captured or killed. I couldn't blame them, maybe I would have done the same thing if I was about to get captured or shot. Just throw up my hands, yell "Chu Hoi"; then tell them lies and pretend to be one of them until I could simply walk away and go back to my unit. They worked our system.

This particular day we were deep within Go Noi in heavy foliage on a platoon-size move. Suddenly we heard two quick bursts of rounds - an automatic weapon. (Marines do not have guns, we have weapons.) It was the distinct sound of an M-16.

I was two-men back from the radio man and soon heard the report. The alert point man had slipped into the tree line and caught two NVA soldiers as they were trying to flee from the abandoned ville. They were shot and killed, weapons and gear captured. Two more confirmed kills for the Company.

Later that night I learned what really happened. Our slippery point man had quietly led us into a dense tree line where he caught two NVA soldiers unaware. They both quickly raised their AK's into the air and shouted "Chu Hoi! Chu Hoi!" The alert point man responded with two quick bursts from his weapon. Then turned to the Marine behind him and said, "What did he say?"

Two would-be traitors were dead. That was the price of being the enemy. The entire Platoon shared the same sentiments as the alert point man. "Chu Hoi - my ass!"

The next day we had a long hump. I popped several salt tabs and passed them around to the troops. The heat was staggering and I was still weak from yesterday's hump. I told no one I was still having problems with my strength, not even Doc Gray or Lt. Rob. I was embarrassed about it, I guess - maybe ashamed. It was a weird feeling. I looked like I was in the best shape of my life, but I wasn't. The combination of that damned amoeba and heat exhaustion resulting from that amoeba was still kicking my ass two months later.

I took all the precautions I could, heavy salt, forced fluids, and the patrol went on. After a few clicks, I was struggling to stay on my feet. We crossed the old railroad and were working our way toward the river. I remember thinking, "I can refill my canteens there."

We got to the rivers edge, and I did just that - also popping more salt. We crossed the river and it felt cool and refreshing.

I woke up looking at the Chief at the BAS who was standing over me, wondering what the hell happened. I had an IV going in my left arm and was very confused. I saw "yellow" in the Ringers lactate and was trying to figure if it was Keflex or potassium, so I would have an idea why I was there. I never got to ask the question. I woke again the next day.

I had awakened with a start, not knowing if I had all my appendages, or why I was on a gurney. The Chief was right there.

"Take it easy, Bear, you will be okay. You had a heat stroke."

I tried to get up but couldn't. I spent the night in sick bay on the gurney and vaguely remember other Corpsmen coming in to say hello and to check on me. I felt guilty as hell not being with my unit.

The next morning I told the Chief I was okay, and wanted to go back out. I told him I had just gotten a little over-heated and was better now. He wouldn't listen. I lay there for three days feeling like 40 lbs of rhinoceros crap. They kept me on my back and pumped IV after IV into me. I wanted to get back to Second Platoon. Oh, make no mistake about it, I would much rather go home for good; but since that wasn't an option, I wanted to go back to Go Noi. I didn't belong here, I was a bush Corpsman.

Finally Chief let me go with a variation of warnings. I had a lot of respect for him and it continued to grow. He had examined my M-16 while I was unconscious, or whatever I was, and saw it was cleaned, well kept and ready for action. Many Corpsmen carried M-16's. We, when at full strength, had eight Corpsmen with our Company. I only know of one that did not carry an M-16. Some used it strictly as "camouflage"- others used it when needed. I looked after mine faithfully. It was yet another tool that could help save the life of another Marine, or perhaps my own life. It was always oiled and cleaned.

I watched the earth below as the chopper descended. We were south of Go Noi now. The chopper landed and it was good to get back to my Platoon. I missed them. I belonged here, at least for now. I hated every minute of it, but I belonged here. Some day, and it was almost April now, I would belong somewhere else - perhaps DaNang. If my guardian angel kept watch, perhaps I would make it out of here. For now, this was home.

We were humping the next day. Stuckey was on point, and we slipped into a ville unseen and surprised a squad of NVA.

The fire fight was over in two minutes and we had killed all but two of them which we took prisoner. We also had captured a stunningly beautiful young woman, who I guessed to be about my age. She was dressed in a black silk pajama outfit and looked very out of place. Her hair was well kept and so were her hands. She practically shined in a world of dull faces.

I could see the guys drooling, just looking at her. At this point in my life, I had no attraction what so ever for oriental women, but that was because of the last five months. There was no denying, however, this was a beautiful woman. I sat her down and tried to talk to her. Guys were jeering and laughing like a bunch of school kids. I looked at her shoulders and they were smooth. She had not been humping a pack through the mountains, nor had she been carrying tons of rice. Probably a nurse or doctor, though I found no medical gear. I mentioned the word "Bacse" and saw her eyes light up. I didn't think it was because she was impressed that I was a Bacse, I think it was because SHE was a "Bacse". I called Rob over and recommended he send her in for interrogation. He thought that that was a good idea.

She joined the two captured NVA as a POW and was flown away on the same chopper.

We started off again, and would set in for the night soon. Tomorrow we were going to reach the Dog Bone.

Hopefully, tomorrow I would see Chi Com.

Chapter 34
<u>Chi Com and Chi-Coms</u>

Our re-supply chopper came in and along with it - mail. There was a visible lift in morale when we had mail call. It certainly improved my outlook and once again I wasn't disappointed. I had a stack of letters. Linda was prepared for our reunion in Hawaii. She had her tickets and flight date. I don't know if I was prepared, but I sure was ready.

I also had a letter from Mike. He was going to DaNang as soon as his bush time was up, and was making sure I would join him there. I had every intention of doing just that. "Casual Company" would unite at First Med Bat; it was just going to be a much smaller reunion that we had hoped for.

We saddled up and were on our way to the Dog Bone. I felt I had developed the ability to think of many things at once. I was thinking about Chi Com, yet was aware of anything that may be out of place, a grass blade, bent banana tree leaves, a stick that could be a warning, a blade of grass not moving just right with the wind, any movement of locals - they all had meaning. Watching the civilians was an art in itself. They told you so much just by the way they moved, looked away from you, or looked at you. If their work-pace quickened at your presence, beware. If they started moving away from you, get prepared for snipers. Everything meant something, yet "nothing was as it seemed".

I had a shit disc in my pocket for Chi Com. The morning after I had treated her I had sent her to her hooch with a can of peaches and a tin of pound cake, wishing I could see her dig into them. Now, I just hoped I saw her. I hoped she healed and didn't get her wound infected. I would soon find out.

Three hours later we were approaching the outskirts of the large ville. We were supposedly going to be in the area for a few days. You could never count on these rumors. Things changed quickly here.

We slowly moved into what we considered the "friendly" ville. I was not naïve enough to believe that the VC and NVA also didn't consider it "friendly". Still, the children were lined up, looking for familiar faces, their favorite Marine who would give them a treat or reward them for a back rub.

I didn't see Chi Com.

We were well into the ville now. The children were running around gathering canteens and promises, and I was unloading my pack into a family hooch when I heard a call, "Bacse, Bacse!!"

I turned around and there she was running straight to me - no longer the shy little outcast. She literally jumped into my arms.

I hugged her and hid the tears forming in my eyes. I tossed her in the air and caught her, totally engrossed in her laugh. I sat her down, and motioned to the wound, so she would know I wanted to check on it. She stood still as I lifted the silk top, and I quickly saw it was doing well - better than I had thought. The sutures had been removed, the wound healed nicely. The scar would barely be visible.

I assumed a Doc from another unit had removed the sutures and this gave me a very good feeling. I wasn't the only one who cared about this special little girl. I would gladly share that smile, but she would always be my Chi Com.

She took the shit disc and three of my canteens which took her a while to return. She had her own special water supply for her "Bacse" and I felt privileged. Once again I drank the sweet, cool water without

320

purification tablets and it was like the "nectar of the gods".

I gave her a can of pears and a tin of date pudding to take with her. Tomorrow, I would give her a can of pork slices.

I went out on the ambush that night with Collins' squad. I liked all three squad leaders now. They were all pretty good, considering a year ago they were in high school.

We set up on a trail west of the Dog Bone and spent the night listening to mosquitoes, out-going artillery and a few B-52 bombers dropping their load a few miles away on the "Canopy".

I had the watch the same time I heard Doc Gray come on watch making his radio checks to us. I recognized his voice and thought I would play with him a little.

He said, "Alpha-2 Alpha, Alpha-2 Alpha. This is Alpha-2. If all secure, key your hand-set twice; if not, key it once. Over!" I keyed it once, waited a minute then keyed it again. He wasn't sure if it was a one or a two.

"Alpha-2 Alpha, Alpha-2 Alpha. This is Alpha 2. If all secure, key your hand-set twice. If not, key it once. Over!"

I keyed it once, waited a few seconds then keyed it again, then pressed the key and whispered, "Nayyyhhhhh, what's up, Doc?"

Doc Gray said, "Damn it! Are you secure?"

"In about ten days I will be. I'll be on a beach in Honolulu." I laughed and so did he, but we were still quite aware that we could see action at any moment.

I loved the Dog Bone area, but when you thought about it, we had a lot of contact around here.

I also liked Doc Gray. I liked him a lot.

321

Nothing happened that night, and we moved back into the ville at first light. We stayed in the area a few days, but moved our position everyday. I was a firm believer in this. It just made sense, a pain in the ass, yes. But we operated as a guerilla unit; therefore, we needed to act like one. Leave little or no traces of the way we set in. Never stay in the same place twice, even if in the same area. I still saw Chi Com a few times so all in all, it was a good few days.

One morning after being on an ambush the previous night, I was taking a nap when I heard someone call my name: "Hey, Doc, got a minute?"

It was one of the blooper men, Terry. He was a squared-away Marine and one hell of a blooper man - young and tough as nails. He stood about 5'11" and weighed maybe 190 lbs. He was hard as a rock. Just a year or two ago he was a star running back in high school.

"Sure, Terry, what's going on?"

He sat down and softly said, "Doc, I'm going to kill that bitch when I get home."

Oh, no, another "Dear John" letter.

He talked to me about it. He was just 19 and his wife had run off with another man and filed for divorce. Terry was pissed, and I briefly thought, I wouldn't want him pissed at me.

"Terry, I know this is tough, man. But all you can do is concentrate on where you are now and get home alive, and then you can deal with it. If she left you, then she doesn't deserve you."

Easy to say.

This was so hard to try to console a man so far from home ands give him really good advice in a situation where he had no recourse. He couldn't call her and reason with her, or try to work out differences.

"I know, Doc, but I'm going to kill that bitch." The hurt was deep and I couldn't blame him for feeling that way. He was doing his duty in a foreign land and was betrayed.

"Terry, try not to worry about it. You can't do anything about it here. Write her and tell her to think things over. Don't do anything just now. Then when you get to the rear we will work it out so you can call her via HAM operator and see if you can get through to her."

What else could I say?

"Okay, Doc. Thanks for listening. I'll do my best."

He would, too. Terry was a picture book Marine. He would have made a good poster model for the "Corps". He was also one hell of a blooper man.

This was so hard. I felt so bad for him, but didn't know how I could help. I gave silent thanks knowing my wife would never be unfaithful to me. It was something I never worried about. It just wasn't going to happen. It wasn't that I was the greatest catch in the world; it just wasn't in her to cheat. It was comforting to know this, but I still felt so bad for those less fortunate.

That afternoon we got supplied and moved out of the area. I got to se Chi Com once more briefly and gave her a can of peaches. A ray of sunshine in a dark world!

We were heading northwest, towards Liberty Bridge, but just short of there. It was an area we called the Cu Ban's and it looked a little like the pictures I had seen of the moon. It was high ground and barren - bomb craters everywhere. The "Bridge" was shaky after being overrun and we were going to the Cu Ban's to run patrols and ambushes and maybe stop it from getting hit again.

We set in and sure enough, we soon heard a 57-recoilless rifle open up on the Bridge compound. Soon it was followed by rockets and mortars.

We were set in not 200-meters from where the NVA were launching its attack. They had no idea we were there.

We were scurrying around like so many rats getting ready to respond and stop the attack, when Terry took off all alone. He had his blooper and was going after them.

My heart sank. We all saw him go and there wasn't a damn thing we could do to stop him. I thought of running after him, but knew I couldn't catch him. He was on a one-man mission he had no intention of coming back from.

Soon we heard blooper rounds flooding the tree line where the NVA where launching their attack from.

Soon we heard AK's and I knew Terry was dead. Such a waste! He was a good man and a good Marine and an undeserving woman would collect his insurance.

We opened up on the tree line and they soon stopped firing their mission and ran. We took off even at night to check it out, because of Terry.

As we expected, he was dead. We got his body, put him in a poncho and the next morning took him to the road where we would send his body to the "Bridge". Everyone was talking about his bravery, and he was brave. But I told no one of our earlier discussion. Nothing would bring him back. It was so unfair.

"...And a rock feels no pain..."

We headed south again and Stuckey lead us through every creek, stream, drainage ditch, and rice paddy between the road and the foothills. It was like watching an artist at work. He looked at the map where we were going, made a mental note of it, and he wouldn't look at it again. He had a picture in his mind where we were going, and he would get us there. We would pick off leeches, drain our filled boots, curse the deep streams, but we once again arrived without hitting booby traps or ambushes. It was a combination of avoiding the disasters and confusing the enemy. He had no equal as a point man.

We had just made the long hump, and I had just pulled my boots and socks off when I learned we were getting a supply chopper in. This was unusual. We usually moved AFTER we exposed ourselves by getting supplies.

I had just put on a dry pair of socks when the chopper landed and three Marines got off. One said, "Is Doc Bear here?"

I said, "Yes, I'm Doc Bear."

"Get your gear Doc. You are supposed to get on this chopper and go to the BAS. The Chief wants you."

It was April 14th, and I was to go on R&R on the 18th. I didn't expect to leave for a couple of days, but I wasn't going to argue.

I said my quick goodbyes, got some good-natured ribbing, and left my M-16 with the radio man and took my Colt .45 with me. We would trade back when I returned.

It seemed like a dream. Four days in An Hoa, then R&R for a week, then one or two more weeks in the bush and I was on my way to DaNang. Is this possible? Was I actually going to beat the odds?

We landed in An Hoa and I walked the mile to the BAS.

The Chief wanted to talk to me about something and I had no idea what. I was always glad to see him and didn't think I was in any trouble or anything like that.

I took my pack into the sickbay and dumped it on an empty rack. It was times like this I realized how dirty I really was - the contrast between my filthy pack and the rack with clean linen.

I asked where the Chief was and was told he was in his office, so I walked that way.

I knocked on the door and he said, "Yes, who is it?"

I said, "Bear, Chief."

"Come on in here."

I walked in and he pointed for me to sit down. He looked more serious than usual. "Bear, I need to talk to you about a few things. First of all, you have another meritorious promotion that has been approved for E-5; you are an HM 2nd class Petty Officer."

"Thanks, Chief."

"As I said, it has been approved, but there is one problem. You are to be discharged in December if you don't get an early out, and you will need to extend your enlistment 90-days to get the promotion."

Well, that wasn't much of a decision. I wasn't extending a day.

"No, thank you, Chief. No disrespect to you, but I want out as soon as I can get out. It doesn't matter to me if I am discharged as an E4 or an E5; I'm getting out as soon as they'll let me."

"Okay, Bear, I understand. You are also up for a couple of medals, and you may be discharged before they go through."

"It doesn't matter to me, Chief. Like I said, my four years are out. If there were more career men like you, it could be different. But as it is, I think I will be happier as a civilian."

"Well, then one more thing: I have a chopper going to DaNang in about a half hour. If you want to go in a few days early, I can get you on it."

I was filthy, totally unprepared, but could get to a few bucks worth of MPC so I said, "I'm ready right now. Thank you, Chief. I'll go look up an old friend at First Med and spend a day or two with him."

I had heard my best friend from the "world" was working as a NP tech at First Med. And I would love to see him.

I could buy civvies at Freedom Hill PX and find a place at First Med to stay until my flight was leaving. I was getting excited.

Soon I was on the chopper headed for DaNang. I was thinking, (always thinking) and one thing worried me. All my life I had woke up with an erection, and it hadn't been happening for a long time. I was hoping it was because I wasn't attracted to hairy-legged Marines, and I knew my ill feelings towards Vietnamese would keep me from getting overly worked up. So maybe it was just due to lack of stimulation. There were always rumors that they put "salt peter" in the C-rats and also food at the chow hall, but being in the "medical field" I thought if that was true, I would know it.

We were under way when I heard commotion in the chopper and I saw we were descending. I had been watching as we flew and was pretty sure where we were. I looked out the window and saw the elephant grass and banana trees and knew it was true - we were landing on Go Noi Island.

I talked to the gunner and asked him what was going on.

"Bravo 1/5 just called in three emergency med evacs, Doc, so we're going in to get them. I'm glad you're aboard - we may need you. They also have a POW we are picking up."

This was not good news. I had always felt I would die on Go Noi, but I never dreamed it may be when I was on my way to meet my wife for a week of R&R. I was scared and pissed. This wasn't supposed to happen. ("Doc, things are never as they seem.") We were going down and our Huey gun-ship escort was working out. It was a "hot" LZ. We were taking rounds and I confess to being scared shitless. I had no weapon; I was in no way ready for this.

We landed and I rushed to the back ramp where the wounded would be brought in. I helped them load the wounded and the prisoner who had his hands tied behind his back. One of the guys bringing the wounded on board was a Bravo Company Doc I had never met. I yelled over the rotowash, "I'm Doc Bear. I will look out for them until we get to DaNang for you."

He said, "Damn, Doc Bear! I have heard a lot about you!"

I was surprised, but said, "Well, nice to meet you! Get your ass out of here."

I checked on the wounded and he had done a good job. I followed up as best I could while we were lifting off and taking rounds, but it was scary as hell. As we got up a little, rounds started coming through the deck of the chopper. "Shit, this is it, I will die here."

I grabbed the POW and threw him on the deck, then piled 2 of the wounded on top of him so the rounds would go through him before the wounded Marines.

We got up and leveled out and things calmed down. I checked for bleeding and shock all the way to DaNang. I hated this place - it was so screwed up. When I got on that chopper I felt as safe as a baby in the womb, then 10 minutes later I thought I was going to die before I got to Hawaii.

We were up and out of range and I realigned the wounded and grabbed the prisoner. I thought about throwing him out the back door and saying, "I don't know what happened, the silly son of a bitch jumped out," but I didn't.

Soon we were landing at First Med Battalion, DaNang. All I had to do was get off the chopper and find someone I knew, which shouldn't be too hard. I had done harder things the last six months, that's for sure.

Chapter 35
<u>A Peek at the Future: Hawaii</u>

I disembarked from the chopper at First Med and helped unload the casualties, then watched as the POW was "taken into custody". "Taken into custody" may not be the appropriate term. He was greeted with a cold Pepsi and a pack of Winston cigarettes, while I carried the wounded to the Operating Room area, where they would undergo surgery removing AK rounds that that scumbag helped put there. I should have thrown the asshole out of the chopper.

Soon I was working my way through the unfamiliar compound, hoping to see a face I recognized. The three wounded Marines from Bravo would be all right, I was sure of it. They were all hit with AK rounds, but I didn't think any of them were in danger of losing life or limb. That's what it had come down to now: can you get home alive with all your arms and legs. It was no longer a matter of whether or not we would win this war. The "Jane Fonda" traitors and protesters had decided that. The politicians would not let us do what we had to do to win. It may offend someone. Well, hell, that's fine! Just get me and my Marines the hell out of here if you won't let us win.

I looked up Eddie Harren, my best friend from Bethesda Naval hospital, who was working the psych ward here. I was still "grungy-looking" and when I walked into his ward he didn't recognize me.

I said, "Hey, ya big-nosed Wop! How does a guy go about getting drugs around here?"

He stood there a minute and said, "Bear?"

I said, "You got it, bubba! But I would prefer a shower to the dope. Can you fix me up?"

"I'm not sure there's enough water in DaNang, but I'll see what I can do." We embraced like the best friends we were and it was hard to let go. I knew I smelled bad, but neither of us cared about that.

Eddie took me to his hooch and gave me a clean set of utilities which actually fit. I made a mental note I was not size 28. When I would go to Freedom Hill tomorrow to buy my civvies for R&R, I'd be looking for 28" waist and 32" length. I was finally longer than I was round!

I lay on his rack and took a nap after the shower waiting for Eddie to finish his shift. This was a totally different world. It was a tent, but had plywood floors and cots with mattresses. It even had sheets, which were the first sheets I had seen in six months.

We went to the EM Club and Carlings Black Label was the beer of the day. It tasted like the beer must taste in Heaven. He introduced me as a "bush Corpsman from the Fifth Marines" and I drew a lot of stares. I felt very out of place but was determined to enjoy this. It was a little like visiting the past, a time when all you worried about was having a nice crease in your uniform and a good shine on your shoes.

Eddie and Sarah, Linda and I were two of the few married couples from Bethesda. We played cards a lot together, and Eddie and I were in the same class at Neuro-Psych Tech School. He was the class clown and probably one of the funniest guys I had ever met. He was the only Corpsman I had ever known of who went to the Psych Department and didn't have to go to the bush. I was not jealous of him, I was thrilled for him. I knew him so well, and he would have been one hell of a good bush Doc. But, at least this way, Sarah had a husband whom she most likely would see again.

It was a bit strange. Here I was tossing down a few beers with a very good old friend, as I talked about old times. I asked about Sarah and he asked about Linda, who I hoped was on her way to Hawaii. The past was all we had in common any more.

I sat across from him and looked into his eyes. I watched the way he moved, looked into what he was thinking, and wondered what he would think if he knew what was going on in my head. I thought, "Does he have any idea that he is sitting across from someone who has shot an NVA soldier through the chest and taken his AK from his hands?"

Does he have any idea how many men I have treated? How many lives I had saved or, for that matter, taken? I didn't even know the answer to either of those questions.

I felt that if he could be inside my head for five minutes he would absolutely freak out. If he could see what I saw when I closed my eyes at night! If he felt what I felt! If he knew what I knew! He would panic. (This would change, in a few months. Eddie would be sent to Delta 1/5, my sister Company and would write me often – "Brothers" again.)

I felt as if I was sitting across from a stranger. He was still funny. It was me that changed. Laughing at a joke no longer was a priority for me.

As I watched him drinking another Carlings, I saw his innocence. I remembered the first man I had ever killed - I mean knew for sure it was my round that put his lights out. I remembered that feeling, that loss of my own innocence. I had done something that for 22-years I had never had a desire to do: Take a life. I remembered the dead NVA's eyes, going through his wallet and finding pictures of what appeared to be his wife and two children. I remembered the feel of his AK-47 as I plucked it from his hands, a superior weapon. I remembered both the sadness I felt and the satisfaction that I got him before he got me. He was shooting at me, but made a fatal mistake.

I decided I would say nothing about those things. He wouldn't understand. How could he? Six months ago, I wouldn't have understood. He was a stateside friend. He didn't need to know my heart, my sorrow, my hopes or my fears. We were now different.

We had probably five or six beers and that was enough for me. I didn't want a hangover. We went back to his hooch and I slept in the cot of a Corpsman that was on night duty - with his permission, of course.

When I woke up, I felt like I was in a foreign environment - which I was. I saw my first "house mouse" (Vietnamese housekeeper) and was very envious of the life these Corpsmen lived in the rear area.

I caught a jeep to Freedom Hill and purchased a nice pair of tan slacks and a brown Banlon shirt. I was looking stronger now, weighed a trim 185-lbs. and was getting some muscle back. I still looked like a Marine, but the flat top was gone. I got a hair cut there, but they didn't do flat tops, so Linda would soon see me for the first time in her life without one.

I was really excited about the R&R and didn't sleep the entire night anticipating it. I had three beers the night before going to bed and awakened with the "fear of not being able to get an erection" now gone. It was environment after all.

One more night at First Med and then I would catch my flight. April 18, 1969, I would meet my wife of two years, four months and one day.

The Continental flight stopped in Guam and I disembarked to go to the PX and bought a fifth of Chivas Regal and a bottle of Mum's Champagne. The price was very reasonable - a fraction of what it would have cost in Hawaii.

Linda was supposed to get to Honolulu a day ahead of me and get our room at the "Reef Hotel". It sat right on Waikiki beach.

The plane landed and we were herded into a bus to go meet our loved ones.

I noticed I had a different walk, maybe an air of confidence; maybe it was a by-product of being more aware. I was aware. No move, nothing out of the ordinary, escaped my attention.

The wives were waiting at a reception hall. Almost all of us on the bus were there to meet wives or lovers. Everyone was very excited and there were several Marines. The wives were told not to worry if the man they were waiting for wasn't on the bus, there could be many reasons for delay.

The bus pulled up and the ladies were lined up on both sides of our exit. I saw Linda as soon as I stepped to the stairs.

She had turned 21-years old January 26, while I was on Go Noi Island fighting for my life and the lives of others. She looked wonderful.

As we walked down the ramp you could hear the women yelling to their loved ones. Some were screaming with joy. Linda wouldn't do that. Oh, she would feel it, but she would express her joy in ways other than a scream.

When we got to the bottom, and walked between the two lines, they were grabbing their man and taking off for what should be an experience of a lifetime. As I walked down the stairs I saw her looking for me. She looked right into my eyes, and then continued her search. She didn't recognize me at all. I was 51-lbs. lighter than when she had last seen me and had a different hair style. I kept walking, passed within a foot of her and kept walking to the end of the line. Then I sat my bag down walked up behind her, tapped her on the shoulder, turned her around and kissed her. She knew my kiss. We were together after six very long, hard months. The first kiss told me volumes. At least one thing hadn't changed.

334

The hotel was beautiful, the beach fabulous, and a southern gentleman doesn't tell the rest. We will leave it at this: when showing pictures from our R&R for years to come we would frequently be asked why we took so many pictures from our room's balcony.

The first evening we did go out for lobster and decided we would have lobster at least once a day for that week.

Linda had already started noticing changes, but the time together was wonderful. The first change she noticed, and I was totally unaware of, was that I seemed mesmerized by the flushing toilet.

I had put the Mum's champagne on ice as soon as we got to the room so upon returning from our first lobster dinner, I wanted to start the romantic evening properly. Not being used to civilization, I tried my best to be gallant and suave. I set out the chilled champagne glasses and removed the champagne from the ice bucket. I worked the corkscrew with nothing on my mind except the next few hours, when suddenly I popped the cork. The pop was loud and before the cork hit the ceiling I hit the deck.

Linda's mouth dropped open in awe as she said, "I have never seen anyone or any THING move that fast in my life."

I tried to laugh it off, "Well, guess I have developed pretty fast reflexes." The rest of the evening went much better.

One night we decided we wanted see a good "show" so we asked around. Don Ho was an obvious choice with his now popular "Tiny Bubbles". But as we asked around, we were told by the locals that the best show on the Island was at the Cock's Roost.

We made reservations and went to the Cock's Roost for both dinner and the show. We were not disappointed. The steak and lobster was fantastic, the

Mai Tais were both huge and delicious, and the show was incredible. Neither of us were big drinkers but we had two or three of the exotic drinks and were in very good spirits. The mood was very stimulating.

The star performed right from the start, beginning with several favorite island songs. Then he came to the song that had made him popular, "Two by Two".

The mood quickly changed as the crowd recognized the song. He began to sing the words that touched my heart more than any song I would ever hear:

"Two by two are four; and four are eight; and eight are sixteen…

Growing by the numbers all are we.
Like a pyramid of broken dreams, while sorrow keeps the score;
In this futile despairing world I…I laugh no more."

It sounded depressing at first, but then the message struck home:

"Teach him, mister! Teach your son! Yes, tell him what to do:
Pick up the gun, boy! Aim the gun, boy! Shoot!
You hit the bird between the eyes and I will understand:
One of these days you'll be shooting……………
Your very first man!
………2……...3………...4……."

I was stunned. I felt deceived, used. All my life I'd learned about gun safety: How to hunt, stalk game and make a clean kill. Had I been in training all my life to fight in a war? Oh, not by my step-dad, brother-in-law or brother - at least not knowingly. But were the wildlife codes conceived in order to produce young men who could quickly learn to kill the enemy? Then the final verse:

"Lord tell me, teach me what to do.
I'm confused and not sure what I'm saying.

336

When my son comes up to me and says, 'Dad, what can I do?"'

Before he sang the verse I knew what I would do, and he sang my thoughts:

"I'll say, 'Run boy, run, before they get you, too!'"

I sat there with tears in my eyes, and deep in thought. I made a decision, something I would under normal circumstances certainly discuss with the future mother of my son. I simply couldn't find my voice.

Our son, when we had one, would never go to war. He would never hear me talk of the "glory" of battle or victories, or anything that glamorized combat or encouraged him to desire it. He would never be a Marine, nor would he be a Doc. Lauren Vincent, if and when there was one, would be a man of peace. He would never go to war. I would see to it.

"Linda, we have to get his album. I would like you to take it home with you and keep it, please, and I don't want to ever forget that song."

We walked back to the hotel, and then took a stroll on the beach. She pointed out to me that I never took a step without watching where I was stepping. I realized she was right and became aware that I would look ahead 20 or 30 meters, mentally clear an area for safety, then watch where I put my feet. Then, I would check out the next 20 or 30 meters. "Creature of habit" was my explanation.

The next morning when I got up I could see Linda was disturbed. I asked what was wrong.

She said I woke up and sat up in bed around 0300 and said, "Is that incoming?"

She said, "I don't know what you mean."

"Did someone holler, 'Incoming'?"

"I don't know what you're talking about."

Still sitting up and appearing awake I said, "Damn it, is anybody hit?"

"John, I don't know what you are talking about."

Then I said, "Awww, fuck it!" and went back to sleep.

My wife had never heard me talk like that in her life. I could see she was worried.

Things had changed; I had changed. It would take a lot of effort from both of us to get through this.

I saw the "worry" in her face and realized that had been her life for the last six months - worry.

Twice she had received telegrams that I had been wounded in action, but they would only tell her as far as they knew I was alive, but wounded.

She never knew how bad, just that last they knew I was alive. It was hard on her. Even in the regular routine of things, she may go two weeks without a letter from me, and then get ten or twelve at once, due to our being unable to mail them. For those two weeks she had no idea whether I was dead or alive.

I was always honest with her, so if I was killed I wanted her to be as prepared as possible.

I wrote and told my mother I was working in a hospital in DaNang, but my wife needed to know the truth. She deserved that.

The week was going by much too fast. All in all, it was paradise on earth. As we were down to two days, I made her a promise I wouldn't make before. I had one, maybe two weeks, left in the bush. I promised her I would make it home intact. Before, I couldn't promise that. Now, my bush time was nearing an end, and there was light at the end of the tunnel. I hoped it would help her not to worry. I had always kept my promises to her.

We rented a dune buggy and went around the island. Time was running out and we hadn't done a lot of sight-seeing.

It was the day before I was to leave and we stopped at a tourist attraction, a huge waterfall at the end of a walking trail. As we were going along the trail, I suddenly realized what I was thinking, "If we get hit, it will be from over there on that ridge. I would set Stuckey's squad in there, put the gun team covering this trail, send an LP over to that point and call in artillery support to be ready to fire on that grid and the one north of it. If we had to call in a med evac chopper, I would make that the LZ right over there."

I was back in the bush and hadn't left Hawaii. I had seen the elephant....and it consumed me.

Chapter 36
<u>Saving Private Brian</u>

The chopper was circling, ready to return me to my unit. I could make out the all too familiar terrain that was Go Noi Island. The Right Guide of each Platoon was waiting below to latch onto the supplies for their respective Platoons. A couple of the Platoon Sergeants were also awaiting our arrival. Supplies, were being brought in - our lifeline, our link to at least a partially civilized world.

As I ran down the ramp I said hello to Sgt. Woody, then went to my unit, absorbing the routine jokes due those returning from R&R. It was good to see the guys again.

I was back in my element, at least for a week or two. It was hard to believe I had been in the bush for nearly six months. It seemed like a week - and it seemed like a lifetime.

I felt the "short timer's" blues; that state of mind where I knew I could possibly beat the odds and make it out of this hell-hole alive and whole. All I needed was my guardian angel to stick close to my side for the next week or two.

I almost felt at home here on Go Noi now. I hated it, yet it had been so much of my life and probably would always be a place I remembered.

I took in the pats on the back, the "Welcome home, Doc!" and knew in a couple of weeks I would miss these guys terribly.

In DaNang I would be just another Corpsman; no one special doing a job anyone with the training could do. I would miss the bonds and the responsibility. Here, I was important, as was each of these men. Here, life and death was in my hands. One wrong decision or one right one, either way a life depended on what I thought was best for the wounded Marine in the brief seconds I had to decide what to do. It was an awesome responsibility for anyone; it would even be for an MD or a D.O. But for a Corpsman herded through the system and given what someone deemed the knowledge we needed to get us and the casualties through any given situation, it was an overwhelming burden. Now more than ever, I felt both the pride and the pressure of being a "bush Doc".

One thing constantly on my mind now, and ever since that day in Hospital Corps School, was having a Marine die in my arms. So far, it hadn't happened. Several were killed instantly, but that fear of having a man I was treating die on me was still just a fear, not a haunting memory.

I wasn't naïve enough to think that luck wasn't involved. I had been very fortunate. Now, with two weeks left in the bush, there were two things constantly on my mind: The ever present afore-mentioned fear, and also the dread that I would lose my appendages.

I was prepared to die, or thought I was; but I wasn't prepared to go through life with no legs.

As I had stepped off the chopper a few minutes ago and saw Sgt. Woody, the first thought I had was, "Damn I miss Sarge!" I did. I could use a long talk with my mentor right now. I could open up to him about my fears and "unload" some of the stress.

There was no doubt at this time that I was still alive because of Sgt. Vince Rios - because of our bond, and his willingness to teach a "squid" how to think like a Marine. I went through those teachings everyday - the lessons, the principles, the priorities. I missed him.

Lt. Rob had become one hell of a Platoon Commander. I still had no intention of getting "close" to him, but in no way did that lessen my respect for him.

"...A rock feels no pain..."

I went out on the ambush that night, and it was an easy one. I would take all the easy ones I could get now. I stood my watch at 0100 and Doc Gray was on the Platoon watch back at the CP. He had done well while I was away and I appreciated him. I crawled around and checked the lines. One man up, two men down, and everyone was awake that was supposed to be.

I sat back down by the radio and listened to the night, looking for anything that wasn't as it should be, a snapped twig, grass swaying unnaturally, a bird crying out in the night.

As I sat there my mind wandered to an ambush several weeks ago. Sarge was there, and I had awakened and no one was on watch. I woke him up and whispered, "Sarge, there is no one on watch, someone must have fallen asleep."

Then I saw it. I had the watch we handed off to the relief on my right wrist. I felt like crawling into a hole. I showed it to him, and said, "Damn!" That was the end of it. I never heard a word about it. I also never fell asleep on watch again, not for a second. I assumed the man who had passed me the watch didn't have me all the way awake, which usually was not a problem. I normally was awake and alert instantly, but I didn't remember being handed that watch.

Sarge didn't rag me or tease me about it. He knew how seriously I took my duties and that it would never happen again. A trait of a true leader.

Sarge didn't hassle the troops. He expected a lot and he got it, but he didn't harass the men. He didn't need to. He got respect by setting an example. Damn, I missed him!

I sat there a while and reflected on the last six months. It amazed me that I was still alive and in one piece. I would never forget that first patrol just two-hours after I got in the bush; the bouncing Betty I stepped on barefooted, just a few days later; chasing Stuckey and that orange mailbag across that rice paddy under fire; the rocket round and the mortar round that hit between Sarge's head and my own - both dud rounds all within a few weeks. How many times AK rounds kicked dirt up in my face as I ran to a downed Marine? So many booby traps! Too many fire fights! During Tet in An Hoa my being picked up TWICE and thrown by an incoming 122-mm rocket! All I had to show for all of this was a couple of scars. Yes, I had a guardian angel, and he or she had been working overtime. I had no idea why I wasn't killed, though; it just wasn't my time. I knew that could change. Sarge was spared many, many times, and then was struck by a 105-round that tore his body, not able to destroy his spirit.

There was no way to figure these things. It could drive a man crazy, and sometimes did. I would just accept it, be grateful and hope my good fortune would continue. That's all you can do…all you can do.

We went back the next morning and through the normal routine, daytime chat and boredom, wondering when we would get mail and supplies. I had the patrol that day, and it too was pretty much uneventful.

That night, Doc Gray had the ambush. They left the perimeter and went toward the river to their nighttime position. It wasn't quite dark when the automatic weapons erupted – M-16's and a lot of it! Rob was on the net and I listened. They had caught some gooks crossing the river and opened up on them. With their pos given away along with the element of surprise, they requested to come back to the Platoon CP. The requested made sense and was granted.

As soon as I saw Doc Gray walk into our hooch, I knew something was wrong. He did not look happy, which when you get them before they get you, would be the normal reaction.

I whispered, "What's wrong?"

"Bear, lets go outside."

We did and again I asked, "What's wrong?"

"It was a God-damned set up! There was no ambush! The point man went down and I looked and the gun teams all got online, so I did too. But, hell, there was nothing there. They had set it up before we left and I didn't know they were going to sandbag an ambush."

Gray was pissed. Sandbagging was just not doing your job and it could also have grave repercussions.

We talked about it, and considered telling Rob, but eventually decided we would both go and talk to the squad leader.

We approached the squad and called him over privately. "If you ever fake another ambush, or sandbag an ambush or patrol, one of us will know and we will turn your ass in to Monty. Follow orders, do what you are supposed to do and be where you are supposed to be."

He wasn't happy that Gray had told me or that we both jumped his case. We pointed out that by faking an ambush you automatically put lives at risk by giving away your position. It was wrong for a variety of reasons.

I liked the squad leader, and he was very good actually, but this war was so different. He was an 18-year old Corporal. I guessed to him it was like playing "hooky" in school. I didn't like it and wouldn't be apart of it, nor would Gray. If I died over here, it would be doing what I was supposed to be doing where I was supposed to be doing it, not playing mind games with the lifers.

The next morning we moved out without getting supplies in. It was a company-size operation with

"Third Herd" on point, then us in the center and First Platoon following up the rear. The Company CP was with Second Platoon. We were in the very heart of Go Noi. Dark, thick, violent, hateful country loomed ahead. The anger of the civilians could be felt with each step. This was Charlie's country we were trespassing. In this particular part of Go Noi, the villes were far apart as were the small rice paddies. The thickness of the dense elephant grass was hard to walk through. At one pause, I put on my cammie top with the long sleeves to keep the sharp blades of grass from cutting my arms. The heat was almost visible. The humidity was thick. I could tell I was regaining my strength finally, at last getting some of the muscle back I had lost. Despite feeling stronger, the 110 degree heat was draining.

"BOOM!!! BOOM!!! BOOM!!!" Three booby traps went off as one - a "daisy chain". Third Platoon point has tripped the one set on the trail, and then two more went off along the trail behind.

They had many wounded, so Doc Gray and I made our way up to help the already very busy Corpsman of Third Platoon. We got to the site and it was chaos. Two were dead from the initial blast and many were wounded. I saw a badly wounded Marine who wasn't being treated so I ran and dropped beside him.

I wanted to see how bad he was hit, check for shock and all that goes with a wound like this, so I rolled him over and said, "Hey, Bud, what's your name?"

He couldn't talk, or breathe. He muttered what I thought was "Private Brian" something or another. He was bad. Shrapnel had hit his throat and larynx, his left leg was gone below the knee and he was bleeding profusely. That was at first glance. I had my hands full

345

with young Private Brian. He was choking to death; he was bleeding to death for starters.

The fear momentarily entered my mind, "This is where you lose one. This man will die on you."

"NO!!!!!!!!!!!!" I quickly put a tourniquet on his left leg just below the knee and went to my surgical kit. I had left my pack behind so everything I needed was easily accessible. I got out my scalpel and the homemade trachea kit I had prepared. I always carried at least two of them I had put together. It was amazing what you could do with a ball point pen and gauze.

I found the third "ring" and cut ¾" deep and an inch wide and inserted the trachea kit. I thought, "Why don't they show us films of this actually being done?" Sure we did it on mannequins and oranges, but doing it on a live man was different. They bled. In Field Med School, there of course was no blood. I remembered the first one I had done or ever seen done in real life and at first I thought I had screwed up because of the bleeding. Now I knew it was supposed to bleed.

I made sure the kit was working and he was able to breathe. Then I went to his leg. It was gone, blown away. I clamped and tied off bleeders and ordered another emergency med evac. I needed to get an IV going. He had lost a lot of blood. The adrenalin was pumping like crazy, my mind working 100-mph.

"Brian, how is the pain, can you handle it?"

"It hurts Doc, but I'm okay."

Good, because I was afraid he would go into shock. I couldn't give him oral pain killers simply because he couldn't swallow.

There was no ambush, no fire fight, at least not yet - just the booby traps. Third Herd had set up a perimeter and Second Platoon had taken over the rear watch. First Platoon was on a sweep. There could very well be more booby traps and probably were.

I had the bleeding stopped and removed the tourniquet so as not to destroy anymore of his leg than necessary. I wanted him to have as much stump as possible. I checked the trache and he was breathing okay, the bleeding was controlled, the IV going. I decided to go ahead and give him ½ of a syrette of morphine. He was awake and alert and since I couldn't give him anything orally, I took a chance.

"Brian, I'm giving you a shot of morphine, but I want you to stay awake, big guy. Don't go to sleep on me. Bitch and moan…for me."

I then checked him out and found other shrapnel wounds, and took care of them as well. Then I went back to the leg, my biggest concern. I had to make sure the bleeding was under control.

He should have about a four-inch stump below the knee, and could lead a reasonably semi-normal life with prosthesis. He would live. I was confident now, he would make it. I applied more pressure dressings and Brian was set. He was going home.

The chopper came in and I was exhausted, more emotionally than physically. I pointed to two Marines and they carried him aboard the chopper. Private Brian had his life and I still had my goal: No Marine had died in my arms.

I also had another week on Go Noi Island………………

Chapter 37
<u>The Longest Night</u>

The Battalion was underway. Alpha 1/5 was sweeping Go Noi Island with a small blocking force set up on what used to be the old French railroad at the extreme north end of the Island.

We were lined up on line and sweeping the dense foliage. It was akin to having 500 point men. We were spaced about 15-meters apart and slowly moving, forcing Charlie to either fight or run.

Every so often someone would spot a tunnel and we would stop while it was checked out by a "tunnel rat". Some of these tunnels were amazing, others just "spider holes". Many were linked to other tunnels making a large complex.

We had captured a few weapons and packs today, took a little sniper fire, but surprisingly had only hit one booby trap, and that was Delta Company, not us.

Elmer Fudd (the affectionate nickname for our Battalion Commander) was with Bravo Company, accompanied by two tanks. They were the blocking force. I had visions of Elmer walking down the old railroad track saying, "Kill duh Commiesssssssss!" He sure wouldn't walk through this crap we were struggling with. He was high and dry surrounded by a whole company and two tanks with 90-mm cannons and .50-caliber machine guns - an act, no doubt, worthy of a Silver Star for gallantry at least. Politics! Even in the Marine Corps, there were politics.

A sniper opened up ahead as I was walking along watching closely for signs and booby traps. Someone was apparently hit, so the column stopped and waited for the sniper to be taken out, and the casualty evacuated.

Soon a chopper came in and took the wounded man away and we were off again.

"Cak. Cak". The distinct "cak-ing" sound of an AK or SKS stopped the column once again. I sat in the grass and took a deep drink from my canteen. God this water never got any better! It was unbearably hot, and we were humping with full packs. My pack was probably over 100-lbs. with medical gear and Marine gear.

"Cak." A round sailed over my head. "Mercy, Sarge!" I always thought about him when under fire - what would the old Sarge do?

A "Cowboy" appeared and was attacking the tree line ahead with 40-mm rockets.
I loved watching the agile planes working out. Diving at the snipers, then pulling up at the last minute and doing a victory roll! So cool!

The decision was made that we would set in for the night. We had been slowed by the tunnels and snipers, and were not going to make it to "Elmer" before dark. We set in and had a decent perimeter, but I would be going out on an ambush that night – Collier's squad.

Contrary to our normal MO, we were getting a chopper in. I was looking forward to the mail and, of course, supplies as well.

I was near the LZ and was watching them land, kind of a, "throw-that-shit-off-the-chopper-and-let's-get-the-hell-out-of-here" type of thing.

The chopper also brought Turner back from his R&R. He was a good man and I was glad to see him. As soon as his squad saw him they came running over to welcome him back and of course find out how he liked Bangkok.

I said, hello and Turner said, "Doc, I need to talk with you a minute."

I replied, "Sorry, man, penicillin won't cure that shit they have in Bangkok," and smiled.

"No, Doc, I met someone you will be glad to meet."

"Who, Elmer?"

"No, as we were leaving the Alpha Company tent," (and I always wondered why it was called the Alpha Company tent, hell it wouldn't hold half of a Platoon) "three squids came strolling in. They will be out tomorrow."

My mind was blank.

"Turner, why the hell would I care about three squids?" I just stood there.

"Doc, your relief is in the Alpha Company tent as we speak. You and Doc Ball are out of the bush as of tomorrow."

My jaw dropped. "Are you sure?"

"Doc, I promise you, right now there are three brand new Docs shaking like a dog shitting peach seeds in the Company tent waiting to come out tomorrow. One is your relief, one is Doc Ball's relief, and I don't know which Platoon the other one is going to. Doc, you are going to the rear tomorrow for good."

This was it, the moment I had waited for. One more ambush and I was out of the bush. I was afraid to think about it, but could think of nothing else. This was going to be a long night. Hell, Britt and his radioman could sleep all night! I would take all the watches because I sure as hell wasn't going to sleep!

"Wow, Turner! Thanks, man! The penicillin shots are on me!" I was on my last few hours in the bush.

The word was soon out and I guess the whole Platoon came by to congratulate me. Stuckey came by and just stood there, tears in his eyes, and walked away. We were close. Doc Gray was very happy for me and I told him my replacement was lucky to get broken in by such a good partner, and I meant every word. I was going to miss these guys.

As we got ready for the ambush my mind was racing. I felt so flaky. So afraid I would screw up on my last ambush and ruin this. We moved out and filed into a small village not far from the Platoon, maybe 500-meters at the most. We set in by a graveyard where we had a good field of fire. Counting the squad CP, there were four three-man fire teams and a gun team. It was pitch black by the time we got there and we quickly set in. I was checking everything, taking no chances. All the fire teams had set out claymores and they knew I was leaving tomorrow - leaving for good. I would not be back. They were happy for me but felt the same way I did, a bit ambivalent.

It was hard for me not to smile, especially when someone patted me on the back and wished me well. I was still scared, but had been for six-months. We had a good ambush site, excellent field of fire and we were as ready as we could be.

(Not tonight, I can't get killed tonight.)

Things settled down and Steve and I were both up as Mac slept. He said, "Damn, Doc, I hate to see you go; but am happy as hell for you."

"Thank you, Steve!" (I had never called him Steve.) "I am going to miss you guys, but it sure will be different in DaNang, not laying out here wondering what will happen next."

It would be strange indeed. I remembered when I was there for that damned amoeba, how everything had changed. How different would it be now? Or for that matter, how different was I?

I searched the darkness for something out of the ordinary, a flash of light, a moving limb, anything unnatural. As always, I was thinking of Sarge while on the ambush.

The night crept by. Finally it was 0100 and time for my real watch, but I hadn't even tried to sleep yet.

I heard something - unnatural, a sudden movement far away. I lay silently watching, M-16 at the ready, an M-26 hand grenade in my hand, with the pin straightened so I could quickly and silently pull the pin and throw it.

It was nothing, probably a rat scurrying.

Fine with me, I would like nothing more than for this to be an ambush without contact.

It was 0300. An Hoa was getting incoming. Nothing unusual about that, I would love to be there in a safe bunker. Tomorrow, I would be.

I let Mac and Steve sleep. I was wide awake and alert, let them rest. I remembered all Sarge had taught me and was impatiently waiting for my "morning star" to appear.

Finally around 0500, it did. That was the sign that most likely we wouldn't have contact unless we happened across a patrol on our way back to the Platoon.

It was nearing first light and I woke everyone up. Five-hundred meters away was our Platoon and we would soon be joining them. I called Sgt. Woody and told him we were coming in.

Those 500-meters seemed to take forever - finally the Platoon perimeter. We approached and I was afraid someone didn't get the word and they would open up on us. I was really flaky - afraid this wasn't meant to be.

We got inside the perimeter and I was home free. We were staying here until the afternoon when the supply chopper brought out supplies and three new Docs, and this meant I had made my last move. I would make it.

All I had to do was take a nap, sit here on my ass and get on the chopper when it came in. I could handle that, but still couldn't sleep. The morning passed as slowly as sorghum molasses. More guys came by and said farewell. I told them to look me up at First Med in DaNang when they came in for R&R or anything else.

This was the hard part, saying goodbye. How do you let these guys go that have been your life for six months? We had been through so much together. Now, I was leaving them. I gave Mac my M-16 and took back my .45 Colt pistol and strapped it on my web belt. The M-16 was spotless, ready for action. I would as soon throw a rock as use the Colt .45.

Carrying the M-16 was a good decision at least for me. Others did better with the .45.

"Chopper!!!" This was it. The chopper was in sight now, coming in. I got my pack and saddled up. I gave Stuckey and Gray one last look as the chopper landed. It hit the LZ and dropped off supplies and mail. A Marine named Johnson also exited. He was the only one.

Johnson walked right straight to me. "I'm sorry, Doc."

"Sorry about what?"

"Alpha Company tent took a direct hit last night by a 122-mm rocket. Six men were killed, Doc, including all three Corpsmen."

My relief was dead. Doc Ball's relief was dead. They hadn't even set foot in the fucking bush and they were dead.

I didn't know what to say. I went numb. All I could come up with was our "attitude check" from Field Med School.

"Fuck it! Just fuck it!"

Of course I felt terrible for the six dead men. I also felt bad for Doc Ball and myself, at least for a while.

We were staying. Our bush time had been extended. I was here on Go Noi Island. The place where I had treated so many wounded. The place where my chopper on the way to Hawaii stopped to pick up wounded. The place where when I was first coming to the Battalion the chopper pilot had said, "Doc, that's Go Noi Island below us. If you are going to 1/5 you will learn to hate that place."

I didn't hate it. It all came together now. This is where I would die. This is where I had first "seen the elephant". This is where Lt. Tommy died. So many more.

I went to Mac and got my M-16 from him. Somehow, this just seemed right.

Chapter 38
Platoon Commanders and Squids

Alpha Company was strong. We had the best Platoon Commanders the whole six and a half months I was in the bush. First Platoon had Lt. John. Second Platoon, of course, had Rob. Third Platoon had Tommy K. (not to be confused with our Lt. Tommy who was now deceased).

In a time when tempers flared and acts of unnecessary violence was common, it is important that I make something clear. Our leaders were (whether I liked them or not) honorable men. Not once in my tour were we ordered to kill innocent civilians.

Did we kill so-called "civilians"? Certainly, but we had no war criminals. They were killed as we assaulted a "hot" tree line, or in a crossfire. And we killed some 10 and 12-year olds who were engaged in battle against us with AK's and SKS's. We probably killed some in our "shoot-anything-that-moves-frag-all-bunkers" assaults when taking hostile ground. We certainly killed hundreds with 500-lb. bombs and artillery when we "prepped" a hostile village. Never did we nor were we told to line up innocent civilians (though I question if there was such a thing as "innocent civilians") and shoot them.

The incident at My Lai happened around this time and I mention this to make it clear. War is truly hell. In any war on your own soil, innocents will die. It is a shame, but with our Company, and I think most Companies, we were not war criminals. Civilians in "free fire zones" were told to evacuate, and usually transportation to relocation villages such as Duc Duc was furnished. They knew that to stay in these villages and mingle with the enemy could mean death. Most who stayed did so because they were Viet Cong. At this point, I had no nightmares about dead civilians. This would change.

Third Herd's Platoon Commander, Tommy K., was the son of a Marine Corps Colonel. He was about my size, 6'2" and maybe 190 lbs. Lt. Tommy K. carried a Remington 870 12-gauge shotgun loaded with 00-buckshot. To say he was "gung-y" would be an understatement. He was also very respected and revered. Six and a half months of bush time had brought a lot of "Second Louies" my way. I'm not being farfetched when I say we were fortunate to have these three.

Platoon Commanders, like Corpsmen, were on a six-month rotation for the same reason. If a lieutenant made it six months in the bush, he deserved the remainder of his time in the rear. Lieutenants and Docs were the main focus of snipers and NVA in general. Platoon Commanders didn't go on every squad-size patrol and ambush, but did go on ever platoon-size patrol and ambush and were always prime targets.

Lt. Tommy looked a lot like the Joe Palooka comic strip dude – tall, muscular and blue-eyed. He was also pleasant to talk to. Doc Gray and I had served a week with him as his Company Corpsmen waiting to be returned to Second Platoon. He was strong and a good leader, as were Rob and Lt. John. As I said, we had the best combination of all the bush lieutenants at this time.

Another matter I have spoken little of is "killer teams". Killer teams were not legal. Any killer team going out was supposed to be a secret. They happened occasionally and were a good thing if run right. They were used to recon the area and also to destroy the enemy, their weapons and morale. They were effective. They usually consisted of three or four, men moving silently in the night. For reasons that need no explanation, these were the best Marines in the unit.

They depended on each other totally and worked together as a team. It may seem scary to think of three guys out there moving all night, taking villages, or checking tree lines with only three M-16's and a few grenades. They had no machine gun team, no artillery support, or no air support. (We weren't supposed to be there, so we couldn't call in artillery or air support.) No helmets or flack jackets – no noise. These teams had to move swiftly, deadly and silently. The burst of three M-16's at night followed by silence brought smiles the faces of those who knew and confusion to those who didn't. Three or four men worked as a team. Scary? Not really. Consider this: These were three or four men who had their shit together. They wouldn't be stumbling around, smoking, talking, sleeping or farting. This was a killer team – not shit-birds. They were true Marines – the deadliest weapon in the world!

Go Noi was made for killer teams. The terrain was dense and plentiful and so was the enemy. Of course killer teams were illegal, so theoretically they didn't exist.

Second Platoon was on a platoon-size ambush along the foothills in eastern Go Noi. We were maybe a click from the First Platoon and 700-meters from Third Platoon. The Company CP was with First Platoon. With three platoons split up on three different ambushes, there was a good chance of action tonight on Go Noi. We were in the center. First Platoon was a click NW of us and Third was 700-meters SW of us. I took my turn on the radio. This is how it works:

The company would call the Platoon CP for radio checks to see if all was secure. The Platoon CP (us) would call the squad CP to see if they were secure. All would key their handsets once if not secure, and twice if all was secure. The Company CP called and asked for a security check. I keyed the handset twice.

Then I heard "Alpha-3, this is Alpha Actual (the Skipper). If all is secure key your handset twice; if not key once. Over." It was followed by one key.

Again, "Alpha-3, this is Alpha Actual. If all secure, key your handset twice; if not key it once. Over." And again this was followed by one key.

"Third herd" was about to hit some heavy shit.

I heard the Skipper get on the net and talk to Lt. Tommy. "What you got, Tommy?"

"Heavy movement, Skipper. Gooks! Looks like a Company headed this way. We are about to welcome them!"

Then all hell broke loose. It was not just an ambush, but a nighttime fire fight. Normally you didn't want to fire the M-16 at night because you had them outnumbered and it gave away your position and drew fire. I heard a Remington shotgun go off - seven fast rounds. Lt. Tommy was getting a grip!

Third herd was outnumbered but they were also set in, which pretty much evened things out. AK-47's, bloopers, M-60 machine guns, SKS's, M-16's, B-40 rockets, LAWS - the whole arsenal was firing from both sides. We were too far away to react and so was First Platoon. The battle went on for several minutes. (The average fire fight was maybe two minutes – this was maybe eight or ten.) The last rounds we heard were from M-16's and the M-60 machine gun. This was a good sign. "Third herd" had won the battle.

Then came the Zulu report. "Lima, Tango, and Kilo" headed the list. I heard the Skipper ask for a repeat. "Lima" meant lieutenant. "Tango" meant Tommy. "Kilo" meant Koster. Lt. Tommy was dead. You hate it when anyone gets killed, but when a truly great Marine gets killed, it strikes you even harder. You think, "Damn! He was so good; and if HE was killed, how can I possibly make it?!!"

Lt. Tommy was a good Marine and a good leader. We wouldn't see them for a few days to get the whole scoop. But what mattered was he and two others were dead and eight others wounded. They paid a price for victory – a heavy price.

Soon there was fire from the NW. First Platoon was now being hit. It was a rocket and a mortar attack mostly, followed by a few small arms. You could hear our bloopers and M-60 machine guns. Weapons Platoon, which was part of the Company CP, was with First Platoon and you could soon hear them return fire with their 60-mm mortars.

First Platoon had a KIA as well. While going to treat wounded that was down, Doc Ball had taken a round in the chest. Ten days ago we were supposed to be out of the bush together and now he was gone. Tommy K. was gone.... Would this ever end?!

I looked at Rob and studied him. Although I had managed to keep a distance, I still worried about him. He was a good Marine and leader. He also appeared not to know the meaning of fear, or if he did, he knew well how to hide it. I could visualize him risking his life to save a man in his Platoon. As it turned out he would do just that.

"Mercy, Sarge!" once again ran through my mind. Doc Ball should not have been here. Sarge was not supposed to be here when he got badly wounded. I was not supposed to be here now! I decided I would just try to do my job and ignore everything else. I would think about my men and my duties and try not to think of where I should be - easier said than done.

Part of me even wanted to be here. I never felt so alive – so alert. This was really, truly being alive. How many people experience this feeling in a lifetime – this total awareness? This adrenaline rush every time a round went off? For that matter how many people were as needed as I was? How many felt the affection of the men each time they saw them? Who had this kind of respect in normal life? How many had 54 men who would pull together as a team to cover for you, and their hearts would skip a beat as one if you fell – watching to make sure you got back up running? Where else could one get this natural high?

On the other hand, where else was life so cheap? Your last breath was a gunshot away. Your life, your family, and future could end in a split second. It was an extreme on both ends. It made you appreciate life, and made death the enemy.

I had received a letter from Mac. He had made it. He was now out of the bush and was waiting for me to join him in DaNang. He was head clerk for the Chief of Medicine at First Med Battalion. Out of the 18 of us "Casuals", I was the only one still in the bush.

I held a cigarette lighter in my hand. Some of the guys in the Platoon had given it to me when they thought I was out of the bush a week and a half ago. They'd had it engraved. One side said:

"Doc Bear
Alpha 1/15
2nd Platoon
68-69
For those who have fought for it
Life has a flavor the protected will never know."

I read it, and flipped it over. The other side read:
"Where God and Marines
Fear to go,
Doc never hesitates.
2nd Platoon"

Well, I never felt I would go ANYWHERE without either God OR a Marine! It was a deeply appreciated gift.

I had another special cigarette lighter given to me by a Marine that I had patched up right before I put him on a chopper. It was the only way he could think of to thank me. And I would always treasure it. It was and is truly special.

I was the last "Casual" in the field. Soon, one way or anther, this would come to an end.

Chapter 39
<u>Whale of a Surprise</u>

We spent the next three days on Go Noi going through the normal daily routines of daily patrols and nighttime ambushes. Sometimes we did this as a squad – sometimes as a platoon. Soon the word came down we were moving out. We didn't know exactly where, but we were heading east and then south. No doubt someone had dreamed up another battalion operation somewhere. Ironically, we passed through the ville where on my very first night in Go Noi Gonzales got shot in the neck.

As we headed east, we came to that huge 1500-meter wide rice paddy and I couldn't help but smile as the column turned to the right and took the tree line at foothills – headed to Razorback Ridge. I will never forget that evening in Go Noi when Sarge set me up at the base of that ridge and said, "Doc, we're going right up the middle of that rice paddy."

Fortunately, we didn't hit any booby traps or ambushes and soon we were climbing Razorback Ridge and turning south.

As usual rumors were flying. The big one was they were moving the whole battalion into the Arizona. But at this point no one on our level knew for sure. We humped most of the day and finally word came down we were headed toward the Dog Bone. As always this lifted my spirits. Chi-com would be there.

We moved down to the base of Razorback Ridge and set in for the night. We sent out a squad-size ambush. The next morning the Company gathered as one and headed to the Dog Bone.

A few hours later, we were moving into the village. As usual, the locals began to gather. I heard her before I saw her. "Bacse!" I saw her running toward

362

me. I squatted down and motioned her to come on and said, "Chi-com! Come here, baby." The only other time I called her baby was the night three months ago when I removed shrapnel from her chest. I had seven-months in the bush now. Word was out that we were staying here tonight, moving to the road and would have road security for a day. This was both good and bad news.

Sometimes you skated on road duty and sometimes not. There were a lot of booby traps and ambushes on that five-mile stretch of road. I sat in the Platoon CP hootch. Chi-com followed me in and I gave her her "shit disc" and sat down and waited for her to come back with three full canteens. I was looking forward to the fresh water so I would not have to add Halazone. What a special little girl. How her life would be? Despite being here and being a racial outcast, I felt good about her. So brave and intelligent! Good genes coursed through those veins. I imagined her Dad was a great Chinese warrior.

That night Doc Gray went out on the ambush. My butt was kicked from the long hump from Go Noi, but I would much rather be here at the Dog Bone. I sat in with Lt. Rob, the right guide, and the radio man, which made up a four-man watch. I could get some sleep tonight.

It was a quiet night and we moved out early the next morning. Since we were going to the road, we would get supplies from the convoy. Stucky was walking point and took us to the road with a few detours. He was still the best point man in the country. I loved to watch him work. He maneuvered his way around those streams and stretches of high ground on pure instinct. He had skill after eight-months. He **NEVER** led us into an ambush and either avoided booby traps or spotted them. It was amazing! We spread out on the road and set up security.

That evening we took off on a platoon-size ambush right at dark and would return at first light. We went out about 500-meters off the road and set in along the trail. Rob had a good site picked out and we had a solid perimeter. I recalled the difference between him and Lt. Tommy. I still missed Tommy and still felt guilty that I wasn't with him when he was hit. But Rob was such a good Platoon Commander. It is just that some people are not cut out for the bush and some are. Rob adapted quickly. Tommy never did. *"...A Rock feels no pain..."*

An Hoa took a few rounds that night, but we didn't. We called in artillery on the site we thought the rounds were coming from, but for the most part we were guessing. For us it was a relatively quiet night.

At day break, we were on the move – just before it was light enough to see - and hit the road. We turned south toward An Hoa going to a designated site as I saw the column slow then stop. I was near the front and I heard, "Man, what the hell are you doing here? I almost opened up on you!" "What are YOU doing here? I almost opened up on YOU!!" There was a miscommunication and we were almost ambushed by First Platoon. They were waiting for a squad-sized ambush to come in from the east and we came walking up the road from the north. Things like this happened every now and then, and we were lucky no one was hit.

We gathered along the road and got the new word. We were marching on into An Hoa and we would be there a day and a night and then choppered out to the Arizona. In my seven- months in the bush, it would be my first time we were ever choppered anywhere as a unit.

I was suddenly dreading that. The Arizona was as bad as Go Noi and similar in many ways, only I didn't know it as well. I pretty well knew Go Noi by now and, even though you never knew where you would contact the enemy, it helped if you knew the area. I just wasn't that familiar with the Arizona.

I was seven months in the bush now – a month longer than I was supposed to be and I dreaded learning another area. It was a long seven months. So many times I should have been killed. It was so hard to figure. We once lost eight men to one squared-away sniper. Another time we attacked a Company of hard-core NVA who were all dug in and had us outgunned and outmanned, and we took that high ground without losing a Marine. You just couldn't figure it. ("Nothing is as it seems in the bush.") Now I had to learn a whole new area.

"...And a rock feels no pain..."

We got inside the perimeter at An Hoa and had a hot breakfast. That alone was almost worth the walk - milk, eggs, bacon, toast, and grits! Then we were herded up and stacked like cattle in a small area where we would wait until morning to catch a chopper to the Arizona. We hadn't changed utilities for over six weeks. They were literally ripped and falling off of most of us. We were a pretty grubby bunch.

That evening we had chow call again, and I ate with Doc Gray. We were very tight now, planning to meet someday when we got back to the world. He was naming his first son after Sarge and me. We decided we would get the two Vinces together and get pictures and somehow find the old Sarge and send them to him. My son would be Lauren Vincent and his would be Vincent John.

That night we bought some beer and had a party. It was nothing special, just a chance to have a beer or three and not worry about an ambush. These were special guys. Johnson was now a squad leader – a squared-away splib who was very bright and a good

Marine. Tom was off to Landmine and Warfare School. Hernandez was another squared-away Marine whom I thought a lot of. I thought a lot of all of these guys. They were my Marines. I only wished they had told us in Field Med School how close you can get out here. Now I knew that was the reason for the "attitude checks".

At the break of the day I was off to the chow hall. I didn't want to miss my last chance to drink cold milk. We would soon be moving to the LZ and were piled in a little corner near some tents. We were still wearing our old grubby utilities. I was laying there taking a nap and I heard, "Where is Doc Bear?"

I thought, "Shit! I'm right here!" I looked up and there was this huge clean guy walking up to me.

He said, "I'm Doc Whale, and I'm your relief! The chief said you're the man and to have you fill me in."

I looked unbelieving for a moment and said, "How much do you weigh?"

"Two hundred and fifty lbs. That's why they call me Whale!" It was like seeing myself seven months ago.

"Well, in three months you will be 190 lbs. if you are still alive. Now sit your fat ass down here and I'll brief you!"

I filled him in as much as I could, gave him my beloved doggie pack, and took his Marine Corps issue pack. I also gave him two trache kits I had made up and all the advice I could think of. These were still my Marines and I wanted them in good hands.

I got up and said my goodbyes. It was very hard. It was the second time I had done this, which made it a little easier. Doc Gray and Stucky were the hardest. I almost cried and so did they. Rob was hard, too. I think it was just that I had such respect for him.

I waved and fought back tears as I turned to walk the mile to the Battalion Aid Station (BAS). I had four technician ratings. I could sit there in front of the chief and name my destiny. In an hour I would be doing just that. In 90-minutes I would be walking away from the Chief's desk thinking, "What the hell am I doing?!"

Chapter 40
Letting Go

The walk to the 1/5 Battalion Aid Station was a long one. Oh, it was just one mile - but as I walked that mile, I took in the last seven months of combat, joys and sorrows. Had I been asked what I would be thinking about on this last mile of bush time, I would have said, "Where am I going next?" or "Home!" or "Getting the hell out of this country!" And all of this crossed my mind. But what I was thinking about most was the Marines, this band of young men with whom I had spent the most emotional time of my life. I thought of how they would have performed in a war where there were no "rules" - going up Iwo Jima Hill or Guadalcanal! They would have fought honorably. Yes, they would have died – many of them – like the true heroes that went there did, but they would have died with honor.

Sarge would have stood out anywhere. Rob was an exceptional leader. The Platoon had changed so much in the time I was there. Seven months ago when I first got there, I had heard of the acts of guys who had no honor. Rumor had it a gun team leader shot himself with a .32 pistol to get out of the bush. Others threw a grenade and it hit a tree, and several were hit who were trying to get out ….and they did, but in much worse shape than they had planned on. I thought I only knew one guy who did this type of thing, and I couldn't even swear to that. But I thought one guy fragged himself. That is one out of the hundreds I had served with. Was this a Platoon of "John Waynes"? No this was a Platoon of 18 to 19-year old kids – some 20 or 21. But most were still in their teens. This was a Platoon that, if I would have had to go up Iwo Jima Hill, I would have wanted to do it with these guys.

I had spent the last seven months with some true heroes. Yes, there were others who were just trying to get through this, and sometimes I felt like I was one of those. We had no expectation of winning this war. It was apparent that our country's leaders were not going to give us the freedom to go in and fight to win. These guys, myself included, were fighting for another cause – each other! The United States of America had lost her innocence and now was exposed to the world. No one who had an open-mind could think we were fighting for these people. We were fighting and dying for big business, oil, and politicians. And even they would not turn the military leaders loose and let us win this war.

No, we were fighting for our units. Alpha Company was fighting for Alpha Company and Second Platoon was fighting for Second Platoon, and God help anyone who would threaten them. They would fight and die in honor, but were they fighting for a cause they believed in? Yes, themselves. The country had deserted us. We had become our own "cause"!

I walked into the BAS compound and saw Smokey. He was second in command and looked just like Smokey the Bear and was probably much funnier.

He said, "Look who decided to come home! Think I could scrape some of that topsoil off of you for my garden?"

I smiled, "Hi, Smokey! Yeah, what are you growing? Pizza toppings?"

He laughed, "Welcome home, Bear! I think the chief is expecting you."

I said, "Okay, is he in his office?"

He said, "Go sit in there and he will be."

"Okay. Thanks, Smokey!"

I still did not have a high opinion of "lifers", but I had found exceptions. Smokey and the chief were two of those. I saw my views changing - but don't hand the re-enlistment papers to me yet. I was a long way from being a career man.

I grabbed a Pepsi, paid my ten cents MPC and sat in the chief's office. Soon he came in.

"Well, the Bear is out of the woods! Welcome back to the BAS!"

"Thanks, Chief, I appreciate that."

"You did a good job out there, Bear. I heard nothing but good things about you from the Marines, the officers and the other Corpsmen. Very well done!"

"Thanks, Chief, but it's not enough, is it? I mean really you can never do enough."

"I guess not, Bear. It is war. And in war men die. You can't change that; you can only do your best."

"Yeah, I guess you're right, Chief."

"Now about your next assignment... You know I would love to have you here, but with your four tech ratings, you can spend your last five months anywhere in country you want: First hospital if you want to do your Orthopedic Tech trade; First Med if you want to be in a plaster room; but I imagine you will want the Neuro-Psych job at First Med. Don't you? It's up to you."

"Chief, I'm having trouble here. Can I go and call my wife and let her know I'm out of the bush and then come back?"

"Sure. I'll call the HAM operator and tell them you are coming."

It was nighttime in Missouri and Linda was home. She sounded so good. She was relieved that I was finally out of the bush.

"Where are you going to be?"

"Well, I'm not sure yet, but I think I may be at Liberty Bridge at the Forward Battalion Aid Station there. If so, it would be just two of us and it would be good duty."

"I thought you were going to DaNang."

"I will be, but not just yet. Liberty Bridge is safe now. It is where we go to recuperate."

"You told me it got overran. How can it be safe?"

"That was Tet. It is safe now and the Battalion Aid Station is inside a bunker that can take a direct hit. I would be as safe there as anywhere. I would be living in a bunker."

"Okay, but you had better come home to me safe after all of this!"

"I will. I promise. My bush time is over. I made it!"

We said our personal goodbyes and I went back to talk to the Chief.

He said, "Well, Bear, what will it be?"

"Chief, I want the BAS at Liberty Bridge. Can I have it?"

"Yes, Bear, I think I can work that out. Greg has been there for a while and I think he would gladly come back here or go to DaNang. Let me call him."

Soon I had an answer. I would be at the forward BAS with Moody, a Corpsman who did his bush time with Charlie 1/5.

We had steaks and beer that night and I had a very long shower and got rid of my skuzzy utilities. I unpacked my gear and got ready to catch the convoy tomorrow afternoon.

I would take things with me that to me were important. I would take my writing gear, my old beat up helmet and flack jacket, and once I was there I would find someone who would trade an M-16 for my Colt 45. I felt relieved yet, strangely, sad.

I knew I was having trouble letting go. I should be on my way to DaNang tomorrow to be with Mac at First Med, but I just wasn't ready. I was honest with my wife in that I felt Liberty Bridge was safe. I didn't have a death wish, but I was having trouble detaching myself from these men I had shared so much with. I was still with 1/5. I would see Alpha Co. when they came to the Bridge.

I caught the convoy on its way back to DaNang the next afternoon. I stood in the back of a six-by and watched the terrain. I knew well the five-mile strip of road between An Hoa and Liberty Bridge. There was where Joe and I had treated the engineer who had lost both legs and his right arm. Joe would receive nearly identical wounds five weeks later. There was where we went in on several ambushes. Right over there to the east two miles away was Chi-Com and the Dog Bone. Right over there to the west two miles from the road was where we ambushed 30 NVA soldiers the first time I heard Sarge say, "Mercy, Doc!" I could still hear that bass laugh. Right over there was Henderson Hill where we had spent many a night on road security. And right over there not far away was where Sarge was hit. I felt the anger build inside of me as I looked out over that area.

We approached the Bridge and went through the gate. I hopped off and walked to the BAS. I climbed down into the bunker that was the forward BAS and I was at my new home. I shook hands with Moody. We would become good friends.

Moody briefed me about our duties. We held sick call from 0800 until 1030, and again from 1400 until 1600. That was it except for emergencies. It was good duty. Moody liked it. I thought I would, too.

We had access to an MD by phone if we ran into something we couldn't handle. But we had nobody looking over us. We were pretty much on our own. It was an easy place from which to evacuate someone with a chopper pad right outside the bunker. There was also a convoy everyday that went from DaNang to An Hoa and back. Compared to what I had been used to, it was a life of luxury. It also gave me a lot of time to think - a lot of time to figure out why I wasn't working in a psych ward in DaNang.

Chapter 41
A Plan for Closure is Born

I lay on the rack after sick call on an honest-to-God cot with a real pillow. My thoughts were still filled with the bush. Where was the Company right now? How was Stuckey? Doc Gray? Rob? Would Frank make it? No, not a chance. He would stumble over a booby trap or somebody would shoot him. Why was I still with 1/5? What was the real reason? I had no closure to my bush time. I wasn't ready to leave it all behind me. What would it take? What was missing? I wasn't sure, but ideas began running through my head – lots of them.

Things were different here – very different in many ways. Race was an issue here, as it was in An Hoa. Splibs hung around with splibs – chucks with chucks. It wasn't that way in the bush – well not completely. Here it was unusual to see a black guy and a white guy walking together as friends. In the bush it was commonplace.

I saw our old Skipper often – Lt. Probst. He got out of the bush about the same time I did and was also assigned to Liberty Bridge. I always spoke to him casually. For example, "Hey, Skipper, what's going on?" He always spoke but seldom slowed down. He seemed to me to be a man with a burden. I remembered the night he wouldn't let Doc Ball call in a chopper when he needed one and the man died that night. I had asked the skipper the next day if that was his first confirmed kill. I think at the time I blamed him for the death of that Marine.

But now I thought about things a little differently. You could never do enough. Like the chief had said, you can't make all right decisions. It was impossible, and when a bad decision was made a man could die.

That was war, and it was hell, but it would happen. All you could do was all you could do – make the best decision you can at the time, and do it unselfishly. That is all anyone can expect of you. We all had regrets – myself included.

That afternoon I got acquainted with an outpatient named Thomas. He had come in to get his medicine refilled. Now to say Thomas was not a handsome man was being kind. I got out his chart and looked it over. He had been on Librium 10 mg. since the Bridge was overrun a couple of months ago. It was a mild tranquilizer and had many uses, but was not a very addictive drug. So I gave it to him. But instead of giving him a supply of them, I made him come in twice a day and gave it to him there and watched him take it. I just wanted to make sure this guy wasn't suicidal. And until I got to know him, he would have to come and get it BID (twice a day).

As I said, Thomas was not a handsome man. In fact there was nothing on him that looked vaguely handsome: huge ears, a Howdy-Doody face with freckles the size of quarters and a nose that went north, south, east and west. His eyes drooped, and well, I'm sorry, but the man was hound-dog ugly!

I had been there on the Bridge about a week and after sick call Moody and I were laying there reading in our cots snacking on milk and cookies when I heard a loud explosion within the compound. I grabbed my unit-1 and ran out of the bunker. It was very loud and I thought maybe a122-mm rocket had dropped in on us. This happened often at night, but was rare during the day. I hit the road and looked, saw the smoke and ran toward it. Moody ran right behind me. But the smell wasn't of gun powder and blood - rather it was of gasoline and shit! A Marine was out burning the crappers and either let the kerosene can get too close to the fire, or was using gasoline to speed things up. I suspected the latter. Well, it all went up and there was a Marine on the ground covered with shit and smoke and half-unconscious. It was Thomas!

I ran to him and said, "Thomas, are you okay? Do you know who I am? Where are you?"

He said, "Doc?"

I said, "Yes, do you know where you are?"

"Yes, on the ground!"

I determined he had a mild concussion and a very good bath would improve both his state of mind and smell.

He looked up at me, "Doc?"

"Yes, Thomas."

"I want you to tell me the truth…"

"Okay, Thomas, what do you want to know?"

"Doc, will I be ugly?"

I lost it. My composure and bedside manner went right out the crapper with the explosion!

"Thomas, you are the ugliest bastard I have ever seen in my life, but this explosion had nothing to do with it!"

I was laughing so hard I could barely get the words out. I felt bad about it later, and, Thomas, if you are reading this, I am sorry. I think I needed an outlet of all of this tension and it came about at the expense of this shit-covered Marine.

Moody and I went back to the BAS. That afternoon Thomas came in for his Librium and I did apologize to him. But every time Moody and I thought about it for the next week or so after that, we would break out laughing.

Three weeks had gone by, and word came that Alpha Company was coming to the Bridge. They were supposed to be here about a week. I felt both dread and happiness. I was afraid to find out who hadn't made it, yet eager to see those who did.   I still thought about Sarge a lot. Where was he now?   Was he getting by? How could he do as he said and raise his son when he had no legs and just one arm? I knew better than to ever underestimate the Sarge, but I worried about him a lot. Some people you are certain won't make it through the bush. I just couldn't see Sarge not making it. Of all the Marines I had seen killed or wounded, this was the one that bothered me the most. Why? Maybe because I knew if right was right, he above all others deserved to make it.   He had the most knowledge.   He did everything right. His attitude was always positive. Still he was gone.

I knew the Platoon had heard I was here and that some of them would come and see me. I may even go over and have a few beers with them on the north side of the river.

A few days later I was holding sick call and I heard a voice outside the bunker. It was obviously said loud enough for me to hear.

"Hey, Turner, let's go in here and con these squids out of some morphine!"   It was unmistakably Stuckey.

I yelled out, "Hey, asshole, you'd better go steal a jeep and drive to DaNang to get that stuff!"

He and Turner came down. Two of the old timers had found me, both now squad leaders. There were no handshakes. We embraced and slapped each other like a bunch of high school football players, and grinned like a rooster locked in a henhouse. Stuckey said, "Doc, seriously, we want to ask you something."

"Okay."

"Let's me, you and Turner go out on a three-man killer team tonight."

"Screw you! I am out of the bush! I'm not going back out there! I don't even go to the crapper without an armed guard now!"

They laughed and we talked a while.

Lt. Rob was doing great....getting short now – almost out of the bush. Stape made it home. Sanford didn't. Bud was dead. Our conversation covered many of our comrades and they asked me to go over to the northern compound that night. I did join them that evening, but I only drank two beers. I had things on my mind. I had had things on my mind for three weeks now.

The next day after sick call, I heard, "Hey, doc, let's you, me and Turner go out on a three-man killer team tonight!"

It so happened that I was alone in the bunker that evening. I said, "Come on down here, guys, I want to talk to you. I have something on my mind."

That was an understatement. I asked Stuckey if he could find the two villes where Sarge had been hit. He looked at me like I had just asked him where milk came from. "Doc, of course I can find them."

I went over a plan with them that had been forming for some time. They listened and agreed it would work. The question was: Should we do it?

I spent the night wondering just that. I lay there for hours, then went out and sat on the BAS bunker looking out into the night. February 6 was on my mind.

By the first appearance of my morning star, the decision was made.

Chapter 42
<u>Dream Team</u>

We climbed aboard the convoy the next morning. Nothing was said. We would have time to go through the final plans after Stuckey picked out the spot where we would bail out of the truck that was bound for An Hoa.

When he gave a nod, we departed the convoy and quietly slipped to the bottom of the ridge, where we would wait seven hours for our friend....darkness.

After our talk the previous night, we had chosen LaMar as the fourth man. On the day Sarge was hit, he was the Marine that kept throwing his M-16 and saying, "Fuck it! I quit! I'm not doing this anymore!!" He was a tough little guy and a good Marine, but I can't say we were the best of friends. I admired his skills and this wasn't a personality contest - this was a killer team.

We went through the plan once again. Stuckey, Steve and LaMar had brought the small arsenal we needed: Two claymore mines each, fifteen M-26 (fragmentation grenades) each, and two canteens. We each had our poncho liners, but no ponchos. If it rained, we would have to abort the mission anyway. The ponchos made too much noise. Soft bush covers, no helmets or flack jackets, and only three magazines of ammunition each. We were only taking those in case we had a skirmish either getting to or getting away from the targeted villages – the two villages where we lost Sarge. It was time for a payback. We had no intention of getting into a firefight or depending on firepower to win this battle. It was based on surprise and terror. We were playing their game.

As we went through the plan, each of us was snapping off the fuses of our grenades – ten each. We had to keep those separate from the other five. When the spoon was released on these there would be no four-second warning, no delay, and no room for error. We left the fuses on the other five. We would be throwing those. One of the most dangerous things we would face in this area was the booby traps, and we would be moving in at night. We all remembered how the five civilians had led us into the booby traps where we lost Sarge.

Stuckey remembered his way to the villes. He was, after all, the best point man in this stinking country and he would have the point. I would be five meters behind watching the portside. Steve five meters behind me was taking the starboard side. LaMar would be covering the rear.

As darkness set in we moved out. It was at least two-hours to the first village, which was the smaller one – the one where the civilians had led us to the booby traps. There was no moon. The stars were our only light. We moved slowly and kept to the tree lines away from the rice paddies. Four Marines, eight claymore mines, 60 hand grenades and 252 M-16 rounds, of which we only planned to use one.

As we approached the village we slowed and listened. It was quiet; settled in for the night. Those who occupied the village were in their bunkers. We gathered together at the edge and got ready. I would take the east side, Steve the north, Stuckey the west, and LaMar the south. It was time to put the element of fear into the game.

We spread out, each to his assigned area. Then we began shouting and getting everyone up and out. "Di di mal!" "Marines bac bac beau coupe VC tonight!" We ran them from their bunkers and didn't let them take anything with them. We wanted them to come back the next day.

We got them in a group, and then directed them out of the village. They were heading just where we wanted them - to the larger village a few hundred meters away. I counted at least 12 VC soldiers making an evening visit. But we didn't shoot or detain them. We were counting on them and the others being at the larger village. We wanted them in a close, crowded area. We pushed and shoved and told them we were there for an ambush and didn't want them to be hurt. We were there to ambush the NVA and Viet Cong. Of course, they were all Viet Cong. When they were gone, the four of us split up and went to our assigned areas. I booby trapped the east side: Ten grenades – each without a fuse. I put one under a cooking pot so when it was lifted, and it surely would be, it would go off without warning. Others I put inside the bunkers in the sleeping areas, also where they would surely go off and do maximum damage. No warning; no escape; no pattern. The only way these grenades would be removed would be in a blast of destruction. Soon we were finished with stage one. The enemy village was a bomb waiting to go off.

We then moved out to the second and larger village. We had to go slow and be very quiet. They may be expecting something, though they were probably laughing at us for being at the wrong place. Before we got to the village, we split up. Again I took the east side of the village, Stuckey the west, LaMar the south. We got close, and then crawled the rest of the way. We had a lot of time before daybreak.

I got to the edge of the ville and picked out my spot - good cover and an excellent place from which to operate. I lay my poncho liner down and took the two claymore mines and set them out. Then I ran the triggers back to the poncho, knowing the other team members were doing the same thing. Altogether eight claymore mines were placed all around the village, each one having a killing radius of 50-meters. At first light there would be thousands of 45-caliber sharp-edged pellets flying in every direction killing anything in the way.

I went back to my poncho liner and covered up. The camouflaged liner also kept the mosquitoes away. I thought about sleeping, but couldn't. Maybe this would bring closure to my tour of duty as a bush Doc – maybe not. All I knew was I couldn't get it out of my mind. It was all I thought about. "Payback is a mother fucker" was a phrase used a lot here. It applied now. I was awake as I saw my morning star. Normally that meant we most likely would not make contact that night. This night was different. It would be light in about an hour.

Movement! I covered my head. An NVA soldier was walking toward where I was laying. "Shit, this wasn't right!" It was too early. I wanted to fire the signaling shot after the first light of day. I lay still and wondered why he was walking around this time of night. He had to take a leak. Damn! He was within five-feet of me. The bastard almost pissed on me. I lay still, hearing the urine hitting the ground beside me and wanting so badly to kill him. He finished and started back to his hootch. I slowly lifted and aimed my M-16. I sighted in the back of his head, but didn't shoot. It was too early. This had to be perfect. I wanted the village to be stirring when we set it off, with everyone up! I wanted the VC and NVA ready to take to the hills nearby and the local Viet Cong ready to start their day. We were hoping to end it.

My morning star was fading. It was breaking day. The adrenaline was pumping heavily now. I knew the other three were ready. They were the best; the men you knew would never let you down. They were waiting for the signal.

I had the remaining five hand-grenades by my side, the pins straightened and ready to pull and throw. My M-16 was at my shoulder, the claymore mine detonators were right in front of my face as I lay there, waiting only for the right moment. When that time came, I would cap off one round – one round only! An automatic burst would send everyone to cover. A single shot would bring them to the ground. Then when there was no more, they would get up to see what and where it came from.

I would fire the initial round. We would all count to ten and then blow our claymores. I watched and the village was alive now. I was aiming, picking the target for my one round when I saw another NVA soldier walking toward me. Closer he came. He had his AK-47 loosely in his hand, carrying it like a suitcase. I sighted in on his chest. This was it. The time was here – revenge, closure, peace at long last. He was within 20 feet of me now. At the last moment I moved my sights to his forehead, as Sarge used to say, "Right between the running lights." I squeezed the trigger slowly and the burst of one single round split the remaining darkness - one muzzle flash. I counted to ten and then blew my claymores. It was as one! All eight went off! Cries and screams rang through the ville. Then the grenades started going off. I had momentarily forgotten about them, I was so keyed in on triggering the ambush. I grabbed one and waited for a target. There! Four NVA were running to cover. I pulled the pin, let the spoon fly and threw it. Then I grabbed another and threw again. Twenty more explosions! Twenty well-placed grenades on a panic-ridden, enemy-occupied village!

Now it was time to make our move. Take advantage of the terror and confusion. They had no idea what was hitting them or why. They only knew they were dying. I was on the east side of the village, the closest to the road to Liberty Bridge. So as I ran I looked behind me. From the left I saw a Marine coming my way – Steve. To my right I saw another - LaMar. Then yes, the third! Stuckey was on the way. There were a few shots fired. I wasn't even sure if they were fired in our direction. They weren't close to us in any event. We were close now, running as a team. I saw smiles, a job well done. As we merged together, I turned and ran, letting Stuckey pass and take the lead. We moved quickly. A ton of emotions went through me on this last leg of our mission. I wanted to laugh, shout, rejoice and cry!

We got to the edge of the high ground, maybe 100-meters from where we would catch the convoy on its return to Liberty Bridge in a few hours. We set in. We talked and were happy with the way it went. About three hours later, they were returning to the first village, the smaller one, the booby-trapped one. "You live by the sword, you die by the sword." We smiled as the grenades went off.

Around 1400 we heard the convoy coming up the road. We shook hands and slowly walked to the road. After that day, we never talked about or mentioned the killer team mission again – ever!

I awoke on top of the bunker sweating; the sandbags where I had dozed off were digging into my back. It seemed so real. I was shaking slightly, and more than a little confused. Had it happened? Was it real, or a plan I had thought so much about that I lived every minute of it in a dream? Before I had fallen asleep, after much consideration, I had decided we would abort the mission. Did I think the plan would work? Yes, the "Master" taught me how to turn the tools of the enemy on themselves.

Would the other three have gone? No doubt. I lay a moment and did what I had been doing since

February 6. "What would Sarge do in this situation?"
He was my mentor; his teachings should decide the
revenge.

Sarge would have resented it. He would not
have been happy that we would have done that. I know
this now and I knew it then. I remember well Sarge
explaining killer teams to me.

Our normal duties included night ambushes.
These were approved and often thought up and
sanctioned by Battalion. They usually consisted of a
squad, a Doc and an M-60 machine gun team with full
gear, flak jackets, noisy helmets, bandoleers of ammo,
etc. They seldom worked for obvious reasons. The
"gooks" would either hear you clanging through the
jungle and ambush or leave the area.

There was, however, a better way. The Marine
Corps had two units, 1st Recon and Force Recon. Force
Recon was the elite of all fighting units. These units
went out in 3 to 7-man teams. They were sanctioned.
They usually took place where the enemy was plentiful
and all "free fire zones". When they slipped upon the
enemy, they killed them. If assigned to do so, they
would spot a larger unit, avoid contact, and then report
to S-2 (Intelligence). These men were the cream of the
crop. They carried claymores, grenades and M-16's.
That's all. No noise.

In a "grunt unit", we also had some exceptional
Marines, men who had confidence in their brothers and
were among the best in the Corps. They were baptized
by blood and knew the enemy well. They were
sometime organized by a squad leader, maybe a Platoon
Sergeant or even a fire team leader. They were called
"killer teams". They were not sanctioned. However,
they did not go after civilians, but only "free fire zones".
They worked. The killer teams would simply notify a
section of the perimeter there would be action that night

and not to fire when they saw movement. These were Marines who were sick of fighting a war with "rules", with their hands tied behind their backs.

I knew this plan I had planned in my mind for so long would work. The Marines I had chosen would go. They were the best. I knew we could destroy this VC stronghold with only four men, 60 M-60 hand grenades and eight claymore mines. The question was this: Would it solve anything? Would it end the nightmares? Bring Sarge back? Restore peace of mind? The final conclusion was "No". Sarge wouldn't approve. He didn't want anyone fighting his battles. He was a professional and he obtained his wounds with honor and would live honorably with them.

After eight-months, I had my "closure". It was time to go to DaNang. That morning, I called the Chief and he made the arrangements. It was time for what was left of "Casual Company" to reunite: All BOTH of us.

Chapter 43
Leaving An Hoa

Chief was making the necessary arrangements. In four days I would be in DaNang. Moody and I did some celebrating. Beer was easily accessed on the Bridge compound – and even a little pot was there to be had at any given time. By now I had smoked pot three times in my life, so I would make it a fourth.

We waited until dark when we knew we wouldn't have any patients come in and we lit up in both senses of the word. We talked a while, both of us about bush time – his with Charlie Company and mine with Alpha. We decided it would be appropriate to leave something behind. So between my creative mind (more so now with the joint burning) and Moody's artistic abilities, we decided to give the Forward BAS a name.

I came up with the name. Moody drew the sign. We proudly posted it at the door: "The Phuc Dup BAS".

Soon I was on a convoy to An Hoa. Once again I watched the last eight months go by on the trip back to the main BAS. Of course I wondered where the Company was today, who (if anyone) was on road security, and of course where the enemy was.

We went within a mile of where Pop's fire team was totally annihilated at the well, two miles from where I gave the rotten eggs to the shit bird. Many memories! Some horrible! Some incredibly funny! We went into the An Hoa compound without incident and I made my way to the BAS. Tomorrow I would check out, get my sea bag and catch a chopper to DaNang. I reported in to the Chief and it was, as always, good to see him.

He had my orders drawn up. I would be working the psyche ward at First Med Battalion my last four months in Vietnam – safe duty.

I went in to the stucco barracks, which was also the building where we held sick call, and found an empty rack. I put my pack and Colt .45 on the end of it. I lay back and was about to take a nap when a Corpsman I didn't know came in.

"Hi! I'm James Berry. Are you Bear?"

"Yes, nice to meet you, Jim."

"I'm going out to Alpha Company in a day or two, and the Chief said I should talk to you before I go. He said you were coming in today. He advised me to take notes."

I said, "Well, what can I do for you?" I remembered the good advice I had received from Doc Norm and all the others eight months ago, and I would do my best to help him prepare.

The questions he asked were the same ones I wanted to know back then: What was it like? Is it really as bad as I have heard? Do you HAVE to go out and treat them, or can you have the wounded brought back to you? I smiled at that one and I remember thinking, "Not this little black duck. They can bring the wounded to me!"

I said, "Jim, you are like a free agent, but you will go out and treat them where they drop, and you will do it because you will want to, not because you have to. You will do it because those men will die for you. They will take care of you. They will lay down their lives to see you are covered."

I saw the fear and doubt in his eyes – the same fears I had eight months ago. We talked a long time and I gave him the straight scoop to the best of my ability. I wanted him to make it. I also wanted to make sure that others made it.

As he was leaving to go on with his orientation, my final words were, "Jim, take good care of my Marines."

I hadn't thought about this. It just came out. Right then I realized they would always be "My Marines". Oh, I would go to DaNang and I would finish my four months in country, but the Marines of Alpha 1/5 would always be "My Marines". That would be a bond that would never end.

The next day I went and picked up my sea bag. I remembered when I checked it in thinking I would never see it again. The uniforms inside would never fit me now and, besides that, I would never again wear navy blues. I had a 28" waist now as opposed to a 38" waist eight months ago. I turned in my Colt .45 and humped my sea bag back to the BAS. I waited around, talked to a few guys, until I got word that it was time to catch the chopper. We had a med-evac going to First Med. I stopped by the Chief's office to say goodbye. I shook his hand and told him I appreciated him. I truly did. He was an outstanding Chief Hospital Corpsman in every sense.

As I turned to go to the chopper, I heard him say, "Bear?"

I turned, "Yes, Chief."

"I want you to remember something. When the nightmares come - and they will come - remember this: You were the best out there. You truly gave it your all!"

I turned and walked toward the LZ, but I couldn't respond to his statement. I would never forget him.

The chopper took off and as we flew across An Hoa basin I was looking for the Dog Bone. I had told Jim to look out after Chi-Com. We flew over Liberty Bridge and then Go Noi Island. I peered down into the dark dense jungle and elephant grass and recalled all the humps, the snipers, the spider holes, my first KIA - so many memories from there. It would be the last time I laid my eyes on it.

Then there was Marble Mountain. This meant we were nearing DaNang. The chopper began descending and I got my gear ready. When we landed, I helped unload the med-evac and stepped off the chopper. I wondered, "Would I ever be on another helicopter?"

I immediately went to the HAM operator at First Med and called Linda. I wanted her to know I was in DaNang. She cried, and I felt bad that I hadn't come here earlier. I assured her that I was safe now. I would be working a psyche ward, but I wouldn't be one of the ones in pajamas. Perhaps I should have been.

Mac was glad to see me, but was a little mad that I took so long in getting there. That didn't last too long. I reported in and got assigned to a tent with a real cot and a little storage cabinet. We also had "house mouses". These were Vietnamese girls who came in everyday to clean. Ours was, as were most, was named Kim.

I looked up Eddie Harren, my old friend from Bethesda, and we went to have a few beers. He was off duty. We talked about the psyche ward and the shifts and I suggested we go as a team and volunteer for permanent night duty. The reason I used was so we wouldn't get "messed with" by the lifers – something that appealed to Eddie. The real reason, for me at least, was I wanted to be awake at night. It was hard for me to feel that we couldn't be hit here, and if we were hit, I wanted to be awake and ready.

I was issued a Colt .45 and also obtained an M-16, which I kept by my rack. I carried the holstered .45 when going outside the First Med Battalion gate, but at night I wanted that M-16 where I could get to it.

It was a new world here. It was as safe as you could get in this country. I just wasn't ready to let go of the old one – not yet!

Chapter 44
"Are you Going to 'San Prancisco'?"

It truly was a different world. It took a little getting used to – not worrying about stepping on a booby trap or into an ambush or taking sniper fire. There were cold beers in the evenings, but working nights limited our consumption, which was no doubt a good thing.

We reported for "inspection" (which was hard to get used to again) at 2245 and work at 2300. We were often able to catch the USO show at the EM club and have a cold Carlings or Schlitz, or whatever the beer of the day was. The USO groups were usually Korean and, other than having trouble with "f" and "r", they were actually pretty good. "I long for San Prancisco with fwowahs in my hair."

Ed and I often got off work around 0700, slept two or three hours, then caught a convoy to China Beach, where we could swim the South China Sea, and even rent a two-man sailboat. This was as close as I would ever get to being a "sailor" in my four-year Navy enlistment.

One morning, I was walking across the compound and I saw a familiar sight. It was Smokey the Bear from the 1/5 BAS.

I said, "Smokey, what are you doing here?"

He said, "Bear! I transferred here last week. Chief Fowler rotated and I didn't care for his replacement, so I decided I would come to First Med."

It was good to see him. He looked incredibly like Smokey the Bear! We talked a while, but because he was a First Class Petty Officer, I didn't see him too often. But it was always a pleasure when I did.

One morning, Eddie and I were going across the compound to catch a convoy to China Beach and I spotted Smokey. Now Eddie didn't care for lifers. As I've said before, as a rule I didn't either. But Smokey was an exception.

I called out to him, "Smokey! We are heading to China Beach for a swim. Why don't you come and join us?"

He said, "Hmmmm...Okay, Bear. But I have to be back by 1500. Will that work out?"

I said, "Yes, we do, too. We have to sleep before we go to work tonight, so go get your tiger shorts and we'll wait for you."

I could see Eddie wasn't happy about my inviting Smokey. "Its okay, Eddie. Wait until you get to know him. He's a hoot!" I was getting really close again to Eddie. We were fast becoming best friends again despite the fact that he didn't have to serve as a Bush Corpsman. I knew his sense of humor was helping me retain my sanity. I talked to him about my tour, taught him what I had learned, it seemed I had a bad feeling - a very bad feeling. Oh, not that I didn't think Eddie would fit right in with the Marines. He was one hell of a good Corpsman and I had no doubt whatsoever he would be an exceptional bush Doc. What bothered me was that they would do that to him? Would they call him to serve his LAST six months in the bush? I thought of the pressure that it would put on a bush Doc. I about flaked out on my last few weeks in the bush; and being in the field my last six months? The worst of it was if that happened, and he was fortunate enough to make it, he'd have no time to adjust in the rear before going home. I had four months to get my head on straight. It would take at least that. I hoped he wouldn't have to go, that he would skate by and be safe and go home to Sarah the very same man he was when he kissed her goodbye. I wanted that for him very much. I

392

knew I had a lot of adjustments to make when my feet hit "Friendly Soil".

Smokey joined us and we caught a ride on a six-by truck heading toward the beach. Eddie and I got on and together rolled Smokey's big ass on board. Soon Eddie was laughing his socks off at Smokey's antics. After a while the truck stopped and picked up yet another hitchhiker. It was a Marine carrying his M-16 who got on board, and it was immediately obvious that he didn't like "lifers" either. Smokey caught that, too.

Smokey said, "What unit are you with?"

The Marine answered, "Third Marines!"

"What are you doing so far from your unit?"

"I just got out of the brig!"

"What were you in the brig for?"

"I threw a grenade at a LIFER!"

"Did you get him?"

"No, I missed him!"

"With a GRENADE!!!!??? How the hell do you miss a lifer with a HAND GRENADE!!??

Eddie and I were cracking up. It was a fun day. We watched Smokey roll around in the surf like a big old bear, and laughed like we were nowhere near a war. It was a very hot day. The mercury hit 115 degrees and it was so humid you could barely breathe.

We caught a convoy back to the base and got off, dragging Smokey slowly off the truck. We were all in good spirits. Walking back to First Med, we passed through Motor Transport where they serviced the jeeps, ambulances and trucks. There happened to be a jeep sitting there that had apparently just been washed. It was dripping dry, and as we walked by it Smokey looked over at the dripping jeep. He said, "Hmmmmm! Don't tell ME it ain't HOT! Look at that jeep – sweatin' like a damn HORSE!" Once again Smokey had brought humor back into my life. That night I would need it.

Eddie and I made roll call and went to our ward for "report". We had a new patient. I sat there listening about him and my blood began to boil. He was from Graves Administration - the Morgue. It is a voluntary job and a way out of the bush for some Marines. I didn't think anyone in his right mind would take that option, but this guy clearly was not in his right mind. He had been sent to our ward after being caught barbequing human flesh at Graves Administration. It seemed to have become a food of choice for him. He was one sick puppy! I read his doctor's orders, which included Thorazine 100-mg four times a day and leather restraints. If given the chance, he would grab anything sharp and stab himself with it. He got off on pain.

I had to restrain myself from wanting to GIVE him a little pain. The thought of him eating Lt. Tommy or Pat, or anyone who valiantly died serving our country was very upsetting to say the least. I admittedly did not have a therapeutic attitude toward this creep. He needed serious help, but I was in no frame of mind to give it to him. If given an injection or anything that hurt, he would laugh like the maniac he was.

Eddie was as pissed off at this guy as I was, but as the true friend he was, he did most of the duties this whacked- out patient required.

I needed OUT of this country!

I wanted to get my old temperament back, but I wondered if I ever would. I felt I could still be effective in psyche, but not with someone like this guy. I was no longer gentle. I was no longer an introvert. I had become Doc Bear and as aggressive as a grizzly.

I had noticed this aggressiveness at the EM (Enlisted Men's) club, too. All my life I would go out of my way to avoid trouble or a fight. Now I found myself looking for a bully or someone who was picking on someone smaller, and I would just wait for a chance to help the smaller or under-ranked guy. I knew I had a lot of hostility inside. It needed an outlet. I was afraid when I left 'Nam in less than three months I would take it with me. I hoped to find a way to get rid of it – soon! Preferably before I was discharged from Travis Air Force Base in lovely "San Prancisco"!

Chapter 45
<u>Stuckey</u>

The elephant grass was cutting my flesh as I ran to the call.

"Doc! Help me!"

I dug in harder, but the load on my back was heavy. What was all this weight? I glanced to my right shoulder and a Marine was draped over it. On my left was yet another Marine. I looked behind me and I was pulling along a makeshift gurney made of sticks and bark. A Marine on each shoulder both badly hit and another on a gurney behind me as I ran to a cry for help!

"Doc! I'm dying! Please help me! It's my spleen, Doc. You can save me!"

I looked through the mist of elephant grass and smoke and saw Lt. Tommy laying there crying for help. He was a mile away and I had three Marines to bring with me – none to be left behind. They were all badly wounded. Yet there was Tommy a mile away crying for me.

"Doc! I have 30 seconds left to live! Hurry!"

I was pulling and pushing to make my way to Tommy, digging my feet in the mud, hearing rounds buzzing by my head. Mortar rounds began dropping in between Tommy and me.

"Doc! I gave you a meritorious promotion! I wrote you up for medals! Please save me!!"

"Hang on, Tommy, I'm coming! Hang on, damn you! Don't you die on me!"

"Doc! Doc! Wake up!"

My eyes eased open and I saw a shadow...."Tommy?"

"Doc! Hey, ya big Bear! Let's cook up some rice and Kool-Aid!"

I quickly sat up, realizing the nightmares had started. Chief had told me they would, but I didn't think so. I was wrong. I could tell by my pounding pulse, sweaty brow, and shaking extremities....I was very wrong!

"Stuckey, what are you doing here? Are you okay?"

"I'm great, Doc. I'm on my way to R&R and thought I would stop by and visit."

"Damn, Stook, it's good to see you!"

I shook my head, got up and splashed some canteen water in my face. The nightmare was much too real. I didn't just dream it, I was living it.

"R&R? Great, buddy! How long can you stay?"

"I leave tomorrow. Can you fix me up with a rack?"

"You can have mine. I'm working nights. There is a shower across the ditch, and you're welcome to use both my rack and the shower."

"Thanks, Doc!"

"Stook, it's so good to see you. Fill me in. Where is the Company?"

"They're around the Dog Bone now. We just got out of the Arizona. It's a bastard, Doc! As bad as Go Noi, only bigger."

I had only been to Arizona twice – two brief patrols and one ambush.

Now for the big question, "How are the guys, Stook?"

"Well, Steve, Felix and I are squad leaders. Did you hear about Lt. Monty?"

I didn't think I wanted to hear this. (I thought: "What did that crazy son-of-a-bitch do?")

I said, "No, Stook. Is he okay?"

"Lieutenant was shot three times in the butt with a machine gun – maybe an AK – not sure. But it was automatic weapons."

"Is he okay?"

"Doc, he is crazy as hell! He doesn't know fear. He was out of the bush with Battalion on an operation in Arizona, and we got pinned down in this big rice paddy. Steve's squad was on point and our new Platoon Commander froze up and didn't know what to do. So did Staff Sgt. Woody. We were pinned down and no one was giving orders. It was crazy, Doc. The whole damn Battalion of NVA had us with our pants down and out of nowhere comes Lt. Monty. Doc, he wasn't even WITH our Company anymore, let ALONE our Platoon! He was supposed to be guarding the Colonel. But when he saw us pinned down he went fucking nuts! He ran out there all alone with just an M-16 and told Steve to send a man to him with some grenades."

I shook my head. This didn't surprise me about Rob.

"Doc, he and the radio man assaulted the whole battalion of NVA. The radio man was killed – head blown clear off. And after Monty threw his grenades and gave us some cover, we were getting to where we could fight back. And he turned to run back toward us and was shot three times. Doc, he's up for the Congressional Medal of Honor, and if fair is fair, he should get it! He sure deserves it!"

He went on to tell me Rob was treated by Doc Gray and was sent out of country. He would be okay.

We waited until the club opened and went for a few beers. It was so good to see this friend. I got caught up on the men of Second Platoon. Tom was blinded by a blooper round. Frank finally was killed. LaMar made it. On and on it went. Doc Gray was almost out of the bush and would be coming here soon.

Stuckey had a little over a month to go. He would rotate before I did.

We had a few beers, but I had to stop. I was working that night, so we walked to my hootch.

Stuckey said, "Doc, I'm not going to make it."

I said, "Stuckey, what do you mean? Of course you are! You have a month left and you are home!"

He said, "My number's up, Doc. When I get back from R&R we are heading back to the Arizona and I won't come back.... I feel it! I know it! My number is up!"

This from the man who walked point five times as much as any other Marine I knew of! This man was no coward. This was a man who was alive and kept others alive by his gut feelings, by his instincts!

"Talk to me, Stook! What are you feeling?"

"I don't know, Doc. I don't think I've lost my nerve. I'll go and I'll do my job. I just know in my heart I won't come back. This is it. The odds have gone against me. I will die before I rotate."

"How are your wounds, Stook?"

"They are okay."

"How's your back?"

"It bothers me some, but it's fine." He had had a little trouble with it when I was in the bush and I had treated him for it.

"Stuckey, when you get back from R&R, come and see me. Okay?"

"Okay, Doc. I think I can swing that."

"No, Stuckey. Don't think it. I want you here when you get back. Alright?"

"Okay, I'll be back here in about a week."

"Okay, buddy, I'll see you then."

I went to work that night and as usual my mind was 23 miles SW of DaNang. Rob was going to be okay. He was hit pretty badly, but he would be alright.

Stuckey had me worried. I and many others had relied on his fine instincts for survival. Now those same instincts told him he was going to die. I couldn't let that happen – not if there was anything I could do about it.

The next day after I got off work, I went to see my buddy Mac at Personnel. He got my service record for me (which he wasn't supposed to do) and let me have it for a day. I took it to a doctor I had seen a few times who held sick call for First Med and I waited impatiently in his office. When he was free, I went in to talk to him.

I handed him my service record and as he looked through it, he said, "Okay. Now what is this about? If you are applying for a job, you've got one. Very impressive service record! But why are you here?"

"Well, sir, I am trying to establish credibility with you. I have something to talk to you about."

I told him all about Stuckey, how he so often - for a full year - volunteered to walk point because he didn't want Marines with families to get hurt – and also because he was the very best.

"Bear, I assume you have no doubt about this man. He is not just trying to get out of the bush?"

"Sir, he has no idea that I am here talking to you. As you saw in my service record, I am an Orthopedic Technician and, Sir, it is my professional opinion that Lauren Alvin Stuckenschmidt has curvature of the spine and should be put on light duty." It helped that what I was telling the Doctor was true.

"Well, Bear, all that I will promise you is that I will see him and talk with him. Is that good enough?"

"Yes, Sir. I would appreciate that very much."

I picked up my service records and went to see Mac to return them. I thanked him and went back to my hootch.

A few days later, Stuckey showed up. He had a great time on R&R and was going back to An Hoa.

"Stuckey, I want you to do something for me."

"Doc, you just say the word."

"I want you to go see Dr. Palmer today. He is expecting you."

"I'm fine, Doc."

"Just go!"

"Okay."

I was waiting outside when he came walking out of the doctor's tent. He looked stunned.

I said, "Well, Stook, how did it go?"

He said, "Doc, I'm out of the bush! I am being put on light duty. No heavy lifting. I am going to be a fucking MP here in DaNang!"

"Good! Come and see me and we'll have some beers when you come by!"

"I don't know what you did, Doc, but thank you!"

"Stook, I am naming my firstborn after you and Sarge. I want you to be alive to meet him someday!"

That meeting took place in October of 1997 – 28 years later. Lauren Vincent was 26 years old. I was 51.

Chapter 46
<u>Sitting on a Dime, Dangling My Feet</u>

I was short. Most pogues and ex-bush Corpsmen as well had a "short timer's calendar." What this consisted of was usually a beautiful woman in suggestive dress which was in 100 sections. When the Marine got down to 100 days, he obtained the "short-timer's calendar" from Freedom Hill, or another creative source.

Upon the 100th day, the short-timer removed a section of clothing each day, usually saving his favorite part of the female anatomy for what was called the "Wake Up". That was the day we all wanted to see - our flight date.

For whatever reason, I didn't have a short-timer's calendar. I don't know exactly why. It certainly wasn't because I didn't appreciate a beautiful lady, nor was it a matter of being aloof or above it all. I think it was probably because I was hiding, letting time go by unnoticed, one day at a time hoping suddenly it would sneak up on me and I would have my orders in hand heading for the air strip. I think it really was just superstition. I was afraid if I got a short-timer's calendar it would be taking it for granted and on the last day a stray rocket would come in and catch me unaware. The truth was it would be hard to catch me unaware of anything. My mind was working night and day. I tried not to think about going home. Oh, it was always on my mind and I would get terribly excited if I let myself think about it. But I tried to go about my duties and let time slowly trickle by.

I was the last Casual left in country. Because Mac came over twelve days earlier, he was gone.

I had seven days left before the "Wake Up" when the typhoon hit First Med Battalion. We had ample warning, and though Corpsmen were seldom called upon to fill sand bags, this was different. We were all asked to report and fill sand bags to protect the tents that housed the patients of First Med.

I was happy to do my share, but, as usual, my mind was working overtime. I had no fear of the coming typhoon, though I had no doubt it was coming. I observed the other Corpsmen filling and carrying sandbags and found I could tell which ones had put in their "bush time" and which hadn't. I tested my observation by asking a few who I thought had spent their bush time. I simply asked, "Who were you with in the bush?"

The answer always came quickly, due to the pride in each unit.

"2/5!" or "Charlie 1/7!" The bush Corpsmen were calmly, methodically doing their job, while the others were frantically filling bags and you could see the fear in their eyes.

It was a typhoon; it wasn't a human wave assault. It was wind and rain, and if it blew a tent down, so what? We would put it up again. It wasn't rockets or mortars, it was rain.

This was yet one other indication that things had changed. Those of us who had been in the bush as combat Corpsmen were very different from those who had not. Even in such a simple thing as a typhoon - our outlooks were entirely different. Many of us were subconsciously looking forward to the storm. We knew deep down in the back of our minds that the enemy seldom attacked when the monsoons were at full force. They couldn't fire their mortars in a heavy rain. Rockets would often misfire. And during this typhoon we had the added luxury of being inside a tent while the storm raged outside.

The typhoon lasted three days and it was pretty much what it was supposed to be: a lot of wind and rain.

Then a disaster much larger than any typhoon hit. Eddie got orders to Delta Company, First Battalion, Fifth Marines - my sister Company. Oh, they were a great fighting unit! They were there when the NVA overran Liberty Bridge during the Tet offensive. Delta 1/5 took the Bridge compound back - one foxhole, one tent, one body at a time. The problem was this: My best friend was going to spend his last six months in-country, in the bush, with the same unit, and under the same conditions as I had just come through. I couldn't hold back my feelings as Eddie packed up to go to the Fifth Marines. I felt I would be there with him - every patrol, every ambush, like I was living it all again. It was so unfair to him.

Three and a wake up!

On the morning my count down was to "two and a wake up", I awoke in a heavy sweat. Nightmares again! Bad ones. I decided to go over them while they were fresh in my mind. The one where I was dragging two Marines and Lt. Tommy was calling for me was easy to figure and also recurring. As I thought about it, most of them were about Marines dying, calling for help, and my struggling to get to them. I dreamed often of the "well" were we lost the fire team of friends - all blown away. Sometimes I dreamed of the ville we blew up, or rather where the Phantoms dropped the bombs, and so many civilians were killed. Sure they dropped the bombs, but who was actually responsible? Yes, it was justified. We were under attack. It was a free fire zone, and we would have had more men killed had we not called in for air strikes. All this was true. Still, women and children perished.

Something significant was missing from my nightmares. I never remembered dreaming of dead enemy soldiers. I saw the faces when awake, or even when I closed my eyes, but I didn't regret that we had killed them. Sometimes, that even made the rest feel better. What is the old saying? "Revenge is a dish best served cold."

The next morning I was once again in a sweat as my rack shook and I was awakened. "Doc Bear, you big ol' squid! Wake up!"

"Lefty, what are you doing here?"

"Me, Shorty, and Turner heard you were going home tomorrow and we were at the Bridge, so we caught a jeep that wasn't being used to come to your going away party."

I said, "Well, I am getting my flight orders today and tomorrow I am going home. So even though I haven't heard about a party, we'll sure as hell have one!"

It was good to see them. I got caught up in the news from the guys, both good and bad, and I was reminded once again, the "bush" was forever a part of my life. I had been here at First Med four months. There were no bonds such as the ones I had with these guys. We had shared so much. Danger, fear, fighting, regrouping, reactionary attacks, incoming, booby traps, ambushes, mosquitoes, leeches, blood, death and conquering the enemy together. What at First Med could possibly compete with emotions such as these?

Nothing!

As it turned out, there was a party planned at the EM Club. Mike, Woody and Doc Gray (the Corpsman who was at 1/5 and now at First Med) had a party planned and had sent word to my old Company. During the day, a few more Alpha Company Marines drifted into the compound. I was overwhelmed. Nothing could have made my last day in-country more pleasant.

I had my orders in hand. I would fly to Okinawa October 23, 1969 - one year to the day of my arrival in-country. From there, I would fly to Travis Air Force Base in San Francisco (why I would be discharged from an Air Force Base was beyond me) and muster out. I was due to be discharged December 16. I would get an "early out". That was fine with me. I was quite ready to put this green mother behind me and go on with my life.

The time had come at last. Tonight we would party; tomorrow I would be on my way home.

We got to the EM Club around 6:00. I had been there many times, but this was different. I had no clue what a shindig they had planned. I usually drank a few beers (enough to get a buzz) and left. I wasn't into hangovers and only on one occasion had I actually been drunk enough to wake up with an ungodly headache. Tonight I planned to find a happy median. I was going to drink more than my routine (yes, I was beginning to realize I planned EVERYTHING in my life) three or four beers, but not so much that I would be miserable tomorrow for my flight home.

There happened to be a Korean USO band at the club that night, which made things even better. Everyone was in a good mood as a few pretty Korean girls began dancing. The beer being served that night was Pabst Blue Ribbon. It was one of my favorites that we got in. Often it was Carlings Black label or Hamm's. Eddie had started a rumor that if you drank Hamm's beer until you pissed sky blue water, they would give you free beer for life. The beer and stories started flowing.

The Marines from Alpha Company stood out like sore thumbs. Most everyone there were Corpsmen who worked at First Med and had on clean, starched and pressed utilities. There were a few Marines there, as well, who worked at First Med as cooks, guards or whatever. My Alpha Marines had been wearing the same clothes for weeks. They were filthy, torn, with residue of blood, mud and gunpowder on them. The other Corpsmen and Marines gave them looks, but wisely kept their comments to themselves.

Listening to the stories was interesting. I was honored how the Marines saw me, but barely recognized some of the situations they talked about. My point of view was quite different and much less heroic. As flattered as I was by all of this, I wasn't enjoying the attention.

I was on probably my sixth or seventh Pabst when the lifer came into the club. There was a Corporal sitting at the bar minding his own business when the Sergeant, who was about my age, started hounding him. My focus switched to that scene. The Sergeant was being a real asshole. The guy was off duty and was being ragged about something he did wrong earlier in the day. I felt my anger rising. The saying "Lifers are like flies, they eat shit and bother people" came to mind. It was ridiculous. If he screwed up, fine chew him out at his job. But hunting him down while he is off duty, trying to relax and forget where he is and will be the rest of his tour is bullshit. The lifer was bullying him, knowing because of his rank, he was safe.

The whole mood changed in the club with the loudmouthed lifer still screaming at the Corporal. Some of the guys who knew me best saw I was getting pissed.

"Let it go, Doc. He's just a lifer - not worth getting in trouble over."

A year before that would be exactly how I would have seen it. Screw him; I will be out of this green momma in four or five days! Hell with him! He will be here 20 more years!

Now, though, I felt my anger rising. I had been fighting for a year and I think I saw before me a "cause":

A bully taunting someone he knew wouldn't fight back. Despite the fact that I had probably been in less than five fistfights in my life, none of which I had started (not counting boxing matches of course), I was ready. I found my feet underneath my ass on the chair, and I sprung across the table yelling "You fucking lifer!" I hit the floor and was flat running down the lifer who had decided to vacate the premises. After my feet hit the deck and I took about two strides, I was hit from all sides, front and rear by my Marine friends.

"Doc, let it go! You go home tomorrow, man! You don't want to go spend a week in the brig over some shit-eating lifer!"

I slowly began to calm down. Oh, God, I had changed so much in the last year!

I was finished drinking so the party broke up and we all went and sat on top of a bunker and talked. There were a lot of tears, mine included. These guys had come so far to see me off, and that was so special to me. We all hugged and I decided I'd better get to bed. I wanted to be up, ready and alert for my big day tomorrow. I didn't think I would ever see that day.

The most important thing about it was, as I remembered Chief Val, I never had a Marine die in my arms because I didn't know what to do. That was 99% luck, but I'll take it. We lost many men - damn good men! Men blown away by mines, shot threw the head by a sniper, etc. But tomorrow my prayers would be answered. I'd go home without a Marine dying in my arms!

I turned back the sheet to my cot for the last time and lay there thinking. I looked to the right, and my M-16 was within my grasp, locked and loaded. My K-bar was under my pillow.

I slept in tiger shorts and a cammie t-shirt. Even now, my last night in Vietnam, I could be engaged in a fire fight in less than five seconds. That, of course, didn't happen. There were no fire fights at First Med Bat. But like most bush Corpsman-turned-pogue, I was ready if it would.

I woke up with a scream in my throat, ready to shout for someone to get their head down, and realized, this was it. I was going to get my dress greens from my locker, load up my sea bag, and a jeep would take me to the air strip where in three hours I would board the Great Freedom Bird.

Kim saw I was leaving and tried to express some sort of thank you. It was a nice gesture, though I couldn't quite make it out. She was a nice little "house mouse", age 15 to 25. It was so hard to tell, and I had never asked. She came in, did her job, and we paid her well, and usually tipped her.

I told her goodbye and wished her luck, though I doubt she understood.

I was in my uniform now, not sure how these medals and ribbons were supposed to go. I realized once again, I may have fit into the bush fine, I may have taken to medicine well, but I still had no desire to learn military etiquette. Monty, a black friend of mine who was also hooch commander, helped me out. By the time he was done, he was laughing his ass off so that not only didn't I know what order to put them in, I didn't even know the names of half of them. I really didn't. I knew two for sure, the National Defense Service Ribbon, which I had for years and the Purple Heart.

I was dressed, sea bag packed, goodbyes said, and jeep waiting. I loaded my sea bag up and we were off to the airstrip.

The driver shook my hand and said goodbye as I unloaded my sea bag and put it where I could keep my eyes on it. I looked all around, taking in the terrain, observing all that was going on around me. The plane would soon be arriving, it would unload passengers, and then we would board. I stood alone, my mind full of thoughts. I never thought I would see this day.

The plane was landing now, flaps down, and turning toward us. There were about 100 of us waiting to board. Some were grab-assing, acting like children. I watched the sky, the plane, listened for noises that were out of place.

Three hundred and sixty-five days ago, I was just like the guys now coming down the ramp - scared shitless and not knowing what I was in for. I stared past them, yet taking them in at the same time. I saw one Marine point and say something about a "bush Doc". Then a few others saw my Navy rank and Corpsman caduceus and medals.

"Damn, a bush Corpsman! He has seen some serious shit."

Yes, I had - dead serious.

I stared ahead and kept aware of all around me.

A black Corporal came down the ramp. He had many of the same ribbons I was wearing. It was his second tour. He had two Purple Hearts. Our eyes met. We were brothers. Bonded by fire! He paused and saluted me and said, "Thank you, Doc." I saw a tear in his eyes and imagined a Corpsman had saved his ass in his first tour.

I saluted back, "Good luck, Corporal!" I meant it. I didn't envy him going back for another tour as a grunt. He was probably from some inner city far away from the Ozark Mountains, but we were brothers. We had both seen the elephant. We knew things others did not know.

Soon the plane was empty and I went up the ramp to find my seat. I sat by a window and was off Vietnamese soil for good. Soon we were airborne and I saw Marble Mountain. Twenty-three miles southwest of there was my unit - Alpha 1/5. Were they in the Arizona still? Back to Go Noi? God, we lost so many good men there! So many fire fights!

It was over for me. I had beaten the odds. Of Casual Company, 1968, I was the last man standing.

I thought of Sarge and Stuckey. Both were gone now - Sarge from severe wounds; Stuckey had rotated with one Purple Heart. Or was it two? I couldn't remember. So many wounds I had treated. So many lives…

I knew I was alive because of Sarge and Stuckey. Our son would bear their names – Lauren (after Stuckey) Vincent (after Sarge). We would call him Vince. Linda had already agreed to that. She had read so much about both.

She knew what Sarge had meant to me, how I relied on him, and learned from him. She also knew how unselfishly Stuckey had walked point when he didn't have to. Two incredible men I would never had known had it not been for this war. Two men I would never forget.

Someday, Sarge would meet his namesake. I would find him. Never had I known anyone like him. The day he lost both legs at the hip and his right arm he said, "Don't worry about me, Doc, I have a son at home to raise, and by God, I will raise him!" He never even lost consciousness!

Now Eddie was walking the same trails I had with Delta Company. I looked at my watch, Marine Corp issue which I had worn through my whole time in the bush. It was an ugly drab green with a canvas band. I made a vow that until I heard Eddie was safe and out of the bush, the watch would never leave my arm. I know that's crazy, but it was a crazy time, and this way, I would never forget Eddie. Every day he would be in my thoughts until he was safe.

It was an emotional time. My thoughts turned back to Sarge.

I could hear him now, "Mercy, Doc, you made it! You are going home." I smiled. He was amazing. We were approaching the sea now, leaving the land below that was Vietnam. I would reflect on the last 365 day and try to bring closure to it all. But first, not caring who heard me, I said aloud, "Mercy, Sarge! Doc Bear is going home!"

Epilogue

Travis Air Force base was very nice. It was kind of cool watching the reaction of these "fly guys" as we walked by. I was there with several Marines to be discharged and no other Corpsmen. I handed my service record over, and we were free to go about the base until we were called. The barracks were like two-man apartments. I had never seen anything like this in the Marines OR the Navy. The food was gourmet. Yet, I wanted out fast. I had my wife waiting for the call of when I would be landing at Lambert Field.

The Chief finally called me and I reported to him. He told me since I had wounds it would take a few days to muster me out. They would have to examine me, determine my disability and so on, unless I would sign a waiver saying I wanted no compensation or disability pension. I about ripped that waiver out of his hand. I wanted to go home.

On October 29, 1969, I was on the final leg of my journey. I would land at Lambert Field. We had all been told of the incidents at the airports, people mocking veterans, spitting on us, calling us names like "baby killers", etc.! I was dressed out in my Marine Corps dress greens and I was ready if that happened. I had done what my country called me to do. I had kept my oath and I had served. I had done my duty and had done it with honor, and God help anyone who spat on me! I had my K-bar strapped to my calf and enough anger to enable me to use it.

Fortunately, the only incident I had was a pleasant one. I was sitting in my seat and noticed a young bearded man two seats away that kept looking at me. He looked familiar, so finally I asked, "Do I know you?"

He said, "I think so, but I'm not sure from where. I see you are just back from Vietnam."

"Yes, I was with Alpha, 1/5."

He said, "I was with the Third Marines, so we couldn't have met there."

Then he said, "I was a Corpsman too. Where were you stationed before Nam?"

That was it! "Mastranardo?"

"Yes! Bear?"

We had been cubical mates at Barracks 12 before I got married. He had been home a year. I didn't recognize him because of the beard and he didn't recognize me because I had lost so much weight.

Mas said, "Well, let me give you some sound advice. When you get home, take off that uniform and don't tell anyone you served in Nam, especially with the Marines. It isn't appreciated here, and it may be a good idea to grow one of these, too."

I had heard this before, but it was hard to believe. The country I went to serve hates me? The people I laid my life on the line for wants to throw rocks at me? How sad! How very sad! What had become of our nation? What on God's earth had happened to the country I loved?

I got off the plane at Lambert Field and immediately kept a promise I had made a year ago. I dropped to my hands and knees and kissed the ground. I never expected to see St. Louis again, or Missouri. Linda was there waiting. God, she looked good! She ran through the ropes and grabbed me and we kissed. Together at last! No more duty stations! We were civilians! I was glad to be home.

We owned a beauty shop in South St. Louis, and it supported Linda while I was gone. She worked very hard at it and it was doing well.

414

There was no pressure on me to go to work right away, since we saved everything I made while in 'Nam. I thought I would wait a week and maybe get my head clear, adjust to this new life, and perhaps enjoy living for a while.

I did spend a lot of time at least thinking about our future. I recalled Capt. Green's promise. He would get me into any med school in the country as long as I committed to Orthopedics. And that was also what I wanted to be, an Orthopedic Surgeon. Though I doubted I could ever be as good as Capt. Green.

The problem was I couldn't see myself sitting in ANY classroom relearning all the sterile techniques, how to put on and remove sterile gloves, contamination, etc., when I had spent seven months in the jungle using the same K-bar and usually the same scalpel blade on multiple wounds on multiple people. Yet, I loved medicine. I had to think about this a lot. I knew I could be a surgeon, not that I was anything special; but because medicine came easy to me. Now repairing a car, forget it! But medicine just came easy.

In November I saw an ad in the St. Louis Paper for part time work: "Seasonal income". It was with United Parcel Service, a relatively new parcel delivery company I had never heard of before. The pay looked good, and we could use a little extra Christmas money, so I decided to go downtown and apply.

I also felt the need to do something. I was glad to be home, but was having a lot of trouble sleeping at night. Nightmares were fast becoming a problem. Anger, guilt, hatred, anxiety were setting in. I didn't have any of these in the bush, but now that I was a civilian, I felt it. It was a hard adjustment. I missed the respect I received as a Doc....and as a Marine. I missed Ed. I got letters from him regularly and promptly wrote back. I could tell he was getting gung ho from his letters, a fact that didn't surprise me, and contributed to my worrying about him making it.

I gathered up my discharge papers, evaluation sheets, and went to UPS at 520 South Jefferson. I found personnel, and went inside. I waited until I was called and was introduced to Jim Bonnell. I gave him a firm handshake, and introduced myself. He seemed nice, and I handed him the copies I had made for him and he quickly said, "We aren't hiring right now."

I held up yesterday's news paper and said, "Then why are you running an ad?"

"Well, we were hiring, but now I have literally thousands of applications to go through. You can fill one out, if you want to."

I filled out an application and left. So much for that!

The next day, Linda was at the shop, and the phone rang. I answered and it was Jim Bonnell from UPS.

"Would you rather work at 520 South Jefferson or at Valley Park?"

"I thought you weren't hiring?"

Jim said, "After you left, I went through your service record. Very impressive! Where would you prefer to work?"

"Valley Park."

He went on to say I would be laid off after Christmas but I expected that, so I agreed.

I worked through Christmas, was laid off with all the other seasonal help, and got a call three days later.

"This is Jerry Odum at UPS in Valley Park; would you be interested in a permanent job?"

"Yes!"

I liked the work. It was very hard and a quick pace, which suited me perfectly. Jerry told me I was the only guy he had ever hired who went to work for him and actually gained weight. I said, "Well, the work I was doing in the Marines was a lot more physical than this," and left it at that.

I didn't tell anyone at work I had been in 'Nam or that I was an ex-Marine. There was another veteran there but he was Army, so we didn't have a lot in common anyway.

I got the phone call I was waiting for. Eddie made it. He was heading home to Sarah, now he, too, would have to deal with the things I was going through. But he was safe! I looked at the battered, green plastic watch and removed it, depositing it into the nearest trash can. Eddie was home! Eddie was home!

December 23, 1970, Lauren Vincent was born. Sarge and Stuckey had a namesake.

On May 20, 1972, we were blessed with a lovely "peaches and cream" daughter, Jamie Lynn. Life appeared to be going great for us to those around us, but Linda and I knew better.

I had developed such hostility and anger. I was always 100% aware of everything - always alert. I drank three or four beers a night, and then could maybe sleep two hours. I knew the dangers of booze and refused to become a drunk. After I slept two hours, I was awake the rest of the night pacing, worrying about my Marines. Who made it? Who didn't? Where were they now? How was Mac coping? Where was Sarge? How was he getting along with only one appendage left? It was endless. We went through hundreds of Marines in my seven months in the bush. I saw only one rotate without a Purple Heart. He was even hit by friendly fire! So, hell, what does that say? For me, the war wasn't over!

My family, other than Linda, knew very little. I had told my mother that I was working in a hospital in DaNang the whole time. They knew something about

Purple Hearts and knew I had them, but I guess they didn't put two and two together. They had seen my picture when I was discharged, medals and all, but no one asked and I assumed, no one cared.

Linda and I had an argument one day. I need this to be clear. My anger and hostility wasn't because of her or the kids, nor was it ever directed toward them. Never once did Linda feel she or the children were in any danger whatsoever from me. We seldom argued. And I wasn't a screamer. My turmoil was within.

One day we had an argument, and it wasn't a big thing, but I guess in a way it was. She wanted to discuss the future and plans for the future. I had a problem discussing the future. It was like if you talked about it, it wouldn't come true. I remember I told her I needed some space and not to worry. I told her I would be back in a few minutes. What I did was drive until I hit blacktop, and floored the Cougar 351 and zoomed 100-mph plus over winding roads until I calmed down.

I returned home safely, and Linda was at the door. She had words for me. She said, "I know the war did this to you. I also know the kind, sweet, gentle man I married is in there somewhere, and I WILL NOT GIVE UP until I get him back!"

In 1973, I was deer hunting with my brother-in-law. I thought a lot of him, and we hunted together every year. I didn't talk about 'Nam to him (even though he, too, had been there while in the Army), nor did I belong to any organizations like VFW or any others.

We had been hunting all morning and decided to make a final "drive" back to the truck. I had a lever action Model 94 Winchester 30-30 that I had since I was 11 or 12.

We went up this ridge that was about two-miles long. We were going to be driving toward the truck. I liked the driving part. I had such fast reflexes. I could often shoot a deer on the jump. I went low on the ridge. Dave was higher up. I loved this. It was good for me. When we got up to the saddle on the ridge, I knew the truck was just below us. I couldn't see Dave, but I went on to the truck and got a drink of water. I was sitting on the front bumper when I heard him shoot. Thinking he may run in my direction, I got down and was walking to a place where I would have a good field of fire when I heard the deer coming. I drew a bead and capped him and knew I had missed the first round. There was heavy brush and I heard my first round hit a tree. I got off three more quick rounds, and I knew I had him. He was down. I was letting him lay there a while when Dave came walking down.

"Was that you?" he asked.

I said, "Yeah, I got him. He is down in that creek bed. Let's give him five minutes."

Dave smiled and said, "I heard those four shots and thought 'That's an automatic. That can't be John!' Then I thought, 'Yeah, that could be John!' I have never heard four rounds fired so fast from a lever action rifle in my life. Who are you? Lucas McCain?!!"

I laughed and said, "I guess I still have pretty fast reflexes."

That night I had my three beers so I could sleep a little while. Dave and Judy didn't know why. They had never seen me drunk, and that didn't happen often, but they had seen me drinking beer a lot.

We were watching the news. It was November, 1973. Walter Cronkite was on and he was talking about the First Marine Division. They were going home. I was overcome! I tried to get up and go to another room, but my sister Judy saw my tears.

"John, what's the matter? That's your old unit, isn't it?"

"Yes."

She said, "It must have been hell! I had no idea. I thought you were working in a hospital!"

I thought silently to myself, "You really thought I was working in a hospital?!" But I didn't say anything.

"John, why don't you talk to cousin Gene?"

Now Cousin Gene was known to the family as "Crazy Gene". He was raised a good religious boy, was a Marine in Vietnam, wounded three times, and then cracked up. Now he thought he was some kind of an evangelist.

Judy and Dave were Baptists, but I had tried the religious route. I had gone to Confession and prayed and came out feeling the same as I went in. I believed in God and for sure believed in guardian angels. I knew I had at least one. But my efforts in religion had been in vain.

I said, "Judy, Gene is crazy, and I don't want to talk to him. I haven't seen him since we were 12." That was that, or so I thought.

In January, 1976, I got a phone call. It was "Crazy Gene" and I knew Judy had been talking to him about me. He said, "John, I'm going to be in your neighborhood on February 15. I would like to stop by and see you. My wife Betty will be with me and you have never met her."

Nor had he met mine, so I said, "Gene, you are my first cousin. You are always welcome in my home. Just don't come here preaching to me. I don't need it."

"Okay, fair enough! I'll see you February 15."

February 15, 1976, was on a Sunday that year and Linda and I went to Mass, which we often did. We came home and got ready for "Crazy Gene". We dusted off our Bible so it looked like we read it, and I popped two Valiums so I would be relaxed in case "the war" came up. If Gene wanted to talk about Vietnam, I would need something to relax me.

The doorbell rang and I was anxious. I didn't want to talk about combat. I answered the door and gave them both a hug (we are a family of huggers). They came in, sat down, and Linda got us all a Pepsi and we began to talk.

Gene had been in the First Marine Division as well a year before me. He was hit by an AK-47 three times. I thought that was the focus of this visit, so I mentioned a few places. Gene said, "I can tell already you were a better Marine than I was. You know what you are talking about. I just wanted to go over there and kill. I didn't know anything about being a Marine."

I said, "Well, neither did I. I had a good teacher. But I didn't want to go over there at all. I had no choice."

Gene said, "Is that your Bible? Can I see it? It's a great book."

I said, "Sure!" And he thumbed through it.

"Isn't it interesting here in this Bible that it says Jesus had brothers and sisters?"

I said, "What? Mary was 'ever-Virgin'! What are you talking about?"

"No," he said, "She was a virgin when Jesus was conceived. She and Joseph had other children." He showed this to me in the book of Mark and then another place. It was there in our own traditional family Bible! "Is this not the son of Joseph, brother of James, Judas and Simon, the son of Mary, the carpenter? Aren't his sisters here with us?" Jesus said, "Only in his home town among his relatives and in his own house is a prophet without honor."

Now "Crazy Gene" had my attention. I felt misled - lied to! It was right there in my own family Bible! If Jesus was the Son of God, He at least had brothers and sisters, the children of Joseph and Mary. So what about all of those prayers to Mary, Mother of God, Ever-Virgin!!?

He went on, but I was somewhat numb. He talked about being saved by grace. Ephesians 2:8-9 stated, "By grace are you saved through faith, and that not of yourselves; it is a gift of God, not of works, lest any man should boast." It is a free gift!!?

I said, "Gene, it can't be a free gift! What about the candles, the praying for the dead? Having to go to Church, Communion? All the things you and I did? What about good deeds? Being good in the eyes of God?"

"John, Jesus was the only perfect man. If by our thinking we can earn salvation, aren't we making what Jesus did on the cross less than what it was, that it wasn't enough? He died once for all - that all could be saved. It is a free gift! We can't earn it, and we would never deserve it!"

"John, let's say I have something for you out in the car. I knew Betty and I were coming to visit, so we purchased this for you three months ago. It was paid for and bought with you in mind. When does it become yours?"

I said, "As soon as you bring it in here!"

He laughed and said, "That's pretty much right. It becomes yours only when you accept it. Jesus died for our sins. Salvation has been bought for everyone, but it only becomes ours when we accept it. It is a free gift."

He then showed me in Hebrews Chapter 10 something that touched me deeply. Linda was very interested, too, and was asking questions. She had let Gene come here because she knew I needed help. She had no idea she did, too.

Hebrews 10 said, "When we confess something to God in the name of Jesus it is forgiven and he casts it as far as the east is from the west, and he will remember it no more."

"John, do you realize what this means? You can say, 'God remember that time in Vietnam....' and confess whatever to him. Then the next day, week or year you may say, 'God remember that time in Vietnam...?' And He will say, 'No, I don't remember that. That slate is clean. I remember it no more.'"

I said, "Gene, do you really believe that?"

He said, "Yes, I have had it happen to me! Do you want that forgiveness? You can have it right here, right now, right in your living room. You don't have to see a priest or a pastor or even be in a church. You can have forgiveness and salvation right here – right now! Do you want that?"

Linda did, I could tell. I said, "Well, I sure as hell have tried harder things!" And we knelt and prayed – all of us. We told Jesus that we were sinners and needed forgiveness. We asked Jesus to cleanse us from our sins with the blood He shed on the cross. Then we asked him to be the Lord (boss) of our lives, and we turned control of our lives over to Him right there. During this darkest time of guilt and anxiety in my life, I had finally seen that sign I had waited for so many times in the bush that told me I could relax and there would be no more battle tonight... I saw my true "Morning Star". The Bible calls Jesus "our bright and Morning Star". I knew the battle was finally over for me.

I got up and felt a peace unlike anything either before or after Vietnam. We were instructed to first read the book of John, that it would tell us about Jesus' love for us. And then find a Bible-preaching church.

We ate the lasagna lunch Linda had prepared and then Gene and Betty left... and the peace was still there!

423

That night when we went to bed, I slept. There was a bad lightening storm with loud claps of thunder. Through the years, Linda had been conditioned to reach out and grab me during storms to assure me everything was okay, that I was home, that the war was over. Tonight I slept through it. Now SHE would have to learn to sleep through such storms. I had the first full night's sleep in seven years, three months and sixteen days! It was a free gift...and it was there all the time. Doc Bear was finally gone...John was home at last!

The year is now 2003 – and the peace is still there. This was the answer for me. I am saying any religion works on the outside with its "do's and don'ts". But when Jesus came into my heart, he worked on the very root of my feelings, changing my attitudes and motivations. He changed me, released me from the nightmares and guilt and made all things new. He threw my sin as far as the east is from the west and remembers it no more according to Hebrews Chapter 10!

I am relating how I found peace, nothing more. If you are a Vet and plagued with nightmares and hatred, this same gift is there waiting for you - the gift of forgiveness, grace, and peace. You sure have done harder things!

John

The Names NOT on the Wall

AFTER WORD

Taking this journey back in time brought back many memories. Most of them were forgotten for self-preservation and good mental health. The events were basically as they really happened as best I can remember.

One important matter, though, is February 6, 1969, the day Sgt. Rios was critically wounded. Yes, it happened pretty much as was written with one exception: Neither "Doc Gray" nor I were in the field that day. I was at the BAS in An Hoa recovering and both of us returned to the bush the next day. I feel this is important to mention for two main reasons:

1. I carried that load of guilt for many years. I wasn't there when my best friend went down.

2. I don't know for sure which "Doc" took my place and actually did treat the Sarge much as I described. He deserves the credit for a job well done. I thank you for being there and assure you Sarge does as well. I'd like to think I would have done as good a job as you did.

We often reunite in San Francisco, and openly welcome any of our buddies we haven't been able to contact. If you were with Alpha 1/5 and would like to join us, please contact me. July 4th is celebrated every year with a parade at Redwood City, CA, and I personally thank the City of Redwood for their kindness.

"Lt. Robin Montgomery" was based on my last Platoon Commander. He was and still is indeed a true hero. There were, in fact, many heroes, but this Lieutenant stood out, a man among men. I am deeply honored to call him "my friend".

The Names NOT on the Wall Author Bio

John "Doc" Hutchings served with Alpha Co. 1/5 1st Marine Division as an FMF Corpsman from Oct. 23, 1968-Oct 23, 1969. "The Names NOT on the Wall" was based on that final tour of duty.

The names of Sgt. Vincent Rios, Lauren Stuckenschmidt, Eddie Harren and Steve Brit were not changed and were used with permission. The events involving them are as exact as can be remembered after 36 years of trying to forget.

"Doc Bear" was based on me and my experiences; though for entertainment purposes, some were enhanced or borrowed from the experiences of other Corpsmen I knew or served with.

Doc has had several songs and poems published including "From a Doc's Point of View", "Dear Field Med Instructor," and "The Corpsman and the Wall", which inspired this novel. Purple Heart Magazine, Always Faithful and Leatherneck Magazine have published his works. Various veteran organizations have used them as part of their programs by either reading them aloud or printing them on the program.

John is a retired business owner residing in Central Florida and is currently working on a second novel, "Point Man".

Post Traumatic Stress Disorder is very prevalent in our returning troops from both current and past wars. I felt compelled to write "The Names NOT on the Wall", which explains how it really was (warts and all) to help both veterans and their loved ones to better understand why the man/woman they kissed goodbye was not the same person they kissed hello.

"GENTLE JOHN" 1966 AT HUTCH'S COLDWATER CAMP, COLDWATER, MO

DOC HUTCH 1969 AT THE DOG BONE ("1000-yd stare")

DOC HUTCH ON THE ROAD TO LIBERTY BRIDGE

DOC HUTCH AND DOC HARREN 1969 (DANANG)

(Eddie taught me it was okay to laugh again.)

STUCKEY'S SQUAD 1969
<u>LEFT TO RIGHT STANDING</u>: KENNY LANE,
WILLIAMS(?), NAKEYAMA, DOC HEMENWAY,
DOC HUTCH, TONY DOWNS.
<u>KNEELING FRONT LEFT TO RIGHT</u>:
(?), RODNEY WILLIAMS, WAGNER, LAUREN
STUCKENSCHMIDT (STUCKEY)

The Names NOT on the Wall

2ND PLATOON 1969 FRONT FROM LEFT: MANDIBLES (?), LT ROBIN MONTGOMERY, HERNANDES, SGT VINCE RIOS. REAR CENTER: DOC HUTCH RIGHT OF DOC: PAT MCCRARY

JULY 4TH, 2005, REDWOOD CITY, CA STANDING LEFT TO RIGHT: PAT MCCRARY (MAC), LAUREN STUCKENSCHMIDT (STUCKEY), LT. ROBIN MONTGOMERY, JOHN HUTCHINGS (DOC HUTCH), AND STEVE BRIT (BRIT). FRONT: SGT VINCE RIOS.

430

MAP OF AN HOA BASIN

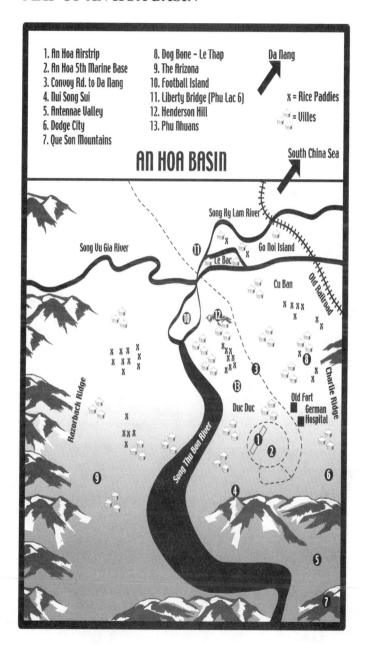

1. An Hoa Airstrip
2. An Hoa 5th Marine Base
3. Convoy Rd. to Da Nang
4. Nui Song Sui
5. Antennae Valley
6. Dodge City
7. Que Son Mountains
8. Dog Bone – Le Thap
9. The Arizona
10. Football Island
11. Liberty Bridge (Phu Lac 6)
12. Henderson Hill
13. Phu Nhuans

x = Rice Paddies

= Villes

Da Nang

South China Sea

AN HOA BASIN

Song Ky Lam River

Song Vu Gia River

Go Noi Island

Le Bac

Old Railroad

Cu Ban

Razorback Ridge

Charlie Ridge

Song Thu Bon River

Duc Duc

Old Fort
German
Hospital